Loving
the **L** word

READING CONTEMPORARY TELEVISION

Series Editors: Kim Akass and Janet McCabe

janetandkim@hotmail.com

The *Reading Contemporary Television* series offers a varied, intellectually groundbreaking and often polemical response to what is happening in television today. This series is distinct in that it sets out to immediately comment upon the TV *zeitgeist* while providing an intellectual and creative platform for thinking differently and ingeniously writing about contemporary television culture. The books in the series seek to establish a critical space where new voices are heard and fresh perspectives offered. Innovation is encouraged and intellectual curiosity demanded.

PUBLISHED AND FORTHCOMING

Loving **The L Word**: *The Complete Series in Focus* edited by Dana Heller

Mad Men: *Dream Come True TV* edited by Gary R. Edgerton

Makeover Television: Realities Remodelled edited by Dana Heller

New Dimensions of **Doctor Who** edited by Matt Hills and David Mellor

Nip/Tuck: *Television That Gets Under Your Skin* edited by Roz Kaveney and Jennifer Stoy

Quality TV: American Television and Beyond edited by Janet McCabe and Kim Akass

Reading **24**: *Television against the Clock* edited by Steven Peacock

Reading **Angel**: *The TV Spin-off with a Soul* edited by Stacey Abbott

Reading **CSI**: *Television under the Microscope* edited by Michael Allen

Reading **Deadwood**: *A Western to Swear By* edited by David Lavery

Reading **Desperate Housewives**: *Beyond the White Picket Fence* edited by Janet McCabe and Kim Akass

Reading **Little Britain**: *Comedy Matters on Contemporary Television* edited by Sharon Lockyer

Reading **Lost**: *Perspectives on a Hit Television Show* edited by Roberta Pearson

Reading **Sex and the City** edited by Kim Akass and Janet McCabe

Reading **Six Feet Under**: *TV to Die For* edited by Kim Akass and Janet McCabe

Reading **Stargate SG-1** edited by Stan Beeler and Lisa Dickson

Reading **The L Word**: *Outing Contemporary Television* edited by Kim Akass and Janet McCabe

Reading **The Sopranos**: *Hit TV from HBO* edited by David Lavery

Reading the **Vampire Slayer**: *The Complete, Unofficial Guide to* Buffy *and* Angel edited by Roz Kaveney

The Queer Politics of Television by Samuel A. Chambers

Third Wave Feminism and Television: Jane Puts It in a Box edited by Merri Lisa Johnson

TV's Betty Goes Global: From Telenovela to International Brand edited by Janet McCabe and Kim Akass

Edited by Dana Heller

Loving
the **L** word

The Complete Series in Focus

I.B.TAURIS

LONDON · NEW YORK

Published in 2013 by I.B.Tauris & Co Ltd
6 Salem Road, London W2 4BU
175 Fifth Avenue, New York NY 10010
www.ibtauris.com

Distributed in the United States and Canada
Exclusively by Palgrave Macmillan
175 Fifth Avenue, New York NY 10010

ISBN: 978 1 78076 424 5

A full CIP record for this book is available from the British Library
A full CIP record is available from the Library of Congress

Library of Congress Catalog Card Number: available

Printed and bound by CPI Group (UK) Ltd, Croydon, CR0 4YY

MIX
Paper from
responsible sources
FSC
www.fsc.org   FSC® C013604

Contents

Part 3: Lineage

Part 4: Legacy

Acknowledgments

Two things occurred that I could not have predicted when Kim Akass and Janet McCabe graciously invited me to edit a sequel volume on the Showtime series, *The L Word*, which would examine the final seasons of the series and provide a follow-up to the 2006 collection, *Reading* The L Word*: Outing Contemporary Television*. The first surprise was Showtime's and Ilene Chaiken's announcement that they were launching a new unscripted spin-off, *The Real L Word*, which would boldly go where no cable program had gone before by following a cadre of young, hip, openly gay women in Los Angeles as they did the things that lesbians do best—"talking, laughing, loving, breathing, fighting, fucking, crying, drinking, riding, winning, losing, cheating, kissing, thinking, dreaming"— only this time, in reality.

The second surprise was that I suddenly found myself in the position of department chair at my university, and was almost immediately sucked into the paperwork vacuum where all new chairs must inevitably kiss their research agenda goodbye for at least one full year in order to learn the administrative ropes.

Therefore, for their heroic patience and fortitude in the face of perpetual delays and long unexplained silences, I want to thank my contributors: Rebecca Beirne, Kellie Burns, Cristyn Davies, Faye Davies, Kim Ficera, Deborah E. R. Hanan, Winnie McCroy, Margaret T. McFadden, Candace Moore, Marnie Pratt, Sal Renshaw, and Heidi Schlipphacke. I also want to thank Tara Shea Burke for hopping aboard the project while it was already in full motion so as to provide much-needed commentary on *The Real L Word*.

Many thanks to Janet and Kim, for their friendship and good humor, and to Philippa Brewster at I.B.Tauris for her stalwart dedication to this project—along with so many others—and her faith in my ability to pull this particular one together despite the obstacles.

And finally—as always—I am happily indebted to my eminently wise and magnanimous better half, Galina Tsoy, for watching television with me and buoying me up through all this with more to come.

Contributors

REBECCA BEIRNE is Lecturer in Film, Media and Cultural Studies, University of Newcastle. She is the author of *Lesbians in Television and Text after the Millennium* and editor *of Televising Queer Women: A Reader* and has written numerous journal articles and book chapters discussing queer representation in popular culture.

TARA SHEA BURKE earned her MFA in poetry from Old Dominion University in Norfolk, Virginia, in May 2012. She is also working towards a graduate certificate in Women's Studies, and has traveled to South Africa and Senegal to work with and offer service to global women's organizations. She has served as poetry editor for *Barely South Review* and currently teaches freshman composition and literature at Old Dominion Univerity, USA. Burke will begin teaching an LGBT-centered creative writing course at The Muse, a community-writing center in Norfolk Virginia, in the fall of 2012. Her poems are featured in *The Quotable* and forthcoming in *Rougarou* and *Switched-on Gutenberg.*

KELLIE BURNS is Senior Lecturer in the Faculty of Education and Social Work at The University of Sydney, Australia. Her research explores the intersections between sexuality, citizenship, and public and media discourses. Her current work explores the ways in which sexual citizenship is produced through the National HPV/Cervical Cancer vaccination program in Australia.

CRISTYN DAVIES is a Research Associate at The University of Sydney, Australia. She is an experienced researcher, writer, editor, and tertiary educator. Her current research interests include the culture wars; literature and new media; and the intersections between gendered and sexual subjectivities with citizenship, childhood and youth studies, and mediated environments. Cristyn has collaborated with academics, writers, performance artists, and digital and new media artists on a range of projects.

FAYE DAVIES is Senior Lecturer in Media and Cultural Theory at Birmingham City University, UK. She is also part of the newly formed Birmingham Centre for Media and Cultural Research. Her specialist areas are television cultures, production processes, and the representation of sexuality in both television and film. She teaches on a variety of courses around the issue of representation and is currently continuing her doctoral research on US commercial television and the representation of sexuality.

KIM FICERA is a northern California-based author, essayist, and humorist, who has been writing about social, political, and LGBT issues since 1997. She has authored one book of humorous essays, *Sex, Lies and Stereotypes: An Unconventional Life Uncensored*, which earned her a spot in *Out Magazine*'s OUT 100 in 2003, and contributed to two others, *Legacies* and *Reading* The L Word: *Outing Contemporary Television*. From 2005–2008, Kim wrote a popular column titled "Don't Quote Me" for MTV Networks/ Logo's AfterEllen.com. "Don't Quote Me" analyzed the ways in which gay and lesbian characters and celebrities are portrayed in the media. Today, when she is not working on her next book, a fictional prelude to the experiences she wrote about in *Sex, Lies and Stereotypes*, she works as a freelance writer, editor, and content producer.

DEBORAH E. R. HANAN is Associate Faculty for Royal Roads University's School of Communication and Culture (Victoria, Canada). A former recording artist, performer, and cultural producer in the music, film, television, and themed entertainment industries, Hanan specializes in entertainment and the arts, media cultural studies, critical media studies, queer theory, and American cultural history. Her work has been published in *Popular Media and Communication: Essays on Publics, Practices and Processes*; *Film and History: An Interdisciplinary Journal of Film and Television Studies*; *Communication Colloquy*; and the two-volume encyclopedia

Disasters and Tragic Events and How They Changed American History.

DANA HELLER is Eminent Scholar and Chair of the English Department at Old Dominion University. Heller holds a PhD in English (Graduate Center, City University of New York, 1989) and an MFA in Creative Writing (Columbia University, 1982) and has been teaching at ODU since 1990. She is the author of numerous articles on topics related to literature, popular culture, LGBT, and American studies, as well as the author/editor of seven books: *The Feminization of Quest-Romance: Radical Departures* (University of Texas, 1990), *Family Plots: The De-Oedipalization of Popular Culture* (University of Pennsylvania, 1995), *Cross Purposes: Lesbians, Feminists, and the Limits of Alliance* (Indiana University, 1997), *The Selling of 9/11: How a National Tragedy Became a Commodity* (Palgrave Macmillan, 2005), *The Great American Makeover: Television, History, Nation* (Palgrave Macmillan, 2006), *Makeover Television: Realities Remodeled* (I.B.Tauris, 2007), and *Hairspray* (Wiley-Blackwell, 2011). Heller is a four-time recipient of Fulbright Senior Lecturing Awards in Russia, Belarus, and Bulgaria, and winner of the State Council of Higher Education in Virginia Outstanding Faculty Award (1997).

WINNIE McCROY is a New York-based journalist who has written about popular culture, queer theory, and the arts for publications including *The Village Voice, The Advocate, GO NYC, Chelsea Now,* and *Gay City News.* She studied with Dr. Heller at Old Dominion University while earning her BA in English Literature with a focus on Women's Studies, and went on to secure an MA in English Literature at Virginia Commonwealth University. She lives in Brooklyn with her partner, and regularly updates her culinary blog, Brooklyn is Cookin', accessible on blogger.com.

MARGARET T. MCFADDEN is Associate Professor of American Studies, and the Christian A. Johnson Associate Professor of Integrative Liberal Learning at Colby College.

CANDACE MOORE is Assistant Professor at the University of Michigan, where her work focuses on queer representation in television. Moore's articles have appeared in *Cinema Journal, GLQ, Production Studies: Cultural Studies of Media Industries, Televising Queer Women, Reading* The L Word: *Outing Contemporary Television,* and *Third Wave Feminism and Television.* Moore has also published extensively as a media critic for *Curve, Girlfriends,* and AfterEllen.com.

MARNIE PRATT is an instructor of Women's, Gender, and Sexuality Studies for both Bowling Green State University and the University of Toledo. She has presented and published her work on *The L Word* in both national and regional outlets, including the National Women's Studies Association Conference and the collection *Televising Queer Women.* More broadly, her research focuses on how members of marginalized communities engage with media and popular culture. Her current project examines the negotiation of identity and socio-political activism that takes place through contemporary pro-queer/pro-feminist independent rock bands.

SAL RENSHAW is Associate Professor at Nipissing University, Canada, and is Chair of the Department of Gender Equality and Social Justice, cross-appointed in the Department of Religions and Cultures. She is the author of *The Subject of Love: Hélène Cixous and the Feminine Divine* (Manchester University Press, 2009), and her research interests range from the philosophy of love to representations of sexuality and ethics in contemporary media. She has previously written on *The L Word* for *Ms Magazine.*

HEIDI SCHLIPPHACKE is Associate Professor of German and European Studies and Director of the Bachelor of Arts in International Studies at Old Dominion University in Norfolk, VA, USA, where she teaches courses on German and European culture, literature, and cinema. She has published widely on issues of gender and family in the European Enlightenment, Critical Theory, and postwar German and European cinema and literature. Her book, *Nostalgia after Nazism: History, Home and Affect in*

German and Austrian Literature and Film, appeared in 2010. She is currently working on a project on polygamy in the German Enlightenment.

Introduction

Loving and Losing:
From *The L Word* to the "R" Word

Dana Heller

Television is a queer thing, and a queerer thing still to be writing about at this particular moment in LGBTQ history. By which I mean to say, it's ironic when we consider that broadcast television, as most of us know it, is generally assumed to be going the way of the dinosaur almost faster than one can say "Hulu." Even television insiders acknowledge it. For example, during the 2009 Emmy Awards show, Amy Poehler and Julia Louis-Dreyfus made light of the industry's demise, announcing that they were "honored to be presenting on the last official year of broadcast TV." Their remark was met with a ripple of urbane laughter that rather quickly evaporated into silence. But queer media advocates and television fans are neither laughing nor silent. Far from it. The mainstream televisual commodification of queerness has made lesbian, gay, and bisexual characters and storylines more visible than ever on both broadcast and cable scripted shows.[1] GLAAD's (The Gay and Lesbian Alliance Against Defamation) 15th Annual "Where Are We on TV" Report, released in September 2010, triumphantly announced a 3 percent increase in LGBT characters, with HBO's vampire-themed series, *True Blood*, leading the pack as the most sexually inclusive program of all. But this simply confirmed the paradox that proclamations of television's obsolescence had already intimated: just as queers gain entrance to the club, the party seems to be moving elsewhere (Stelter 2010).

Indeed, television may be fading fast, but queer television fan communities remain cautiously optimistic in the face of this slow death, optimistic and serious about the power of television—and in particular television studies in dialog with queer politics—"to re-describe and thereby necessarily change the world" (Chambers 2009, xiii), despite the lack of any conclusive evidence that television can mobilize the world in our favor. Reading between the optimistic headlines, the indisputable fact remains that LGBTQ people remain woefully under-represented in the mass media, and non-white queer and/or transgender people remain scarcely visible at all. Our recurring characters are still largely limited to gay white men. Not that I'm complaining—I can relate to Cameron and Mitchell on *Modern Family* as well as any middle-aged lesbian. But at times I can't help but wonder how campy "cream puff" gags and *True Blood*'s stock metaphor of sexy vampirism will help topple the heterosexual status quo. Queer theorists and civil rights activists may have rightly abandoned a facile politics of identity, but might we have become nostalgic for the satisfactions of unambiguous identification? Or are we simply nostalgic for television itself, even before the final network logo sign-off? Could that be why we continue to watch, talk, and write about queer television narratives and characters as if our lives depended on them?

Take *The L Word*. When the Showtime series premiered in January 2004 hopes ran high, even if tempered by awareness of the enormous stakes involved in such a project. Never before in television history had there been a series exclusively focused on lesbians, or in this case a well-groomed, glamorous cohort of lesbian, bisexual, and queer women who live, work, and consume endless cups of latte in the gay Mecca of West Hollywood. Never before had queer women been granted the opportunity to see their lives, communities, and relationships reflected week after week in dramatic story arcs that place recurring lesbian characters at front and center, rather than to the side. And never before had an openly lesbian producer, Ilene Chaiken, garnered the industry clout to tell the kinds of stories that resonate with queer women, stories that both network and cable television have traditionally suppressed or watered down to the point of utter dilution. Originally titled "Earthlings" (a slang term for lesbians), the idea of a cable series made by lesbians for lesbians seemed almost too good to be true. And of course it was. Chaiken acknowledged as much when she cautioned viewers against outsized expectations for the show: "I do want to move people on some deep level," she explained. "But I won't take on the mantle of social responsibility. That's not compatible with entertainment. I rail against the idea that pop television is a political medium. I am political in my life. But I am making serialized melodrama. I'm not a cultural missionary" (Glock 2005).

While *The L Word*'s initial reception was positive overall, and while the show rapidly acquired a dedicated fanbase composed of women and men, gays and straights, heated criticism of the series' representational strategies did not take long to register. The vast majority of objections focused on the series' traffic in conventional feminine gendering. Glamorously employed, impossibly svelte, and chicly coutered, the scripted lesbians of *The L Word* seemed without exception positioned as wanton eye candy, which prompted some viewers to wonder whether the show was targeted at straight male audiences rather than dykes. Where were the butches, the women of size, working-class womyn? While Chaiken could be credited with minimally acknowledging racial difference in the characters of Bette Porter and her straight sister, Kit Porter, the series was clearly populated with lesbians who seemed designed not to offend the sensibilities of straight viewers, and to provide (as Winnie McCroy put it) "pud Fodder for Joe Sixpack" (2003). While it opened a space for lesbian representation the likes of which we had never seen before, *The L Word* struck some as a masturbatory fantasy that too willingly catered to hackneyed porn industry clichés and pulp fiction sensationalism, rather than acknowledge the decidedly unglamorous, non-scandalous realities of most lesbians' work-a-day lives and engagements with community.

But this was precisely the point, and—dare I say it—Chaiken's unparalleled achievement. For all that was questionable in the series' disregard of authenticity, one thing was certain: *The L Word* was determined to generate debate about its own representational practices and politics. In other words, the series demanded that viewers confront the lack of continuity between pop culture's commercial aesthetic and the ethics of identity politics. Showtime renewed *The L Word* for a second and a third season, and with each hyper-dramatic story arc and campy plot twist the series increasingly highlighted the contradictions of its own watchability, placing its evasive signifier—"The L Word"— within quotation marks. You could cringe at the theme music and laugh at the inane dialog but the series had something undeniably intelligent at its core, a flamboyant self-reflexivity that marked it far less as an earnest queering of *Sex and the City* than as a "complicitous critique" of the pitfalls of lesbian visibility and visualization.[2] More than "pud fodder," *The L Word* provided some serious brain fodder for LGBTQ media critics and fan communities in the post-Lawrence vs. Texas era, as the state of Massachusetts introduced same-sex marriage and as *Queer Eye for the Straight Guy* took the entire nation from "drab to fab" in a ratings blitz that stunned television executives at Bravo. Surrounded by such signs of visibility and progress, viewers both loved and hated *The L Word*, but, more importantly than that, viewers *loved* talking to one another about how and why they loved and hated *The L Word*.

This was confirmed with the 2006 publication of *Reading* The L Word: *Outing Contemporary Television*, a collection that collectively undertook an examination of the series' dynamics and its potential contribution to the larger history of queer media. That volume, nimbly edited by Janet McCabe and Kim Akass, and with an introduction by Sarah Warn (founder of the entertainment website AfterEllen.com) became one of I.B.Tauris's most successful publications of that year, a tribute both to the quality of chapters included in the book and the dedicated fan culture that the show had generated. Above all, *Reading* The L Word demonstrated the extent to which the series had become a critical flashpoint for discussions about LGBTQ television marketing and production practices, discussions that had advanced well beyond the question of why *Ellen* was canceled after its lead character and star came out, both in the series and in real life. Moreover, writers realized that the show was becoming a catalyst for online communities and a participatory media culture that was changing the nature of television viewing practices and audience engagement through media convergence. This owed as much to the fans as it did to Chaiken's strategic (some might even say crafty) marketing of *The L Word* brand, her entrepreneurial vision of the series as a community-enabling franchise. With its publication only two seasons into the series, the contributors to *Reading* The L Word (myself among them) agreed that the series was doing something important—it held promise, even if it was too soon to say exactly what that promise was or whether it could be fulfilled.

Loving The L Word picks up where *Reading* The L Word leaves off, with that giddy sense of possibility, apprehension, and cautious optimism, in order to reflect on the series in its entirety and its quantum contribution to the ongoing evolution of queer television. Originally, my intention was to canvass those writers who had contributed to the first collection (as well as some newcomers to *The L Word* party) to find out if their opinions and analyses had changed in the course of the series. Did *The L Word* live up to expectations or did it disappoint? What were the principal pleasures and pitfalls of *The L Word*? What had the series achieved in the larger context of lesbian politics and popular culture, and what might we say of its legacy? These questions were meant to provoke disagreement, and that they did, as the structure of the volume reflects. In Part 1, "Lamentations," Kim Ficera, Rebecca Beirne, and Faye Davies contend that for reasons ranging from lack of substance to fan betrayal the series ultimately failed to deliver on its promise. Sal Renshaw, Heidi Schlipphacke, and Margaret T. McFadden, on the contrary, demonstrate in Part 2, "Laudations," that, despite its weaknesses, *The L Word* managed to break important new ground in its discussions of art, sexual politics, and lesbian stereotyping. In Part 3, "Lineage," Marnie Pratt, Winnie McCroy, and Deborah E. R. Hanan remind us that the series' originality is rooted in pop cultural, literary, and media traditions that make it heir to a long history of representational practice. And in the book's final section, "Legacy," Cristyn Davies, Kellie Burns, Candace Moore, and Tara Shea Burke consider what the series has bequeathed to us and where it may lead us next.

Throughout the volume, there are points of broad consensus that guide the discussions. First, this volume proceeds from the recognition that *The L Word*, for good or ill, transformed the lesbian television landscape as we knew it and reshaped the discursive communities that follow queer television, talk about it, and care about the narratives and characters that drive it. It fulfilled a long-neglected, visceral desire for lesbian stories and images, and served as a critical flashpoint of cultural anxiety and debate about the wages of lesbian stories and images in mainstream media.

At the same time, many writers acknowledge that the series ultimately sank somewhat under the combined weight of community expectation and producer hubris. In January of 2009, *The L Word* aired its final season amidst controversy—and countless expressions of viewer vexation—about the killing of Jenny Schecter (a character who had morphed from fragile *ingénue* into a cartoonishly wicked uber-diva), the ripped-from-the-tabloids pregnancy of transgender Moira/Max (with the rendering of his queer body as both a gesture of inclusivity and a site of abject spectacle), and a host of disjointed narrative twists and plot contrivances that seemed as hastily scripted as they were implausible.

And finally, this volume proceeds from the understanding that while *The L Word* ended in 2009 it manages to live on. Imaginatively, it lives on in the aforementioned discursive communities that continue to generate dialog, gossip, fan fiction, and buzz. Industrially, it lives on in the form of a spin-off reality show, *The Real L Word*, which premiered on US Showtime in the summer of 2010. Boasting the promotional tagline, "The truth is hotter than fiction," and described by Tara Shea Burke in the final chapter of this book as *The L Word* meets *The Real World*, *The Real L Word* follows a recent trend in television programming where scripted shows spawn reality-based shows (e.g. ABC's *Desperate Housewives* and Bravo's *The Real Housewives of* ...; HBO's *Big Love* and TLC's *Sister Wives*). However, the path from *The L Word* to *The Real L Word* is unique in that both projects are the properties of the same cable network, Showtime, and the brain-children of the same producer, Ilene Chaiken.

So while *The L Word* may have run its course, it continues to perform significant work on behalf of queer television culture in general and Showtime/Chaiken in particular, who have turned ensemble lesbian domestic drama into a titillating cottage industry. The chapters in this volume are a testament to that ongoing work. Indeed, even beyond *The Real L World*, I would dare say that the LGBTQ-inclusive programming we enjoy today would be unthinkable without *The L Word*'s influence. We can recognize it in comedic contexts. For example, Jane Lynch's incandescent performance as Sue Sylvester in *Glee* undeniably carries the trace of *The L Word*'s trafficking in a certain type of "A" personality queerness that, although not named *as such*, doesn't really need to be named *as such*. Naya Rivera's portrayal of Santana Lopez, a villainous baby-dyke whose conflicted sexual identity and desires cause her to wreak havoc with other students' relationships, seems nothing if not heir apparent to the cold-hearted Jenny Schecter, whose own conflicted coming-out narrative organized *The L Word*'s first season. The series' influence is apparent in dramatic contexts as well, such as *Desperate Housewives*' soapy season six lesbian subplot involving Katherine Mayfair's (Dana Delany) and former stripper, Robin Gallagher's (Julie Benz) discovery of same-sex attraction and their consequent escape from the meddlesome neighbors of Wisteria Lane to the anonymity of Paris in order to explore their feelings for one another. To the extent that *The L Word*'s camp aesthetics of lesbian desire have become part of mainstream broadcast television's roster of programming, *The L Word* lives on.

Of course, this is not to say that television's stock inclusion of sexually diverse female characters and the occasional sensationalized lesbian-themed episode is grounds for a victory lap around the National Mall. Indeed, many of these representations continue to be virulently homophobic. Take, for example, one of NBC's more recent dyke enticements: a lesbian kiss between the comedian Kathy Griffin and the actress Mariska Hargitay, who plays detective Olivia Benson on *Law and Order: Special Victim's Unit.* Griffin, who has a large LGBTQ fanbase, makes a guest appearance as the lesbian activist Babs Duffy, a righteous advocate for lesbian victims of sexual violence. But in the end, viewers tuning in to watch the encounter between the two women were disappointed to discover that NBC cut the kiss scene altogether. What they were treated to instead was a catalog of the most clichéd and offensive stereotypes known to lesbiankind, including strident feminist politics, man-hating butches, predatory sexual behavior, and—to top it off—a *Chasing Amy*-styled dénouement that reveals Duffy to be harboring a secret male lover, much to the outrage of her fanatical followers. In the face of such a blatant bait-and-switch, it is hard not to become cynical about the progress of lesbian representation on the small screen. Or as the title of one (now-defunct) video blog on "AfterEllen" bluntly concludes, it would appear that "We're Getting Nowhere."

But where exactly was *The L Word* supposed to get us? When all is said and done, when all the actors and writers have moved on to other projects, and when we finally admit that we'll never really know who killed Jenny Schecter, was *The L Word* good for lesbians or bad for lesbians? Before anyone accuses me of my own bait-and-switch, I should say upfront that the contributors to this volume do not promise to deliver definitive answers to that tangled question. But I will say unequivocally that *The L Word*, and its noteworthy expansion of lesbian and queer televisibility, has been very good for LGBTQ television scholarship. Book-length works such as Akass and McCabe's *Reading* The L Word, Rebecca Beirne's *Lesbians in Television and Text after the Millennium* and *Televising Queer Women*, Samuel Chambers, *The Queer Politics of Television*, peer-reviewed articles in top-notch scholarly journals in media, cultural, gender and sexuality studies, book chapters, dissertations, and numerous academic conference panels and presentations at meetings around the world probably speak less to the novelty of a television series "in which lesbians exist, go on existing, exist in forms beyond the solitary and the couple, sustain and develop relations among themselves of difference and commonality" (Sedgwick, in Akass and McCabe 2006: xvii), than to the sense of urgency experienced among scholars and graduate students, gay and straight alike, who had previously only dreamed of such representational fullness and dramatic continuity in the television treatment of women, let along a group of women of whom most are openly lesbian. Whether good or bad, *The L Word* made history simply by being what it was: the first television series to put lesbian and genderqueer characters in the spotlight and render their lives with mannered gravity and narrative spaciousness.

What we know now—and what we did not know in 2006—was that *The L Word* would make history for becoming the first *long-running* series to put lesbian and genderqueer characters in the spotlight. With that longevity, as the show's dedicated viewership grew to know these characters and anticipate the rhythms and rituals associated with the short-season model of cable series production, fans acquired not only a sense of cultural ownership over *The L Word* but the influence to make their wishes and protestations part of the planning, marketing, and scripting of the series. That passionate level of interactivity, and in particular its exercise and management via online communities, is a central theme that connects many of the chapters in this volume. Indeed, *The L Word* was a series notable as much for the penetration of the series into the real lives of fans as for the penetration of fans into the fictional world of the series. And the value of these exchanges over time was marked less by expressions of audience satisfaction— although there was always plenty of love to go around—than by rigorous debate over questions of lesbian authenticity that the series seemed intentionally to provoke. The audience critique of Chaiken's mass-marketing approach to lesbian representation and its pronounced disapproval of certain storylines, the stereotypical gendering of female characters, and exclusions of ethic, racial, class, and generational differences, are part of *The L Word*'s lasting legacy. And equally a part of that legacy is Chaiken's executive skillfulness in keeping a step ahead of the debate, at times even setting the terms of debate by deftly drawing critical dialogs surrounding the show into *The L Word*'s *mise-en-scène*, thus aestheticizing viewers' attempts to politicize the series in a manner that both reflected and deflected viewer frustration. By the end of the series fans could no longer debate the *ethics* of lesbian authenticity in *The L Word* as much as they could debate the *aesthetics* of lesbian authenticity. Yet in the process, *The L Word* registered distinctive tensions that had arisen from the culture's growing acceptance of queer stories and characters, as well as from the mass appeal of queer televisual performances that did not so much promise to capture the reality of lesbian gender as to transform it in accordance with the subscription cable network's perceived limits of tolerance.

And yet, for all of its shortcomings and artful maneuverings around audience demands for social accountability—for all that it did not ultimately give us, or live up to—*The L Word* drew complicated, contradictory characters, women who struggled within themselves and with one another. It tried to depict something simmering beneath the surface of all that frivolous West Hollywood jouissance. It dealt—or tried to deal—with real issues, like the US military's policy of "Don't Ask, Don't Tell," and the hypocrisy of Christian right-wing propaganda, and breast cancer. It spoke, eloquently at times, to our inner desires for lives of beauty and creativity. It showed us a living community and its erotic economy warts and all, and in doing so reflected the communities that remain central to our social sustenance and psychological survival. Certainly, that would explain the powerful symbolic resonance of "the Chart," Alice Pieszecki's graphic constellation of lesbian sexual connections, which she maintains as evidence of her belief that everyone is related to everyone else through a complex web of erotic contact. For many viewers, "the Chart" summed up what the series was all about: the links and intimacies that are part of a common history, a shared body of knowledge. If *The L Word* was a successful series it was because there was always an "us" at its center. Individual characters were always inexorably connected to something larger than themselves, no matter how remote or self-absorbed. And if we were never entirely sure who killed Jenny Schecter, it was because no individual character held a monopoly on motive: blame for her murder was a shared holding, our community asset.

This helps explain why reports of television's death (to quote Mark Twain's response to the premature publication of his obituary) are "greatly exaggerated." Television appeals to us because even in its current state of decay it continues, at its best, to animate the sense of connection to something larger—the sense of "imagined community" that was (for Benedict Anderson) as instrumental to the popular development of the modern novel as it was to the rise of nineteenth-century nationalism (1983). And this may also help to explain why Chaiken's new project with Showtime, *The Real L Word*, has thus far failed to generate the same level of critical enthusiasm and audience support as its scripted predecessor. Although *The Real L Word* is similarly based in Los Angeles and promises to follow the unfiltered daily lives and relationship challenges of an ensemble cast of real gay women as they plan expensive same-sex weddings, pursue high-stress careers, fight and reconcile with lovers, and engage in drunken one-night stands, the première season of *The Real L Word* lacked one essential lesbian ingredient: the Chart. In other words, the subjects of the series emerged as lost and fragmented pieces of a formless jigsaw puzzle. Their "segments," edited as if with a machete, lacked connections, complexities, or recognizable contexts. There was no community, no "us," and as one fretful blogger observes, no stories. "I know the conflict in Sammi & Ronnie's relationship from watching twenty minutes of *Jersey Shore*," she writes. "[But after one season] I've still got no clue what Rose & Nat are ever actually fighting about" (Bernard 2010a).

As tempting as it is to describe *The Real L Word* as "*Jersey Shore* meets Dinah Shore," spellbinding sordidness of the "guido/guidette" variety was not Chaiken's stated intention with the series. Her goal was lesbian authenticity. "We wanted to make an authentic show that expanded the premise of *The L Word*. … I'm not about to put on a show about lesbians that pushes us forward as trashy, ridiculous, vulgar people that behave badly all the time" (Bolonik 2010). Notwithstanding such claims, it would be difficult to credit Chaiken for taking the high road, especially considering the first season's sustained emphasis on debauchery, hot party weekends, infidelity, and major emotional blow-outs. Chaiken acknowledges that one of the things she had to get used to in producing *The Real L Word*—one of the biggest differences between the scripted original and its reality spin-off—is that she had to cede control over the stories that get told. But ironically, what's most striking when you watch the first season of *The Real L Word* is how narrowly constrained and conspicuously "typed" the personalities are, and how clumsily the narrative arc rises and falls when guided by the imperatives of lesbian authenticity, which in this case seems above all to mean uncensored girl-on-girl sex.

The second season of *The Real L Word*, which premiered on US Showtime June 5, 2011, seems determined to bear this out, beginning with the season's tagline (captioning an image of the new cast scantily dressed and coated in mud) that reads, "This time they're getting dirty." It is also worth noting that all of the first-season cast members have been retired except for Romi Klinger and Whitney Mixter, who distinguished themselves largely through their mismanagement of multiple, complicated affairs and their willingness to cross the "porn" line by granting Chaiken permission to use graphic footage of them having wild, drunken sex with a reportedly unwashed strap-on dildo at a "white trash" theme party. No judgment, but it's hard to imagine how season two could get any dirtier than that. And not to demur, but I'll set aside for now the controversial question of whether that moment was grossly and unnecessarily exploitative or socially revolutionary in its depiction of female sexual agency and pleasure, or an unsettling combination of both. The question for the contributors to this volume is how *The L Word* helped advance the codes, conventions, and community negotiations through which lesbian reality has come to acquire cultural legibility and commercial currency in contemporary media culture.

Lesbians are sexual beings, after all, and we've too often been neutered and desexualized by pop culture myths that depict us as cat-loving victims of "bed death" desiring little more than herbal tea and a cuddle at night. There are thrills to be had in watching "authentic" lesbian sex on television, no matter what one's gender or sexual orientation. But I'd hate to think, after all is said and done, that reality television killed Jenny Schecter. It would be unfortunate if Jenny—and all those florid, entertaining characters—died at the hands of the disingenuous promise of authenticity and "never-beforeness" that reality television is obliged to serve up. It would be sad but not unprecedented, the reason being that for queer folk authenticity has always been dangerous, a fraught and hazardous minefield. On some level we know that authenticity is a social luxury that history has not afforded us. But more bluntly, authenticity is a hammer that's been used to beat us into submission and conformity in the name of religious morality and community standards; it is a hammer that we have used to beat one another into conformity and submission in the name of identity politics. And a significant part of queer history, or the establishment of what we could call modern gay identity, involves the conscious subversion of authenticity through the stylized exaggerations and self-conscious hyperbole that are the properties of drag, gender parody, and camp.

The L Word is now a part of that history. The series placed the very possibility of lesbian authenticity in quotation marks, recognizing that authenticity is a performative contradiction, both a longing and a myth, a state of being that is as much individually produced as it is culturally constructed and socially conferred. *The L Word*, in this way, takes a page from post-identity-oriented theoretical practices, evident in the way that the series assiduously avoids association with either one of the two camps that result from evaluative media assessment— the (we're getting nowhere!) despairers and the (we've come a long way!) boosters. What *The L Word* told us is that these camps miss the point—the bigger picture—that queer politics and cultural products are far richer, more diverse, and internally inconsistent than debates over whether an image is positive or negative—good for queers or bad for queers—can ever capture. And despite all protests to the contrary, *The L Word* also reaffirmed the unmistakable sense that television, generally speaking, continues to live and loom in our minds as the great guarantor of queer visibility—a place where pleasures and politics converge in the instance of seeing ourselves—but not really ourselves—on TV.

Notes

1   ABC's Emmy-winning *Modern Family* depicts a monogamous gay male couple raising their adopted Vietnamese baby. *Nurse Jackie*, on Showtime, is set in a New York City hospital and focuses on an Oxycodone-addicted ER nurse, along with a medical staff that includes a gay male nurse, a bisexual, and a prominent young doctor whose parents are a lesbian couple. HBO's *True Blood* is a vampire saga with lavishly diverse sexual and racial overtones. Fox's *Glee*—with its exuberant cast of outsider teens belting out pop and Broadway show tunes—may simply be the queerest show ever to appear on any major television network, at least since ABC's *Ugly Betty* was unceremoniously canceled due to a precipitous decline in ratings. And the UK continues the trend, with *Skins* and *Sugar Rush* normalizing the experiences of LGBTQ youth in a manner that would have been impossible only fifteen or even ten years ago.

2 "Complicitous critique" is Linda Hutcheon's term for describing the
   critical ambivalence of postmodern art that perpetuates the very
   conventions that it ostensibly condemns (1989).

PART 1

Lamentations

"Slip under my cloak of boringness. No one will even know we're gone."

Kim Ficera

Like a longtime lover who one day went out for milk and never came back, the final episode of *The L Word* left me hanging.

In a word, I felt cheated. In a lot of words, watching the finale was like having been read a story by someone with Alzheimer's, who purposely set the book on fire before reaching the last page. Just seconds after the credits rolled, I wanted the hours and hours and hours and hours I'd devoted to the show, the characters, and the storylines back. I wanted to hang Ilene Chaiken in effigy with the rope left over from all the loose ends she failed to tie.

But did I expect more than I got? Did I expect, for example, an answer to the question, "Who killed Jenny?" No, not really. But I have to admit I held out a sliver of hope that the finale wouldn't be as abrupt and careless as it was. So when it failed to live up to even my low expectations, I was angry.

On March 9, 2009, the morning after the finale aired, I wrote the following on my blog, "Pimp My Wry":

> To sum up the way many, if not most, viewers of *The L Word* finale feel this morning, I need only steal a line of dialog from Alice Pieszecki: "Thank you and fuck you."
>
> Alice said those words to Jamie last night, but today unhappy lesbian viewers are saying them right back to the woman who wrote them, the woman responsible for last night's debacle, Ilene Chaiken.
> …
>
> The past six years haven't been a total waste of time … we owe a lot to Ilene and Showtime. Increased lesbian visibility on TV is good, even when it's mediocre, and, yes, even when it's downright

cringe-worthy ... [But], unfortunately, Chaiken remained true to form and gave us in the finale exactly what she's given us the majority of the past six years, a jumbled and irrational hour that left us shaking our heads ...

For the record, I didn't enjoy writing those words then, and I don't enjoy revisiting them now, because it's never any fun to be reminded of a love affair gone terribly wrong. And a love affair is exactly what I'd call my relationship with the show.

(Cue *Leave it to Beaver* theme-song-like music.)

I can vividly remember the moment I was seduced by the mere idea of *The L Word*. It was an average day in Suckerville and I was walking home alone when Ilene pulled up beside me in a Subaru. "Excuse me, Average Lesbian, my friends and I have a great idea for a show," she said as she handed me a picture of Jennifer Beals holding the cutest puppy I'd every seen in my life! "Will you ride with me to find more puppies and hot brunettes if I promise to tell your stories?"

"Yes! Yes!" I said. "I love brunettes! I love puppies! I love my stories and they do need to be told!" And I got in her car, and she drove me to hell.

Okay, so it didn't happen exactly like that. The truth is, I fell in love with the show of my own free will after reading all the hype and seeing the pilot episode. I was hooked from the start, infatuated and charmed by the entire package, but especially by Alice's "Chart."

As I wrote in *Reading* The L Word, this book's companion text, the Chart was something any lesbian with a sexual past could identify with:

[It] served to provide viewers with a not so subtle representation of the characters' sexual ties to one another. ... Lesbian viewers understood. We laughed out loud. We've all taken similar paths, after all; only the names of our pit stops were different. Regardless of our ages or accents we saw ourselves in the Chart and we each reacted similarly, as if a long-lost friend had finally gotten the huge break she was waiting for in Hollywood. (112)

I so wanted that friend to make it, and by midway through the first season I was head over heels in L Word love-lust. So smitten was I that

I didn't only look forward to my Sunday night dates with show, but also planned my life around them.

"I'm sorry," I said to any and all who invited me here or there, "but I can't do whatever fabulous thing you want me to do tonight because *The L Word* is on and, well, you're not Marina."

I also didn't notice other dramas as much as I used to. *Law and Order?* Not tonight. Sure Mariska Hargitay was and is a hottie, but no matter how hard I prayed or how long, she never kissed a woman. And that so-called lesbian on *ER?* The one with one cane in her hand and another up her attitude? The one who obviously never had any sex? Please! I laughed in NBC's homophobic face! I was finally able to turn on my television and watch a program I could actually relate to, a show that was as out as I am, a show that celebrated lesbians, the incestuousness of our lives, and the sex games we played out of necessity or even boredom. Why waste time on teases when I could enjoy the real thing?

For two years I was happier than Max at a computer convention sponsored by The Hair Club for Men. But as the third season came and went, something changed. Ilene had told stories, true, but she hadn't told my stories. Could it be I'd been duped? Had I fallen not for *The L Word*, but for its potential? I wondered.

The show was groundbreaking, sure; that would never change. And, yes, there were entire seasons of greatness (one and two) that proved attempts at excellence were made. But the series had developed a superiority complex, an unrealistic and exaggerated opinion of itself. Also, not-so-little things, like Dana's death and Tina's obsession with men and real penises (season three), had come between us, and I was frustrated by the fact that Shane, a grown woman, rolled around LA on a skateboard. What lesbians had *The L Word* writers channeled for material? None I knew.

So I questioned Ilene, and did so publicly. In January of 2007, I wrote her an open letter and included these words: "I'm not angry; I'm concerned, and like many who watch your show, I'm disappointed in the last two seasons. Did you fall and hurt your head?"

She never answered.

I grew more and more disenchanted. I felt increasingly appeased instead of loved, tolerated instead of valued, and, perhaps predictably, I felt that I was trying much harder to make our affair work than I should have to. I felt as if I was being taken advantage of and that my relationship with *The L Word* was becoming (insert scary music here) unhealthy.

If only I could find a lesbian therapist!

One major concern was that after having been introduced to characters that I quickly grew to love (or hate), and after having become invested in their lives, their behaviors went from fascinating and somewhat believable to infuriating and downright preposterous. At least two characters never stood a chance of escaping the one-dimensional prison that the writers locked them in. Loyal viewers need only to recall the story arcs of Moira/Max and Kit for proof that rational character development wasn't exactly a priority for the writers. In fact, it was so unimportant that by the end of the series both Max and Kit became caricatures—not of themselves, but of the transgender and African-American groups they were supposed to represent.

More troubling, I felt that Ilene wasn't delivering on her promise of substance, of art imitating lesbian life. She tried, I suppose, by feeding me storylines that were pulled from the day's headlines—Max's pregnancy in season six, and Tasha's "Don't Ask, Don't Tell" military court battle in season five. But for the most part, instead of quality storytelling I got daytime soap-like nonsense—Jenny's adopting a dog just to euthanize it in season four, and Jodi's humiliation of Bette in her payback-is-a-bitch art sculpture-cum-magic show in season five—stories so far-fetched that even the craziest, most dysfunctional lesbians in West Hollywood probably deemed them implausible. (Did Ilene really think I'd believe that Jodi just wished all that footage of Bette into existence?) Chaiken, I thought, was only one bad idea away from having Jenny enlist help from the Cassadines to build a weather machine that would freeze LA.

What was a priority? What had replaced the substance of the first two seasons? What did I get in return for my devotion? A lesson in—get this—brand promotion.

The Chart, the very thing I loved most about the show, went from prop to character to product when Ilene turned chunks of the very first episode of season four into an advertisement promoting the launch of her now-failed "OurChart.com." The Chart, the one "character" that had stayed true to that point, was now turning me off, and Ilene was making it perfectly clear that I was nothing more than a consumer in her eyes. Consumer—the least sexy word in the entire dictionary, next to congeal.

That move was, apparently, just part of her long-range plan.

In August of 2008, the summer before the sixth and final season, Advertising Age published an article titled "On Ad-Less 'L Word,' Brands Become Part of the Plot" (http://www.commercialalert.org/issues/culture/product-placement/on-ad-less-l-word-brands-become-part-of-the-plot) in which writer Claude Brodesser-Akner penned the following:

> Ilene Chaiken, the creator of *The L Word*, has obtained something unprecedented among Hollywood's writers—the power to control all brand integration for the show's final season, as well as for a spin-off series launching on the network next year. ... Those with knowledge of the matter say that for $300,000, consumer brands can buy an "integration package" that will either incorporate a brand into existing "L Word" storylines or allow the brand to work with the show's writers to create customized storylines, participating in one episode or across several. Ms. Chaiken is also offering brands opportunities for integration around Ourchart. com, the largest social network for lesbians on the web. ...
>
> The "L Word," [Chaiken] notes, isn't just about and for gays and lesbians; it's about "affluent, avid consumers plugged into pop culture," which Ms. Chaiken said makes the series "a rare, perfect opportunity for showcasing brands" to women, lesbian or not.

An "opportunity for showcasing"? Uh, no. It was more like an opportunity for Ilene to punch me in the face while insisting she's kissing me with her fist.

Right then and there I should have changed the channel. While product placement happens all the time on TV, being subjected to blatant infomercial-like scripted dialog in the middle of show was a first for me, and I hated it. In my mind it was an unprecedented infringement on our sacred relationship—the marriage, if you will, of story and audience. In fact, it was more than just a betrayal of trust and a barging in on of personal space; it was an undeserved and very overt flipping of the bird. Through that ad stunt Ilene said, point blank and without apology, *I interrupt this program in this very shameful way because I can, and if you don't like it, lump it. I'm the only game in town, sister, and therefore I've got you by the short hairs.*

The clincher? She was right. I didn't move.

I continued to watch despite having been used, despite the ridiculous scripts, despite that the theme song was annoying, and, yeah, despite that it was clear that the powers-that-be were setting the stage for the eventual rupturing of the global lesbian spirit—the event otherwise known as the finale.

Why? Maybe because mediocre sex is better than no sex. Or maybe it was just fate. Maybe, as Alice said in season one, "we're all connected, through love, through loneliness, through one lamentable lapse in judgment."

The T Word:
Exploring Transgender
Representation in *The L Word*

Rebecca Beirne

In 2007, Representative Barney Frank proposed a bill to the US Congress, the Employment Non-Discrimination Act (ENDA), which sought workplace protections for those being discriminated against on the basis of their sexual orientation. This bill, however, did not include legislation barring workplace discrimination against transgendered people. While many among the LGBT community protested such exclusion, others saw it as a necessary measure in order to have the bill passed. Indeed, at the time "Frank criticized groups for demanding that gender identity be included in the bill, saying that, while such inclusion might make it stronger, such critics 'rarely are helpful to us in getting the votes to get it through'" (Keen 2009: 13). In effect, the debate can be seen as an opposition between those promoting inclusivity and those in favor of the strategic exclusion of individuals who might present "too much otherness" (to quote the character Tina in *The L Word* 1:1) to a possibly homophobic and transphobic congressional audience. This debate is by no means a new one. From early gay and lesbian rights groups that promoted gender normativity among their members (such as the Daughters of Bilitis), to more contemporary groups such as the Human Rights Campaign, the question of the best ways for LGBT communities to present themselves to both political bodies and mainstream heteronormative audiences has often divided queer communities. Something that has been common too is the frequent exclusion of transgendered individuals. As gay and lesbian life has become more accepted within legal and cultural venues (for example via gay marriage laws or gay characters on mainstream television), the rights and representation of transgendered people have sadly lagged behind.

It is precisely such a tension that rages in *The L Word* in its representation of the transgendered and others of non-normative genders. In its narratives, casting, and rendering transgender bodies as spectacle, one can see that *The L Word* shares Rep. Frank's 2007 anxiety about audiences, and what it was perceived they would be willing to accept. Much as Frank sought to make what he perceived to be necessary compromises in order to contribute to the acceptance of homosexuality, the creators of *The L Word* attempted in several different ways to create a show that would disassociate lesbianism from any characters or communities that might make it less palatable for a mainstream audience. As the first big-budget show dedicated to depicting a diverse lesbian community, *The L Word* was faced with significant challenges in representing such a population. How it responded to such pressures indicates not only the strictures of commercial television industries, but also political choices, and a series of compromises that some saw as necessary, and others saw as fatally flawed.

Just like the proponents of the original ENDA bill, *The L Word* from the very beginning displayed a distinct consciousness about its intended audience. In a *New York Times* interview, creator Ilene Chaiken admitted that "if Showtime expects her to tweak and repackage and make lesbianism hot, hot, hot then she is happy to comply" (Glock 2005: 38). If such an attitude is to be followed to its logical conclusion, one must assume that the writers and producers of the series were likewise willing to compromise on other matters in order to appeal to both Showtime and their audiences. During later seasons, with a dedicated lesbian fanbase established, *The L Word*'s particularly noticeable investment in its audience could also be seen by such activities as the establishment of the "OurChart" website[1] and competitions such as the "fanisode."[2] Certain narrative developments, such as the shift in the representation (and eventual death) of the vastly unpopular character Jenny, could also, arguably, be seen in the context of responding to the audience's attitudes. Of course, a desire to attract the widest possible audience comes as no surprise from a premium cable television series where ratings are a key issue. It is clear that the producers did have both certain pressures and clear assumptions about what they thought would be deemed "acceptable" to both the mainstream and lesbian audiences they hoped would watch their show (with the transgender audience no doubt being considered too small a demographic for them to attempt to please).

Television has had an ambiguous relationship with transgendered characters. While drag has long been a staple of television comedy, unambiguously transgendered and transsexual characters have been few and far between. With the advent of unashamedly queer television, such as *The L Word*, there were hopes for a growing representational prominence of diverse gender identities. During the first season of *The L Word*, this took the form of two genderqueer characters, the bi-gendered drag king Ivan Aycock and the "lesbian-identified-man," Lisa. Neither of these characters was treated with great seriousness, and the show was criticized for the lack of gendered diversity among its characters. A response to such critiques arose in the third season in the form of female-to-male character Moira, who quickly transitioned to Max, and remained a character for the rest of the series' run. Faye Davies (2008: 180) has argued that *The L Word* "prioritizes one form of sexual identity and gender over another," defining lesbianism against bisexuality. Such a rhetorical practice is also evident in *The L Word*'s representation of Max. In this depiction, the "queerer" specter of transgenderism has been narratively utilized to redefine the series' feminine, gender-normative, Los Angeles lesbians within a space of "normality." This is in keeping with contemporary assimilationist political perspectives that seek to normalize gay and lesbian individuals, at times through disassociation with those who are deemed to be outside of potential normalization. Just as in the world of politics, in the world of television narrative, polarity is often a key feature of both comedy and drama. And as a result of such choices of representational politics, transgender or genderqueer characters appeared on the margins of the world of L.

Lisa, the "lesbian man," is perhaps the first character who is indicative of gender transgression in *The L Word*. Lisa is also demonstrative of an oppositional characterization that renders gender ambiguity suspect while acting to render cisgender lesbian characters as comparatively normative.[3] Appearing in the episodes "Lies, Lies, Lies" (1:4) through to "L'Ennui" (1:7), Lisa insists on hir identity as including both male and lesbian elements, stating: "I'm a lesbian-identified man" (1:4). In Jacqueline Zita's provocative essay "Male Lesbians and the Postmodern Body" (1992) she considers how to define "lesbian" in order to attempt to account for such a positionality as the male lesbian. Opening up discussion of how lesbianism was redefined by lesbian-feminists in the 1970s, she argues that in this modality of understanding lesbianism:

> "Lesbianism" becomes a role, a positionality open to insertion. This is especially true if "lesbian" is defined as an ideological, ethical, or political posture: a way of being in the world and relating to others, a way of seeing the world which is "woman-identified" or "woman-seeing," a special way of loving, preferring, or "sexing" women – any number of political oppositional practices engaging or disengaging the domination of heteropatriarchy. (110–11)

The presentation of the character of Lisa certainly resonates with this earlier, politico-emotional mode of understanding lesbianism, despite Lisa's bodily positioning as male, which no doubt would have proved troubling to 1970s lesbian-feminists. If one is to evaluate Lisa's lesbianism through the above framework it is easier to consider the character as lesbian due to hir positioning as woman-identified, dislike of heteropatriarchy, and engagement in sex acts understood as lesbian. It soon becomes clear, however, that Lisa has not been included in order to engage in a discussion of what constitutes the category of "lesbian," but is rather primarily utilized for comedic value. These moments of intended humour, by offering older stereotypes of lesbianism, make the more mainstream lesbians of *The L Word* seem less transgressive by comparison, most obviously through their parodic disassociation from perceptions of lesbian feminism.

In these scenes, it is incongruity with gender norms that produces the humor. But far from undermining gender norms, the attitudes of the characters in fact reinforce them. In "Losing It," for example, Lisa remarks of Tina's pregnancy: "This is such a beautiful and crazy time in a woman's body. I'm jealous my body will never experience what you're experiencing right now" (1:6). Tina and Alice both respond to this with (somewhat veiled) hilarity that an individual they read as "male" could express such identifications and desires. Such a reaction indicates that there is little room in the series for feelings or behaviors incongruous with birth-gender. The comedic status of the character is undermined when we see Alice and Lisa about to engage in a sex act. When Lisa brings out a dildo in order to engage in sexual relations with Alice, Alice insists on the use of "the real thing" even if it "goes against who I am" (Lisa in 1:7). Lisa is clearly distressed by this insistence, and its dismissal of hir identity, and the scene that follows reads as a sexual violation, after which we never see Lisa again: this non-normative character and identity have been wiped from the screen. Just as Rep. Frank proposed to make transgender individuals invisible in the first iteration of non-discrimination legislation, *The L Word* here too elides the visibility of those who may not fit into traditional norms of gender and sexual identity. While Alice seems to have been able, at least to some limited extent, to accept Lisa's asserted identity, when it comes to sex, her insistence upon the physical body, at the expense of identity and sexual desire, is insurmountable.

This persistent refocusing from identities to bodies can also be seen with the two other main transgender characters in *The L Word*. From the very beginning, the tasteless name of Ivan Aycock (based on that of real-life Canadian genderqueer Ivan E. Coyote), indicates the attitude of the series towards his gender-transgressive behavior. Ivan was introduced in the first season, with his wooing of heterosexual Kit culminating in his performance of Leonard Cohen's "I'm Your Man."[64] While Kit is clearly taken with Ivan's performance of gender, those around her have quite different ideas. Sister Bette in particular is quite troubled by Ivan's male identity, insisting that "she is in love with you, and she wants to be your husband" (1:12). Jennifer Reed (2009: 170) contends that *The L Word* takes full advantage of mass media's oft-used strategy of a split and contradictory address, trying, as Susan Douglas argues, "to please simultaneously the 'lowest common denominator' and the more rebellious sectors of the audience." While such a split address is indeed used in *The L Word*, as is to be expected in an ensemble drama, the narrative and characterization is often utilized to define one of the positions as "correct," most commonly via placing it in the mouths of ongoing and thus narratively dominant characters (as can be seen in the previously discussed interactions with Lisa). This also occurs in *The L Word* in relation to Ivan, who, as a minor, non-continuing character, is barely given dialog to respond to the identities others thrust upon him or sufficient screentime to prompt audience investment or identification.

A scene during season two, which sees Kit accidentally walk in on a partially naked Ivan, also undermines a reading of *The L Word* as presenting multiple points of view on this subject. In the eyes of Kit, this view of Ivan's body shatters her perception of his maleness. For Kit, as for Bette, and indeed Alice, gender identity and performance are insignificant in relation to the physical, material body, which they define as the "real" gender. Ivan becomes an unambiguous woman in the eyes of Kit due to a brief glimpse of his breasts. And this glimpse of gender atypicality not only causes Kit to lose romantic interest, but also provides the excuse to virtually eliminate Ivan from the series. While quick and unexplained disappearances of seemingly ongoing characters are certainly not unheard of in *The L Word*, the elimination of genderqueer characters from the narrative would seem to resonate with an approach to production that is conscious of appealing to potentially homophobic or transphobic viewers—offering an "issue of the week" aesthetic to genderqueer characters and identities. This is extended to having each of these characters narrativized through the perspective of a primary, gender-normative character (Alice/Kit).

Such recourse to the body occurs not only with secondary characters Lisa and Ivan, but also with the ongoing transgender character Max. Like Lisa and Ivan, Max is originally introduced as a romantic interest for a primary character (in this case Jenny), and this affects the extent to which the audience can be given a direct representation of this character. Introduced in 2006, shortly before the ENDA bill was initially proposed, Max is an interesting case study of the series' attitudes towards transgenderism. Historical representations of transgender characters on-screen have frequently been demonizing, with these characters represented "as either killer, sexual predator, or deranged psychopath" (Rigney 2003: 4). Even later, more positive representations, such as that seen in *Boys Don't Cry* (1999), still fit transgender individuals into a modality of victimhood. As an ongoing character in a queer-centered television series, the character of Max promised a different scenario. Introduced in season three, when the series was already well established, the initial episodes surrounding the character engaged with some key issues faced by transgender and genderqueer people. These included potential violence during a stopover as Jenny and Max traveled to Los Angeles from the Midwest, as well as facing the attitudes of *The L Word*'s lesbian community (see, for example, Carmen's immediate and vocal dislike of Max).

Following his initial introduction in season three, however, Max's character arc changes. As soon as his transgenderism becomes a non-issue, has lost its "issue of the week" status, he seems to disappear into the background, primarily reappearing in roles that are supportive to the major characters. While this kind of absent-present character positioning was not unique to Max within *The L Word*, one wonders if the character ceased to be interesting to the writers after this storyline was complete, in the famous fashion of queer characters brought into a series in order to come out, face the reactions of others and then leave again. Or was this due to a desire not to diminish focus on the lesbian narratives out of concern that "too much otherness" would be detrimental?

Regardless of the reasons behind it, the representation of Max did not deviate from the previously criticized depiction of genderqueer characters Ivan and Lisa. A scene from "Lez Girls" (4:5), featuring Max, mirrors the gender undressing undertaken with Ivan in season two. As I have written previously (2007), the episode opens with a scene of Max undressing in front of a mirror. This scene could have been utilized to great effect to undermine conventional and ideologically ascribed notions of sex as naturally dimorphic, by demonstrating the real-life masculinizing effects that hormone therapy can have on an ostensibly female body. Indeed, if *The L Word* had wished to make an attempt at realism in its depiction of a transgendered man who has undergone hormone treatment, it could have utilized digital technology to superimpose Sea's head onto the body of a real-life transman. Instead, we see Sea's clearly female body, and the camera focuses on a hairless chest (unlikely given the amount of testosterone Max is reputed to take), breasts, and even freshly waxed legs. This narratively unnecessary scene acts as if to deliberately reaffirm viewers' skepticism of transsexuality, suggesting that Max *really* is a woman. This acknowledgment of "womanness" is implied as necessary for him to defend a female colleague, as he proceeds to do later in the episode. Once again, this can be seen as a mediated representation, one in which the depiction of a transgendered man can only take place in this popular cultural format if it is seen to offer a voyeuristic insight, and play into dominant conventions of gendered representation.[5]

The very real capacity for bodily transformations between genders is undermined by such a scene, which implies that gender transitions are purely performative, and can be taken on and off like a set of clothing. For those viewers with little other knowledge or experience of transgendered individuals, this is both an inaccurate and a troubling message to send, and reflects that the educational elements *The L Word* offers to its audience about lesbianism do not extend to transgendered characters and identities.

This is part of a tradition of representing transgender men in which "The female (and feminized) body must be kept under control, rigidly stylized, and differentiated from that of the male/masculine body" (Rigney 2003: 7). This quotation could almost have been written of *The L Word*, which displays such "rigidly stylized" bodies regularly, and in fact promotes the show on this basis (as can be seen in group publicity shots for each season). That the producers were unable to show a hairy-chested Max (or even one with unshaven legs) is part of the series' need to permanently and irrevocably differentiate maleness and femaleness as a binary pair, and then place transgender men on the side of the female. This demonstrates that *The L Word*'s view of gender is based upon an antiquated culturo-scientific tradition that fails to take into consideration not only the gendered diversity that is seen both among humans and other species,[6] but also medical advances that allow more complete sexual transformations than were previously possible.

Indeed, *The L Word* is almost at pains to ensure that the permeability of the border between genders is erased, via regular reminders of Max's physical body. This occurs not only via the scene in "Lez Girls," but also via constant reinforcement on the part of other characters. For example, Max is portrayed as aggressive and violent during his initial transition (see "Latecomer," 3:8)—his body, and its hormonal changes, seem to have overtaken his otherwise gentle nature. While early transition is certainly an emotional time due to hormonal changes, by focusing upon this element, and also on his treatment of girlfriend Jenny, which quickly goes from sensitive to aggressive, instead of on his own feelings regarding this intense time, *The L Word* casts a negative light upon transition from female to male. It renders the interior experience of transition irrelevant despite its rich potential as a plot device, instead relocating this experience within the realm of the character's relationship with, and indeed domestic abuse of, a woman.

Furthermore, Max is on multiple occasions called upon to defend his transition—almost as if he needs to justify his identity to women, who appear to view his gender identity as some kind of betrayal that requires explanation, in a fashion reminiscent of such authors as Janice Raymond (1980). Examples of such conversations include Max's interaction with Dana Fairbanks in "Latecomer" (3:8), with Kit in "Lead, Follow, or Get Out of the Way" (3:9), and even with new romantic prospect Grace in "Lacy Lilting Lyrics" (4:9). This is perhaps indicative of what Reed observes (2009: 177): "Even as the show steadily de-queers Max, it distances itself from Max's straight FTM position. The perspective of the show, through the point of view of major characters, leaves Max sitting uncomfortably in hegemonic masculinity." A perception of FTM masculinity as unproblematically hegemonic fails to account for the very real experience of many transgender men who never experience any kind of male privilege, and indeed are key victims of hate crimes. The assumption that Max is able to attain male privilege in the world of *The L Word* is additionally made laughable by the costuming and voice of the character, which would make passing as male extremely difficult at best.

In this post-postmodern age, having been through the sex wars and years of queer politics, why this constant definition of sexuality and gender identity in relation to physical birth-gender? For is not lesbianism itself—the feature, topic, and title of *The L Word*—in contradiction with what the majority of the world's inhabitants would consider natural and gender normative? Are we not past this by now? If *The L Word* is anything to go by, it seems we are not, and this dimorphic view of gender is a boundary too firm to cross.

Some might ask, how is one television series to represent such a diversity of identities and still remain coherent? Which makes it particularly curious as to why *The L Word* writers and producers did not choose to include a male-to-female lesbian transsexual, rather than the female-to-male Max. Such a character would have allowed more flexibility for a representation of transgender identity to be integrated into the lesbian "world" it features: such a character could even potentially be a romantic prospect for one of the existing lesbian characters. By including a female-to-male character instead, *The L Word* effectively sidelined the transgendered character from the dialectic of lust and melodrama that held the series together. As Reed (177) puts it, Max "is available for babysitting, moving help, and computer searches, but he holds no sexual charm on a show driven by sexual energy. He is clearly not part of the lesbian community anymore." Surely in an era where an openly transgender actress can play a transgendered character in prime-time on Disney-owned ABC (granted commencing in 2007 during the fifth season of *The L Word*—see Baber 2008), a cable series dedicated to representing the queer community could do better than including a transgendered character as some kind of odd-job handyman, who only appears in the series from time to time.

Whether this was simply a narrative choice, inspired perhaps by the increasing awareness within lesbian communities of the time of an FTM transgenderism, or a conscious decision not to include a transgender lesbian whose relationships may have sparked complaints from some elements of the lesbian fanbase, is difficult to determine. Perhaps this character choice was again seen as a "necessary compromise" caused by a perception that audiences would be less comfortable with viewing an MTF transgendered character than an FTM one. While transgendered lesbian characters have occasionally appeared in film texts, such as in the enormously successful *Better than Chocolate* (Canada; Anne Wheeler, 1999), television's female transsexual characters have generally been presented as heterosexual.

Or was this choice of characters perhaps a deliberate political decision? There are certainly gestures in these representations towards *The L Word* inhabiting a political modality that I have identified previously in relation to other aspects of *The L Word*, of a politics more akin to lesbian-feminist separatist politics than to the kinds of inclusionist practices more common in contemporary times. While the characters of *The L Word* never visited the Michigan Womyn's Music Festival (MWMF) (certainly an event that would display some very different kinds of lesbian bodies and identities than the slim, trimmed, shiny face of L due to its lesbian-feminist heritage and associations) one cannot help but wonder whether similar exclusions occur in this case. MWMF's policy of not allowing transgender women access to the women-only event implies a patronizing attitude that the event coordinators know better about what really constitutes someone's gender identity than that person themselves. And this is certainly what we also see in *The L Word*, where all the major characters seem to feel entitled to freely express even negative opinions about Max's identity.

No doubt inspired by real-life transman Thomas Beatie, who gained media prominence in 2008 due to his pregnancy, Max's key storyline in the final season of the series is that of an unwanted pregnancy. Unlike Beatie, whose chosen pregnancy undermined dominant conceptions of maleness and femaleness, Max is depicted as ensnared in his pregnancy, trapped by the residual femaleness of his body, completely without agency. In his homosexual relationship with the gay sign-language interpreter, Tom Mater, Max not only becomes pregnant, but also does not realize this until it is too late to have an abortion performed. Clearly not a lot of research was undertaken for this storyline, as prevailing medical knowledge (Gorton, Buth, and Spade 2005: 58) specifies that it is necessary for a transgender man to cease taking testosterone in order to become pregnant:

> If a transgender man has not undergone oophorectomy, he may regain fertility on cessation of testosterone. … However, with the ovarian changes produced by long-term androgen therapy it may require months of cessation of testosterone and possibly assistive reproductive technology to regain fertility and, if desired, become pregnant.

Max has certainly been depicted as taking testosterone for longer than the few months required for fertility to cease, and it is also not suggested that he has gone off his testosterone at this point. Instead, he is depicted as expressing a clueless surprise that such a thing is possible, while he is chastised for being so foolish as not to use birth control.

This is perhaps *The L Word*'s most grievous example of associating transsexual men with the female body, and Max ends the series alone and pregnant with a child he does not desire to carry or raise—a strange fate for one of the longest-running transgender male characters on television. Just as occurred during his transition, Max's pregnancy causes him to once again become aggressive towards his partner, this time Tom (6:4). The effect of hormones is depicted as eliminating all rationality in Max, and more curiously so because Tina was not depicted in this fashion when she was pregnant and also going through hormonal changes. Such differential depictions do not gesture only towards the differences between intentional and accidental pregnancies, but to a naturalized, essentialized view of gender and reproduction that places a positive experience of pregnancy firmly in female hands. It also offers a curiously heterosexualized view of sexual relationships between a gay man and a bisexual man (albeit with female genitalia). Such a perspective of associating Max with the female body also explains the curious throwaway fashion in which the narrative shifted from Max's proposed mastectomy.

Perhaps the most visually disturbing scene in relation to Max over the course of *The L Word*'s run is that of the Willy Wonka-themed baby shower Jenny arranges for Max (in "Lactose Intolerant," 6:6). Even here, the primary narrative purpose of this scene is to allow Jenny to be portrayed as "malicious" (Alice) and "completely and totally evil" (Bette), and thus give various characters a motive for her murder in the final episode. During this sequence, a clearly uncomfortable Max is subjected to a variety of party games, including the measuring of his pregnant belly. While it is a scene ostensibly about Max, and it seems the audience will finally get to find out more about Max's inner world, it is more clearly about the lesbian characters and their interpersonal relationships. Max is barely allowed to speak, and is shown as terrified when the women start discussing childbirth, asking questions that display a lack of knowledge and education about the mechanics of the situation, and is again placed in the position of being educated by the more powerful female characters.

During this scene, the women, and Jenny in particular, show little sensitivity to Max's clear discomfort with the way in which the pregnancy reconfigures his body, and even exhort him to breastfeed. With the kitsch, pseudo-childlike decorations inspired by the 2005 Tim Burton adaptation of *Charlie and the Chocolate Factory*, and Max clad by the women in a purple coat and top hat, allusions are drawn between Max and Johnny Depp in his performance as Willy Wonka. The somewhat creepy, mentally unstable and slightly effeminate nature of the character as played by Depp is drawn into viewers' perceptions of Max during this scene. Just like Wonka, Max is isolated from the population of the real, surrounded by, and seemingly dependent on, individuals who care little about him. Max's discomfort, and that of the viewer, is palpable in this scene, which serves to infantilize the character, undermining his masculinity and reclassifying him as "mother." Max's pregnancy, most clearly and grotesquely represented through this scene, functions as "a graphic visual assertion of who is 'male' and who is 'female'" (Rigney 2003: 9).

The scene, through a zoom in on his panicked face, implies that the reality of the situation is dawning on Max. He soon thereafter is shown topless in an extended pedestal shot that moves from his swollen stomach up to his enlarged breasts. After staring into the mirror, Max proceeds to shave his face, consenting finally to removing his only obvious signification of gender ambiguity in order to placate societal mores that insist on biology over identity. This gesture, perhaps more than any other in the series, demonstrates a reluctant yet firm affirmation that some societal boundaries are unable to be crossed: that it is necessary to abide by certain rules in order to gain acceptance. From a narrative perspective, this episode seals the fate of Max: to subsume his own identity as a man in the face of disapproval from the lesbian community as represented by the major characters of *The L Word*.

"Lactose Intolerant" was first screened in February 2009, the same year as the ENDA bill was reintroduced and *The L Word* concluded its six-year run. This time, the bill included gender identity as a protected category along with sexual orientation. That such an alteration took place over the course of only two years is indicative both of the hard work undertaken by the transgender community and their allies, and also of a certain cultural shift, no doubt at least somewhat facilitated by increasing representational prominence. For during *The L Word*'s five-year run, television slowly began to include transgendered characters in more positive ways than were previously apparent. Many of these took the form of biographical narratives, such as *Opposite Sex: Jamie's Story* and *Opposite Sex: Rene's Story* (Showtime 2004), *Danny: Escaping My Female Body* (BBC 2007), and two reality television series: *Transgenerations* (Sundance 2005), a six-part reality television show about the lives of a diverse group of four transgendered college students; and *Transamerican Love Story* (Logo 2008), a Bachelor-like dating show, in which, unlike its forerunners such as *There's Something About Miriam* (Sky 1 2004), contestants were aware of Calpernia Addams's gender history prior to signing on. While representation in scripted series has perhaps been more ambiguous, transgendered characters have featured on *Dirty Sexy Money* (ABC 2007–2009) and *Ugly Betty* (ABC 2006–2010), with transgender characters also appearing in one-off episodes of *Two and a Half Men*, and *Queer Eye for the Straight Guy*. Even *Oprah* has screened an episode featuring transgender families (October 12, 2007).

Within such a context, why such timidity on the part of *The L Word*? Looking back at the series, now a franchise with conventions, accessories, and even a reality spin-off (Schneider 2009: 1), was this popularity attained at the cost of problematic attitudes towards transgender representation? And was this perhaps, like the original ENDA bill, a deliberate measure, born of a perception that a more positive attitude towards transgendered individuals would compromise the pro-lesbian-rights agenda of the series? Calls for more diverse kinds of queer representation on *The L Word* were often countered with the contention that such diversity would not, as Frank might put it (in Keen 2009: 13), be "helpful to us in getting the [audiences] to get it through" (to either network or viewers). With the revisions to the ENDA bill, and implied acceptance that gay and lesbian rights should not come at the exclusion of transgender rights, does this new attitude now extend to representation? When will television be ready for The T(ransgender) Word? For as we look at where transgender representation on television today stands, it is much where lesbian and gay representation was twenty years ago. Within such a context, one must look at *The L Word*'s tentative steps with Max, forwards and back, and hope for a brighter future for transgendered representation on television. Here's to waiting for *The T Word*.

Notes

1   See Elizabeth Jensen (2006: C5).
2   See James Hibberd (2005).
3   "Cisgender" refers to non-transgendered individuals.
4   This scene and relationship is discussed by Kim Akass and Janet McCabe in "What is a Straight Girl to Do?" (2006).
5   See also Beirne, "Lesbian Pulp Television" (2007).
6   See Bruce Bagemihl (1999).

The End of *The L Word*: Fan Pleasure or Fan Pain?

Faye Davies

Whenever a successful TV series ends, fans react in a variety of ways; with nostalgia, sadness or even anger. The end of *The L Word* (Chaiken 2004–2009) was no exception. A reaction from lesbian viewers was understandable; after all *The L Word* was *the* seminal lesbian drama series of the early Noughties. From its first broadcast, and given its representation and narrative, many lesbian fans considered the show was about them and, perhaps more importantly, *for* them. Speaking personally, this was an exciting time—a lesbian show with lesbian characters at the heart of the narrative! Given that the show generated excitement and intrigue among gay, lesbian, and straight audiences, but ended with more of a blip than a bang, it is important and relevant to explore the fan reactions to the cancellation and ending of the show.

This chapter explores fan reactions to the end of the show, and seeks to understand why viewers, unhappy with its cancellation, continued to watch, even if it was through gritted teeth and with trepidation about the direction of *The L Word*'s final season. To achieve some understanding of audience pleasures and anti-pleasures I looked to Showtime's fan forum (http://www.sho.com/site/lword/interrogation.do). What became apparent from an analysis of postings and responses is that any enjoyment of the series came from non-traditional viewing perspectives that embraced the openness of the storyline or a celebration of the lesbian culture the show generally portrayed. The celebratory position was rare on the forum. Instead there were more negative posters who framed their lack of enjoyment within what they considered was the increasingly consumerist nature of the show's production. But what is interesting is that viewers kept on watching, even though a number of them were not particularly enjoying the storylines or final outcome of the series.

This particular forum was useful because it was consistently used by fans and was focused solely on the show. The forum contained 11,980 posts up to March 1, 2010. Other forums online did have a general show focus but often discussed other matters related to the lifestyle of lesbians and so would detract from the subject at hand. The forum was located on the Showtime website where the weekly appearances of the season six "interrogation tapes" were hosted and these also form the topic of some of the analysis of audience readings of the final season. These "tapes" (even though they were of little use in terms of storyline!) followed on from the season finale and generated animated discussion online.

What became immediately apparent on the forum was that the fan relationship with the show had soured somewhat in the light of what were perceived as rather odd storyline developments in season six. It became clear that some lesbian fans were immensely disappointed with the lack of an answer to "who killed Jenny?"[1] They were instead rewarded with a return to the traditional lesbian screen death seen throughout film and television history and discussed widely through the work of Russo (1987), Wilton (1995), and Tropiano (2002) among others. Some viewers felt this portrayed lesbians as untrustworthy at best and murderous at worst. This is interesting, as such a focus emphasizes how the cultural and social experience of lesbians can impact on what they actually want from television portrayals of lesbian life. Perhaps it can be posited then that the initial and distinct focus on social and cultural issues which impact on the lesbian community fueled the need in *The L Word*'s lesbian audience to feel considered by producers in the closure of the final story arc. Initially this could also have been due to a general lack of lesbian-focused drama and positive portrayal in the media.

After noting this key mood change I really wanted to uncover why lesbian audiences kept watching *The L Word*, and why they felt the need to comment and vent their thoughts on the show in, often, vehement ways. What was clear from my initial reading of the forums is that there were clear trends around the declining enjoyment of the series and expectations from lesbian viewers to see positive lesbian characters and culture on-screen. What is blatantly obvious though is that this audience was "active," showing key insights into production contexts and cultural politics. The notion of the active viewer is one long held in the cultural studies tradition. Stuart Hall (1997) argued that the cultural background of an individual media consumer impacts upon their reading and understanding of a media text. With regard to *The L Word* varying readings of the text are expressed through postings by "cult" fans who often critique, and display annoyance, with producers via online spaces (Hills 2002). This makes the focus on an online discussion board useful for exploring these propositions, as it provides detailed and relatively easily available data.

"I thought it was an excellent finale"

As stated earlier, it was quite clear when reading the forums that viewers were generally unhappy with the end of season six both during and after broadcast. But there were a small number of postings which did show that viewers found some pleasure in the ending of the show, and attempted to be fairly positive about the general existence of *The L Word*, rather than the much-maligned plotlines of season six. There were distinct reasons alluded to when discussing how the finale of the show was a pleasurable event,

> I thought it was an excellent finale. I think it was true to life – you can't have things neatly wrapped up – that is why I like the L Word so much because it seems real to me. The relationships aren't perfect, the friendships are up and down and each character you like and dislike.
>
> BBNash, March 11, 2009

> I think we all feel this a great series and we all would love more … but why does a series have to answer questions for you. Leave it to your imagination. Great job by the writers!! [sic].
>
> Jeremy, March 12, 2009

Postings similar to these support the point that a few fans enjoyed the non-traditional ending that *The L Word* gave to us, where the narrative around the death of Jenny Schecter was left open and unanswered. These viewers embraced the sense of "realism" that the lack of answers provided. They define this by comparing it to the kind of realism they experience in their own lives, one that is ongoing and doesn't give resolution to every problem. What was most important to these viewers was that the lack of resolution is vastly different from the so-called classic realist narrative that has all loose ends tied up and gives answers to any ideological questions. It differs from the theoretical understanding of media realism that "imposes coherence and resolution on a world which has neither" (Fiske 1987: 105). For these particular members of the audience the final season's pleasures are related to *The L Word* being what we could term a "writerly text" (Fiske 1987: 75) that allows them to continue in online discussions and fantasize about what actually happened to any of the characters. They embrace being able to use their imaginations to end the series for themselves and celebrate the openness of the storyline. This is also perhaps reflective of the growing culture of fan fiction about contemporary television drama and a sense that the text continues on beyond its initial network run.

Those viewers who did appreciate the lack of traditional closure arguably reflect a postmodern viewing position, as this particular season of *The L Word* seems to "eschew the codes and conventions of realism and narrative" and has a "significant tendency to tinker with television's earlier and more sacred realist traditions" (Calvert 2008: 172). Although rare, this pleasure in non-narrative closure appears to be a growing aspect of contemporary television and mirrors approaches to narrative seen in *Twin Peaks* (Lavery 1995) and, more recently, *The Sopranos* (Miklitsch 2006). Nevertheless, these pleasures appear to be limited to small numbers of the audience analyzed in the case of *The L Word*.

Postings also seemed to show that viewers liked the ability of the show to create discussion and draw attention to both itself and lesbian culture, and it didn't seem to matter whether this attention was positive or negative. It was clear that some forum contributors believed this made both the series and executive producer Ilene Chaiken an "artistic" success.

> You really need to respect the artist's concept for the L Word. Like it or not, and obviously we loved the series!! And whether you approved of the ending, it has gotten more comments and attention which is what any artist wants [sic].
>
> Aimee Gaston-voss, May 5, 2009

Ileen Chaiken says to form you own opinion about the end. I think the last season was a creative jump that stands alone. It was intriguing, earth-shattering but what can I say, it mirrored life and sometimes there are no happy endings [sic].

Lucas DeLeon, May 14, 2009

Again, these fans celebrate the openness of the storyline and also take real pleasure in Chaiken's online interview (Showtime 2009a [online]) where she encourages viewers to make their own decisions about the end of the show. Posters refer to Chaiken's artistic creativity, as though she is an auteur who has produced something unique and groundbreaking in terms of both television drama and lesbian representation. These postings celebrate Chaiken as a creator and a producer who is creatively unique. In order to help explain this sort of audience position Jonathan Bignell (2004) considers why contemporary audiences refer to television in this supposed critically aware way. He links this to what he also regards as the contemporary nature of an audience's experience of televisual culture. Taking this point as a foundation I would argue that these postings reinforce the position that "everyone is now a critic." Television is so much a part of viewers' lives. It is also relevant to consider that, due to technological advances online, public spaces have become available for them to express a critical position. The very existence of online discussion forums makes viewers and fans feel like reviewers with opinions worthy of being shared and in this very act they find pleasure. Television in particular is discussed so widely and heavily that it has become part of an artistic discourse.

"... be grateful we had 6 years of 'our moment in the sun.'"

In terms of what lesbian viewers enjoyed about the show, their pleasures were focused more on the visibility of lesbians on television than on particular issues of narrative. Lesbian visibility, support, encouragement, and a sense of community are matters that are politically and culturally important to lesbians in contemporary western culture, especially as lesbians have a relatively recent emerging identity in mainstream culture.

LEAVE ILENE ALONE!!! yall should be happy we even had a series devoted to us ... just thank ilene and all the beautiful people for making this happen [sic].

kms, March 12, 2009

Who cares "who killed Jenny"? Get on with real life and be grateful we had 6 years of "our moment in the sun."

Barb, March 11, 2009

These were typical comments and suggested that whilst it was understandable for both lesbian and straight viewers to be disappointed and angered with the lack of a solid story, for lesbian viewers there was a factor that should never be forgotten: that *The L Word* centered on lesbian characters as its main focus. The defense of executive producer, Ilene Chaiken, was focused on her bringing, arguably, the first lesbian ensemble drama to mainstream television screens. Although it can be argued that lesbian audiences have had a number of overtly lesbian characters to identify with since the early 1990s, and many of these representations dealt with lesbian topics and, more usually, problems (Becker 2004b), *The L Word* differed from other prime-time shows in that it focused on "lesbian life" and everyday culture. Lesbian characters are not just an add-on to the show to be tortured about their sexuality or disappear after a single supplementary storyline. *The L Word* managed to get beyond the treatment of lesbianism as a social problem, issue or deviation from the norm. Lesbians on the forum celebrated this. Arguably, this perspective demonstrates that the show was both a (sub-) cultural success and, for Showtime, a successful commercial entity representing lesbians in a prime-time narrowcasting environment.

The pleasure for lesbian audience members was not just in the watching of the show, but also in its impact and integration into their own lives. Much of the enjoyment seems to have been linked to personal experience and this can be explained through Hall's claim that the decoding of media texts can be related to audiences' understanding of "meaningful discourse" through their own "frameworks of knowledge" (Hall 2006). The gratification of the viewers quoted is often explained in postings via their own social experiences. This seems to add to their sense of inclusion and exclusion in both lesbian culture and wider society. Specifically, many audience members described how the show allowed them to begin a discussion of their sexuality with family members, how it encouraged them to "come out" publicly, even relating the show to their own acceptance of their sexuality.

> I just want to thank the L word because it was a show I got into as I came into my acceptence of being gay. I relate most to Phylis confused all her life and than discovering something that she never saw before. Watching this show with my partner of now almost two years has been so wonderful [sic].
>
> Suzy Yaqub, April 29, 2009

> But I have to admit that it played an enormously huge role in my life ... You guys pulled me out of the closet and continuously giving me courage to be out [sic].
>
> Ryuuen Zhou, May 1, 2009

These postings exemplify audience pleasures that came from "experiencing" *The L Word* as a site of recognition, identification, and community support rather than just a television show. They suggest that *The L Word* was important because it made lesbianism acceptable, everyday, and normal. This certainly seems to be the case in a posting from another lesbian viewer who responds with vitriol to a fellow poster's claims that the representation of lesbians in *The L Word* lacks diversity.

> There is no way to depict every "kind of lesbian relationship and every lifestyle" and to believe so is extremely closed minded. What this show succeeded in doing is presenting lesbians to people who had no access to them. And shame on you for thinking to deny them. This show has been a life line to many people. People like me, who grew up in the bible belt, who were taught that homosexuality would damn us. In short go fix your screwed up relationship and stop hating [sic].
>
> J.R., March 16, 2009

Pleasure for this viewer is explained through a solid understanding of the limits of any kind of representation on television. Clearly this poster understands that representations are framed, selected, and constructed by television producers, and that they can never be "realistic" for every viewer's individual experience. This viewer finds comfort in the support and acceptance *The L Word* offered in the form of a challenge to the social experience of religion that they had personally encountered. Arguably the pleasure here was one that was formed from *The L Word*'s production of a representation of lesbianism that expanded and added to the viewer's existing experience. In a Foucauldian sense, this could be seen as a challenge to "force relations" (Hekman 1996) or what can be termed dominant stereotypes and ideas about homosexuality. For this viewer *The L Word* was a welcome addition and challenge to the society in which she existed, an important change in how she considered her own lesbian sexuality.

"I've never felt more betrayed as an L word fan"

There were a number of very negative responses to the end of *The L Word*. But my purpose in discussing these points is not to engage in an argument about whether or not *The L Word* is a good or bad TV show. Instead, I seek to understand the reasons for negative audience readings, or what we could see as anti-pleasures explained through a socio-political and commercial context. What actually became evident was that viewers had to put aside their anger and negativity about various production issues in order to continue to watch *The L Word* and still enjoy it.

As mentioned previously, the negative commentary on the forum is focused distinctly on the narrative and character development of season six. This is a vastly different focus from the previously discussed positive posters, who commented less on the actual TV show and more on the "bigger picture" of *The L Word*. Much of the anger about the show was anchored in the lack of resolution around the death of Jenny Schecter. This was due to the promotional material that promised: "This season one of our favorites will take her last breath ... and one of her friends will take the fall" (Showtime 2009b: [online]).

Both straight and lesbian viewers alike shared an angry response to the lack of closure:

... although only a recent (straight) fan (have only seen 2 seasons, all in 2 months!), i am tremendously disappointed in this lazy, imitation sopranos ending. i don't need everything wrapped up tidily, but when your tagline for the season is "who killed jenny schecter?" i expect and await the answer with glee. this was the complete opposite of glee, i feel totally ripped off and i've never seen a worse series finale [sic].

spitfire, March 12, 2009

How could such a "break through" show that helped so many people be shown in this world. Have a place, come out, and be even more proud than we were before end like this? There are soooo many more questions than anwsers. I've never felt more betrayed as an L word fan [sic].

Yoziie, March 16, 2009

What seems to fuel anger in these instances is a betrayal of audience expectations. Of course, serial drama has generic qualities that typically put off complete narrative closure and "happily ever after" stock conclusions. This is usually considered the best way of keeping the audience interested and watching. And it appears that *The L Word* managed to maintain interest through the expectation that questions would eventually be answered, rather than merely posed by the end of the final season. The subsequent lack of closure to that particular narrative strand caused the audience to feel cheated and led astray by the well-advertised plotline. The audience still wanted resolution after the end of the show:

"Can't you just have like a miny series to rap it up?" [sic].

Let Down, March 12, 2009

There were many posts asking Showtime and Ilene Chaiken for an *L Word* movie or for the series to continue, suggesting that viewers wanted the comfort and clarity found in the usual "season finale" of serial drama. One way to read this is that the producers had fulfilled the generic quality of narrative deferment excellently and had left their audiences wanting more. Sadly for the audience this was at the wrong time in the lifespan of the show: the end. A possible explanation for this production decision, and for the posters' request that *The L Word* continued in some form, may be found with Mary Ellen Brown, who writes, "Resistance to narrative closure provides an opening for speculation by auditors as well as by creators as to how the case itself may be reopened" (1990: 56). Thus, not only did the open ending offer a potential comeback for the producers; it also fueled a fan call for continuation of the series. There was still a curious group available for the producers' commercial focus.

Interestingly, many audience members vocalized this particular viewpoint of why such a narrative decision had been made in the case of *The L Word* and why they had been subject to such a mass narrative deferral. This, for me, highlights the notion of the "savvy" television viewer who isn't merely concerned with the broadcast of his or her favorite television show, but also wants answers as to why certain production decisions are made in the broadcast, thus demonstrating a growing general awareness of the commercial imperative in relation to broadcasting among television audiences.

But the decision to leave the show open has potentially backfired in a commercial sense as a number of the savviest fans made it clear that this experience would stop them from consuming any further productions related to *The L Word*:

> As you sit back, calculate residuals, begin scripting the now inevitable film and spin-off series, and gloat over what a fantastic money-maker your little "stunt" has proved, I hope you're well satisfied with yourselves.
>
> Who cares if loyal fans have been sorely disappointed, who cares about artistic integrity, heck, who cares about the communities you were supposedly meant to represent— all have been sold out in favor of the Almighty Dollar. Now, the "L" word is, apparently, "lemmings," as we are supposed to continue blindly following you (while you swoon over the incredible number of website hits) in desperate hopes that we just *might* get the answers we crave. Thanks for playing us for suckers—makes me feel oh so warm and fuzzy for having dedicated six seasons-worth of my time to you.
>
> Anyone else thinking that a boycott might be in order?
>
> S, March 15, 2009

What is interesting about this particular strand of audience reaction is the clear criticism of commercialism. The fans who express these kinds of opinions want to know if they are being primed for further commercial opportunities. They want an explanation and they feel maligned. Many fans and audience members understand the nature of the commercially driven television industry and this is seemingly acceptable to most fans much of the time. But what makes this particular viewer angry is that s/he feels the decision not to reward fans with the typical closed ending has a *purely* commercial motive. Furthermore, a number of postings described Chaiken as "calculating" and driven by the need for the prison-based spin-off pilot "The Farm" to be picked up by Showtime (it was subsequently rejected by the cable broadcaster). The reason for dissatisfaction is that fans feel that their viewer loyalty has been fruitless in terms of their own satisfaction.

> Then after all of the money we as people have spent on buying these seasons, you would screw with it so badly that you go away from the original backbone of what the series portrayed. I am completely writing off anything else that comes out from these people [sic].
>
> Karen Rogers, December 29, 2009

Some audience members outline that they will no longer participate in the commercial aspect of *The L Word* in terms of buying DVDs, merchandise or subscriptions to Showtime. Their response is to punish the producers in the only way they know how. In these instances the producer–viewer relationship has failed. This highlights some interesting considerations made by audiences in a narrowcasting and commercial "pay for access" environment. These fans believe that they have power, particularly as they can withdraw their subscription, interest, and investments in merchandise when they feel disregarded or unrewarded with the kind of well-rounded narratives that they consider essential in a quality television product.

> Yes, I agree. No Movie. I would have loved to have an L-Word movie before I saw the ending. But seeing the ending and seeing this last season would lead me to have serious reservations about the quality of the movie.
>
> Lynn, March 16, 2009

This is one distinct example of the problem of studying fans and represents the mercurial consequences of betrayal after heavy investment in the text. This, according to Matt Hills, gives rise to the

traditional notion of the "resistive" fan or cultist. *The L Word* fans quoted
are devoted to the text and have very particular expectations. Any
deviation from that expectation is at the peril of producers, as they will
disrupt the very trust "placed in the continuity of a detailed narrative
world" (Hills 2002: 28). Still, as Hills further explains, such a position
doesn't allow for the consideration of a fan culture that appears to be
commercially averse and yet still continues to participate in commercial
activity in relation to the chosen text. What is most interesting about
the discussion board is that for as many fans who expressed that they
wouldn't continue to consume or be involved in *The L Word* in an
economic sense, there were those who outlined their unhappiness but
also admitted they would participate in the merchandising and any
further productions, even if the position was a little contradictory!

> Ilene seems to know that most people will take anything at this
> point, Jessica, and that's the problem … I refuse to pay for a movie
> when I was led all season to believe that there would be a resolution
> during the last show. I will also be getting rid of SHO if they are
> not going to air The Farm.
>
> Facebook user, May 4, 2009

The wider context of this posting shows that the decision made by
this poster appears to be based on the reasoning that there is so little
lesbian-focused television material available. Although they have had
their fill of *The L Word* they do want to see a pick-up of a related TV
series. This was justified as being due to the significant amount of
investment through time (six years) that fans had made in the show.
However it is certainly arguable that such fan responses should be a
consideration for commercial producers in a continually fragmented
media market where there are more products competing for audiences
in terms of viewing figures, subscription, and merchandising.

Other reasons for negativity towards the show were based much
more around issues of lesbian identity. What further compounded the
sense of betrayal for many fans of the show was the fact that it was
about lesbians, and they considered it should have been "for" lesbians.

> Is that really what you all want, for the show to go on? We all know
> now that season six is a segue to the farm, which is why it doesnt
> make any fucking sense. Ilene Chaiken doenst give a shit about you,

dont give her any more money to make any more rediculous drivel. I realise we will all miss the characters but i think that credit is more due the actors, not the 'Masterbatory opus' that the L word eventually became. Ilene Chaiken has shown that she doesnt need us, we have to realise that and move on. something else will come along, and we will now be ready for it, but thats all the credit she deserves [sic].

adele, March 13, 2009

The excerpt above suggests that although Chaiken is "one of us" (in a lesbian sense), now that she is successful she no longer needs "us." The very terms of reference used by the poster suggest some sort of "break up," which is emotional but has to be faced! There is a critique of the sexualization of the show as it continued and a sense that lesbians now need to actively look elsewhere for their community to be represented in what constitutes a more satisfactory fashion. For this poster, her lover has become more interested in other matters and she's never going to have her needs fulfilled in this symbolic partnership.

Chaiken is discussed in many of these vitriolic postings as individualistic and commercially driven, using the final season of *The L Word* to advertise and promote her new pilot. But what is clear is that the majority of these negative postings contain a sense of betrayal that further compounds the sense of community lost and disconnection from *The L Word*. There seems to be the rather unique expectation that Chaiken, as a lesbian, should have focused on the community, and that an ethical and thoughtful lesbian representation should have been at the forefront of her mind. For some it seems that betrayal has placed her outside of the lesbian community on a number of levels:

Way to piss off every lesbian on Planet Earth. Good job, Chaiken. I'm sure you'll EASILY be able to find more work again in this community. *eyeroll* [sic].

Krystina Kraus, May 20, 2009

Ilene Chaiken responded to this perspective during *The Final Word: The End of The L Word* hosted by Showtime's website (Showtime 2009a), stating that she didn't intend for the show to be purely aimed at a lesbian audience as this would marginalize its appeal and, one would assume, its potential for pulling in a wider audience. For these posters, her comments indicate that the lesbian community was not at the top of Chaiken's priority list, something that many find shocking. This potentially led to Chaiken's further ostracization—something that the release of the "interrogation tapes" only fueled further.

"... why are you violating us with these tapes?"

Postings to the Showtime forum evidence a detailed understanding of wider narratives and more traditional and accepted ideological representations of lesbians in both cinema and film. As noted earlier, the history of homosexuality in film is well summarized in a variety of key gay- and lesbian-focused historiographies and theoretical frameworks such as Russo (1987), Tropiano (2002), and Wilton (1995). What is pertinent about notations on Hollywood representation is that lesbianism was often constructed as perverse, murderous, and often the cause of suicide until the early 1990s. In relation to these representations many audience members of *The L Word* signaled dismay at similar negative characterizations within the broadcast version of season six and also in the follow-up "interrogation tapes" which appeared on the Showtime official website for a few weeks following the end of the season. This is rather surprising given the ongoing success of the show and prior warm reception by lesbian audiences.

One particular issue that related to the end of *The L Word* concerned the characterization of lead characters as potential murderers. For some this was a clear move backwards in terms of lesbian representation, constructing lesbians as unbalanced, vengeful, and angry.

> Thank you Ilene Chaiken, for turning the women we could relate to into murderers. By leaving your little "whodunnit" question unanswered, that's what you essentially did.
>
> Facebook user, May 9, 2009

For these viewers the potential for one of the characters to be murdered by a lesbian was unacceptable. The comment above corroborated a high number of postings that clearly objected to Chaiken's construction of lesbians as at best unbalanced in a variety of ways and at worst as potential thieves, cheats, and killers. For the lesbian audience the fact that there was no narrative resolution to the actions of the characters and no explanation for their immorality only caused further concern and upset.

These concerns were further underlined by the creation of the "interrogation tapes" which appeared on Showtime's official website for four weeks after the end of the televised show. Again, with regard to characterization the key issue for audience posters was the interrogation tape of Tina Kennard, who when asked if Bette Porter was her first lesbian lover responds with the revelation that her sister (who has since become a born-again Christian) was the person with whom she had her first lesbian sexual experience. The response of the audience postings was mainly negative:

> … why are you violating us with these tapes?
>
> Silver Main, April 6, 2009

> Murders and committers of incest. The writers have completely gone to pot. I am deeply offended and they have lost their vision completely [sic].
>
> Facebook user, March 12, 2009

> … with Tina's footage I'm reminded why I loathed the show on-and-off. What would be the point to introducing her relationship with her sister??? I have my opinions but would hope that they just made a mistake and wasn't trying to explain why she is a lesbian [sic].
>
> Nicole, March 11, 2009

These examples evidence a distinct worry about what wider audiences will construct from both the broadcast show and also the additional "interrogation tapes." Again there is a questioning of why generic narrative inclusions were not present in the televised version of the show, and why producers would want to introduce further narrative information that seems inconsequential. There is also a distinct sense of discomfort with the revelation that Tina had an incestuous lesbian affair with her own sister. There is awareness that representations tend to construct wider social meaning about particular sub-cultural groups, and this interrupts any form of escapism or enjoyment for lesbian audiences in this instance. Lesbian audiences express keen awareness of the potential implications for "the lesbian" to be constructed as perverse or immoral "other" through attributes that are seen as socially problematic. It's clear that lesbian audiences do not consume in a vacuum and are aware that there are few mainstream lesbian representations available. There is a clear fear that these portrayals may have real and distinct consequences for how they are considered in social circumstances. Their worry and fear is a distinct example of Hall's position (1997) on reading and consuming media texts, but for this minority group the consequences may go far beyond a misrepresentation of or discussion on the merits of *The L Word*.

The greatest problem for these posters is the number of loose ends that remain at the end of *The L Word*. All the narrative work that had been undertaken to create rounded characters those viewers could identify with through their interactions as couples, as friends, and through their developments into what constitutes a family life, were undermined. Factors that could never have been imagined were introduced, but could go nowhere and seemed fantastical. From the responses it seems that, due to the lack of secure and distinct lesbian narratives generally in television drama, this development was a step too far.

The end?

To conclude then, there were a number of positions taken up by fans of *The L Word* in relation to both the finale of the show and its general direction over its six-year run. It seems that audiences enjoyed the "creative difference" of the show and felt that this was a unique artistic quality of American television. Arguably, this way of reading the show put the power to create meaning in the hands of the viewers. You could decide on your own ending!

For lesbian viewers, enjoyment was not specific in terms of the narrative of the show. Potentially this suggests that minority groups that have been traditionally under-represented find pleasures in being represented in any way whatsoever. This is certainly something worth exploring in relation to lesbian representation and adds another dimension to our consideration of minority audiences and their expectations. Indeed, a key defense of executive producer Ilene Chaiken was that she had been responsible for bringing the first lesbian-focused drama to television screens. For many lesbian viewers that fact nullified their disappointment over anything else to do with the show; again, this links audience pleasure to cultural position. There is an integration of *The L Word* into lesbian social experiences—viewers use it as encouragement to come out, and as a basis for a more positive representation of the self. Thus, *The L Word* was not just a television show to be watched, but was also something these viewers experienced in other areas of their lives.

Negative audience responses dominated the forum and were mainly focused on the lack of narrative closure. Viewers felt they had been promised answers. Basically Chaiken "jumped the shark" in not providing answers! It appears that there was a distinct misjudgment on the producers' part of how viewers would react to the outcome of the show. Whether or not it was intended to provide the foundation for a spin-off, lesbian viewers saw it as a betrayal fueled by economy and greed, with a number of posters declaring their refusal to take part in any further economic consumption of *The L Word*. This confirms that generic convention is still central to the enjoyment of television texts. It also reveals that modern audiences can feel empowered through online discussion and their willingness to withdraw their financial investment in the show, although what is clearly questionable is whether these are merely empty threats.

Issues with the characterizations of immorality further compounded negativity, especially the morally perverse and potentially murderous. Not only could the audience see no end in sight, and no narrative resolution; they were also disturbed by the characterization of lesbians as a dangerous "other." The sexual identity of these posters had a distinct impact on how they read the text.

There are a number of key conclusions raised by this analysis. The first is that creating television that represents lesbians to lesbian audiences has a weight of political expectation that is not found in relation to heterosexual audiences. For *The L Word*'s lesbian audience, loyalty and consideration of the lesbian community was a key factor in the reading and enjoyment of the text. When this didn't happen the cultural position of the lesbian viewers became an impediment to the enjoyment of the show. For lesbians to fully embrace the show they felt that their political needs should have been addressed through positive portrayals. When the show didn't portray lesbians in a positive light there was a distinct sense of betrayal. This work indicates a need for further investigations into the commercial nature of lesbian-centered television and the audience's political expectations of the serial drama genre, as these appear to be the factors which have impacted the most on audience pleasures surrounding the show in its final season. Such factors should be of consideration to producers of lesbian-centered serial drama and wider televisual portrayals.

Whilst *The L Word* didn't suffer in terms of viewers dropping away from the show, perhaps these reactions highlight a disparity in the expectations of lesbian-focused drama between the audience and production. What seems difficult is Chaiken's claim that this was never a drama for lesbians, but for all audiences. This claim is problematic for many lesbians, especially as there is so little content made for or singularly about us. Ultimately this has been seen as lesbian portrayal by those who are sometimes labeled in the forum as "taking ourselves too seriously."

What is also highlighted is that producer considerations of lesbian audiences may be a requirement in the production of any future lesbian-focused dramas. The experience of "The End of *The L Word*" may have heightened expectations for lesbian viewers the world over. The first lesbian drama has now been and gone, leaving behind some disaffected viewers in its wake. Next time the bar may be set much higher and lesbian loyalty may not be as kind with difficult narratives that never find any conclusion.

Notes

1   "Who Killed Jenny?" referred to Jenny Schecter and was the lead
    tagline for season six of the show in a variety of promotional
    material prior to broadcast.

PART 2

Laudations

4

Queering *The L Word*

Sal Renshaw

This will be a contentious claim: *The L Word* was nowhere more politically edgy, more progressive, and, I would argue, more subversively feminist, than when it attempted to tackle the issue of sexual identity through the overtly gender non-normative characters, "Lisa," the lesbian man, Ivan, the drag king, Billie Blaikie, the very genderqueer manager of The Planet, and most especially through Moira/Max, the character who, over four seasons, transitioned from female to male. Bracketing any critique as to the quality of these attempts, we can see that there was a sustained commitment—conscious or otherwise— on the part of the producers to explore complex questions of sexual identity right from the fourth episode of the very first season with the introduction of Lisa all the way through to the last episode of the last season.

Contentious claim number two: If, for the purposes of argument, we accept the blunt instrument of the wave theory of feminist politics, then it seems fair to say that *The L Word* rides two waves simultaneously with respect to the politics of sex, gender, desire, and sexuality. If the representation of genderqueers like Lisa, Ivan, Billie and Max falls into the category of third-wave feminism, then it seems all too obvious that with the ensemble of middle-class, mostly white femme lesbians, the show predominantly and strategically rides the second wave. The producers took very few political risks with this group. Instead they consistently held out the assimilationist handful of sugar to their ostensibly spookable straight audience, always on the verge of kicking the top rail and galloping back to the safely gendered pastures of the likes of *CSI* where the men are men and the women are mostly dead. No surprise that if this imagined straight audience was the one the producers and Showtime were most concerned to be courting, then the sustained representation of the main cast would be committed to not rocking the gender boat. In terms of the representation of the core ensemble, *The L Word* is fairly accused of trading on blatantly normative assumptions about sex and gender, and even more so was this the case when it came to depicting relationality. Merri Lisa Johnson's incisive chapter on the politics of compulsory monogamy in *The L Word*'s first two seasons remains apt at the conclusion of the sixth season (Johnson 2006). While the configuration of the couples changed considerably over the course of six seasons, there was never any genuine threat to the underlying assumptions about the supreme value of heteronormative monogamous coupledom. Being gay was more often than not a difference that didn't make one. Regardless of how well each of the individuals managed it, and frequently they didn't manage it well, monogamous coupledom was the only relational model the series truly got behind. The few token nods towards any alternatives amounted to strategic buttressing for monogamy, there only to convey the idea that if you think monogamy is hard, the alternatives are so much harder, best not even consider them!

But, if a more radical gender politics is what we're interested in, something we might think of as a queer genealogy in *The L Word*, then we can't ignore the fact that alongside this dominant heteronormative representation of "the gay girls" there ran a decidedly riskier one with respect to some of the more marginal characters. With these marginal characters we often saw an image of gender that disrupts the supposedly natural nexus of sex, gender, and desire. At the very least, more politically interesting work is done with these storylines, and at best, they're also more subversive. And this representation of gender-queerness got a lot more complex and a lot more interesting as the show went along. If Lisa the lesbian man is the first kick *The L Word* takes at the queer can then they came a long way by the time they told the stories of Kit Porter, an older, het woman who falls for a drag king, and Max, a lesbian woman who transitions and gets pregnant by his same-sex male partner. To be clear, I am not suggesting that the queer politics were central; they weren't. On the contrary, the queer critique was obviously marginalized, mostly played out through tertiary storylines and characters. Nor am I suggesting that it was intentional; it might not have been. But, regardless of queer theoretical literacy or authorial intentions, a queer critique of normativity is nonetheless there, persistently. As such, it functions politically as the internal contradiction that unsettles the otherwise all too comfortable norms of gender and sexuality which defined most of the characters, in most of the story arcs, most of the time.

Framing the issue

Turning now to a conceptual framing of my initial claim that nowhere is *The L Word* more progressive or subversive in its feminist politics than in its explicit efforts to tell gender non-normative/queer/trans stories, I take my lead from Samuel A. Chambers. In his essay on heteronormativity in the first two seasons of the series, Chambers intellectually aligns himself with queer thinkers like Michael Warner, at the same time as he stands on the shoulders of queer feminists like Judith Butler (Chambers 2006). When Chambers urges us in our analyses to "shift away from the question of representation and towards a queer politics that considers the problem of norms" (2006: 82) he is declaring both his theoretical and political allegiances. In emphasizing norms, Chambers positions himself within a set of debates about the complex social conditions in which we are all produced. The norms to which he refers are those elusive everyday rituals, beliefs, and practices that often unconsciously shape so much about all of us, from who and how we desire to the beliefs we hold, even to the ways we consume. They are not reducible to the rules per se but they are enshrined in them; they are not the laws, but again, they are often embedded in them (2006: 84). Norms are the often-invisible architecture of our social worlds, our moralities, our becoming, and they are inescapable, which is not at all to say that they are unchanging. They are nothing if not endlessly shifting targets.

Chambers also notes that from the outset a very rich debate concerning the representational politics of the show emerged, a debate not lost on anyone, fans or producers alike. No surprise that in being the first show to center on lesbians, *The L Word* provoked questions about representation, visibility, authenticity, and reality: Whose stories are being told? Where are the real butches? Why are even the women of color so white? Do any of these women actually work? Why are they so conventionally beautiful?[1] To quote the show's executive producer, Ilene Chaiken,[2] "I always knew it would be a contentious audience, that everybody would claim ownership. Everybody would feel that her story wasn't getting told, that there aren't enough butch lesbians and there aren't enough women of color, or this or that" (2005). Leaving aside the question of just who makes up this "contentious" audience, Chaiken's response alludes to the shortcomings of a taxonomic approach to identity; i.e., the everybody fits neatly into a category approach. And Chambers identifies one face of the critical failure of this approach when he cautions against attributing too much political significance to visibility alone. "'Representation' … can provide absolutely no political guarantees. Norms of gender and sexuality may be changed by a show about lesbians, or they may not be. To get at the political level of the show requires both a different approach to it (no longer fixated on representation) and a clearer conception of norms" (2006: 83). Before taking up Chambers' challenge to articulate a clearer sense of the norms of gender and sexuality, and even while taking seriously his observations about the political limits of representation, I do want to draw attention to the representational significance of the character of Max. If, as Chambers does acknowledge (81–2), there is some political significance to the very existence of *The L Word*, if it is politically meaningful to have a show which represents lesbian lives that don't end in suicide, or lesbian loves that don't end in a retreat to heterosexuality, if it is politically meaningful to see lesbians depicted in communities and with families, across a range of social contexts as complex and whole human beings, then it's equally, if not even more meaningful in a homophobic, heteronormative, transphobic culture to recognize as politically significant the positive representation of a transgender/ transsexual character integrated within this community. However, as readers of this volume will clearly see, this is by no means an uncontested view, as evidenced by Rebecca Beirne's important critique of the show's representation of transgender and genderqueer characters.

Returning now to the politics of norms, in revealing the extent of the social and subjective effects of a binary understanding of sexual difference, heteronormativity is connected to but a complication of heterosexuality. For Michael Warner, who coined the term in his 1993 book *Fear of a Queer Planet*, heteronormativity finds its roots in the assumption that "heterosexuality is normative in terms of identity, practices and behaviors" (Chambers 2007: 663). But beneath this assumption lies the deeper commitment to the two-sex model of sexual difference which, significantly, stands as the biological bedrock of gender expression, roles, and performance, and also then of opposite-sex desire. It's the all-too-familiar story of human identity where biological males "naturally" develop into masculine-gendered men, who "naturally" desire biological females, who have developed into feminine-gendered women, who, unsurprisingly, "naturally" desire those men. This bio loop finds the proof of its essential nature in reproduction, where we end up with children as evidence of the "nature as destiny" story of opposite-sex human desire. Ironically, this ostensibly biological story of human relationality and human desire is deeply tethered through the very dynamic, ever-shifting social notion of normality. So the concept of heteronormativity helps to disrupt this bio-normal story about the natural relationship between sex, gender, and desire by revealing the elaborate social practices and institutions that turn heterosexuality into a norm that defines what it means not only to be human but to live a supposedly good life. Heteronormativity, as Chambers notes, is best understood as the concept of heterosexuality when it is operating as a norm (Chambers 2007: 657) and central to this operation are the norms of gender. "Heteronormativity is a regulatory practice of sex/gender/desire that thereby alters or sometimes sets the conditions of possibility and impossibility for gender intelligibility" (2007: 663). So in defending my claim that *The L Word* is never more politically subversive than it is with the storylines of the gender non-normative characters, I am accepting Chambers' premise that subverting the norms of heterosexuality, disrupting traditional conceptions of femininity and masculinity, queering binary gender, and destabilizing the connections between sexed bodies and desiring subjects are fundamentally progressive political strategies.

Essential bodies: "Lisa" the lesbian man

Few would likely disagree that the storyline involving Lisa the lesbian man was problematic. But if we accept my hunch that the storyline is better understood as part of a continuing exploration of the sex-gender-desire nexus, then, perhaps, we can think of it as the antecedent of an examination that got much more interesting over time. Lisa was introduced in the fourth episode of the first season as an alternative love interest for the bi-identified, Alice Pieszecki ("Lies, Lies, Lies," 1:4). At this point Alice is exasperated with what she refers to as "dyke drama", and going back to men looks appealing. Alice is consistently the voice of the normative despite, on the surface, appearing to be the most open in her willingness to engage with difference. If the simultaneous conversation running throughout season one about gaydar opened onto a space for reflecting on the unstable, unreliable relationship between gender expression and sexual orientation, then the Lisa arc adds to this the sexed body, at the same time as it foregrounds the problematic suggestion that the body is the final arbiter of the truth of identity. This is a point Rebecca Beirne makes in this volume about the show's response to transgender characters, when she notes that the show persistently refocuses attention from "identities to bodies" (27). In taking for granted that sex and gender are inextricably linked as well as readable off the surfaces, Alice reveals her underlying attachment to the heteronormative story of sexual difference. However, at least in principle, the character of Lisa offers the opportunity to queer this story. Despite being a relatively soft version of masculinity, baby faced and gently spoken, we are never seriously invited to question this lesbian man's presumptive sex. Lisa might well be a hippy boy with a girl's name but, as Kit says at a later point, Lisa is pretty clearly a dude ("Losing It," 1:6). So while I agree with the sentiment expressed by Eve Sedgwick, when she said she wished that not all the characters in season one "came equipped with a handy sexual label" (2004), in presenting as unquestionably male while self-identifying as a lesbian, Lisa creates a vertiginous sense of category confusion for everyone, cast and audience alike. The blogosphere and fansites were sparking with reaction. How can you have a lesbian man? Aren't these mutually exclusive terms? Aren't lesbians by definition, women? What on earth were the writers thinking? Is this a joke?

The treatment of the storyline around Lisa has rightly been criticized for giving far too much support to the last question, but, while the transphobic undertones are palpable, the loudest outcry came from lesbian-identified viewers. This posting from Michelle Jones's blogsite "On the Path" captures the spirit of incredulity and indignation, and in so doing reveals something of the anxieties around the politics of identity categories and how they get deployed.

> Alice (the bisexual one in case I hadn't mentioned that) has a crush on a man who calls himself a "Lesbian identified man." Excuse me? What the fuck are you talking about? If I heard correctly he also calls himself Lisa. Lisa the lesbian identified man. Let's just repeat

that to ourselves for a moment ... "Lisa the lesbian identified man." Apparently I missed the update to the definition of lesbian from "of or relating to homosexuality between females" to including men. I swear when the character spoke the line about being a lesbian identified man I really just want to hurl. I mean we don't get any solid words to describe our relationships and commitments (spouse, partner, girlfriend all have other meanings as well as in the lesbian context) and now the one word that actually has a solid definition for us is being used by/for a man? I'm really not a psycho militant lesbian but come on! (http://michellejones.net/onapath/2004/02/the-l-word-week-4.php)

In a pattern that was repeated throughout *The L Word*, the queer, politically subversive impulse found itself disciplined by a reactive heteronormative response. A closer examination of a couple of scenes which bookend the political tensions in the Lisa arc will illuminate the queer interpretive possibilities that were contained in this figure of the lesbian man.

Let's turn first to an exchange that took place soon after Lisa was introduced ("Losing It," 1:6), when "the girls" are gathered at one of their homes playing cards and Lisa leaves to go to the bathroom. Once out of earshot the questions begin, starting with Dana Fairbanks, who teasingly gives voice to the category anxieties provoked by Lisa when she facetiously asks Alice if he pees standing up or sitting down. The absent/present referent underlying Dana's question obviously concerns the relationship between Lisa's penis and his self-identity. But in reality, as previously noted, Lisa's sex per se is never seriously put in question. While the question of transsexualism is briefly raised by Lara Perkins, it is just as quickly shut down. Lisa isn't trans, neither transsexual nor transgender, and as such trans is not going to be a category option to make sense of the lesbian man. Not willing to let go of this line of inquiry, Dana follows up with another crack, which more explicitly gets at the underlying issue concerning the limits of self-identification and the truth of sex. She teasingly asks Alice if the "lesbo man is really dating the fake bisexual." Following up right on her heels, Tina rolls the category dice again by asking Alice if she is dating Lisa "more as a lesbian or as a man?" Each of these questions takes aim at different aspects of identity but all are in the service of a normalizing impulse. All are attempts to stabilize the instability Lisa has introduced through his non-normative self-identification. While Lisa can be seen as adopting certain gender non-normative behaviors—he is nurturing and attentive—this is not where the non-normative politics bites down hardest with this character. The real challenge to heteronormativity and, indeed, the subversive political potential, lies in the disconnect between Lisa's visual presentation as undeniably male and his insistent self-identification as lesbian, a category, as Jones's blog entry makes all too clear, typically understood to be dependent on femaleness.

It seems obvious that in hanging this arc on the issue of self-identification the writers were referencing, albeit in a problematic way, the very fraught tensions that surrounded the emergence of the trans rights, trans equality movement, especially in its early-stage collision with second-wave feminist understandings of sex and gender.[3] So there's something intriguing about the politically paradoxical way the card-game exchange is resolved. Kit ends up closing down the conversation, smoothing the ruffled gender feathers of what we are clearly invited to think are the "real lesbians" when she turns to Lisa and says, "If the dude wanna give up his white man rights to be a second class citizen then hey, welcome to our world" ("Losing It," 1:6). So in the language of second-wave debates about the relationship between equality, oppression, and privilege, and even as she adds to the whole arc the critical issue of the operations of race, Kit offers the most politically progressive if somewhat paradoxical reading of Lisa. Kit affirms Lisa's maleness and whiteness as the bedrock of his identity—the white man's privilege—at the same time as she also affirms his right to self-define, at least to the extent that she supports the notion that these were things he could "give up" by way of his gender identification. She doesn't question the stability of the categories of either race or sex, but she holds out the possibility that Lisa has some agency in determining what these categories will mean and how they are lived. In other words, she affirms his right to self-identify.

In a later scene Alice and Lisa are having sex and Lisa momentarily pauses in the heat of the moment to get his dildo ("L'Ennui," 1:7). When he breaks it out, Alice responds with incredulity, asking him if he's kidding and reminding him that he has "the real thing." In Lisa's response we glimpse a truly queer moment for television, one that puts to the test the seemingly progressive affirmation of self-definition that was hinted at in the resolution of the card game scene. Lisa insists that, despite the fact that he has a penis, he is indeed a lesbian and he doesn't want to make love to Alice "that way." In amazingly short order the subversive political potential of this remarkably gender-disruptive moment is powerfully disciplined by Alice's response. Once again we are offered an example of the oppositional structure that sees queer moments provoke normative responses. Alice's reaction does the normative work of defiantly inscribing the limits of self-identification by re-suturing Lisa's identity to his body, simultaneously reducing maleness to the presence of a penis and lesbianism to the lack of one. Forcefully topping Lisa by flipping him on his back Alice straddles him, looks him in the eye and states, "Listen! You're a man! You're a man named Lisa, but you're definitely a man" ("L'Ennui," 1:7). Bracketing for a moment the egregiously heteronormative assumptions surrounding lesbian sex that infuse this representation of dildos as "fake" penises, just as significant is the way this scenario realigns the normative sex/gender/desire triumvirate by relying on the presumptively immutable body as the final arbiter of truth. In effect Alice's unspoken dialog looks more like this: Hey dude boy, you can say whatever you like about who you are but in the end they're just words and it's that erect penis that is going to have the final word, a word which won't begin with an L![*] In effect Lisa's body is presumed to make a lie of his self-identification.

Just in case any ambiguity around subverting gender norms remains, the Lisa arc ends in the next episode when in utter exasperation at just how complicated her life has turned out to be with Lisa, Alice aggressively pursues an even more normative version of masculinity in the form of Andrew. Lisa, now ironically the spokesperson for second-wave feminist politics, is shocked that Alice would be drawn to this kind of man who, he says, "represents everything that is wrong with the world!" Hammering home her normative commitments Alice responds: "You know what Lisa, when I first started seeing you I wanted something simple and easy and instead I end up with the most complicated interpretation of sexual identity I've ever encountered. You know, you do lesbian better than any lesbian I know, Ok? And I don't want a lesbian boyfriend. I'm sorry. I want a boyfriend who's straight or I want a lesbian who's a girl" ("Luck, Next Time," 1:9). With this deafening shout out to heteronormativity, Lisa exits stage right, as in politically right, leaving all of us clear that when push came to shove, despite her ostensible openness to difference, Alice really desires a normative performance of gender that can be reliably stitched onto a stable sexed body.

Dragging Ivan, queering Kit

Given that Lisa was really the first significantly non-normative character
the show attempted, and in light of how poorly executed that plotline
was, audiences could be forgiven for worrying about future attempts.
But Lisa's departure did not mark the end of genderqueer on the series,
and his immediate successor was a considerable improvement. Ivan,
the drag king, was introduced late in the first season as yet another
unlikely love interest, this time for Kit, Bette's very heterosexual half-
sister ("Locked Up," 1:12). While Ivan managed to survive into the
second season, curiously transformed from drag king to transman
along the way, in the end this was also a storyline that was not well or
extensively developed despite this time at least being popular with the
fans. In the end the politics more or less repeated the same structure
as with Lisa: the subversive queer potential of a character was set
up, thereby opening an important political space, but the resolution
of the arc saw the disciplining of the queer and the affirmation of
heteronormativity. As with the Lisa arc, the body functioned as the
site of both the truth and problem of identity. Whereas with Lisa it was
the presence of his penis that inscribed sex as the bedrock of identity,
and thereby contained and constrained his ability to self-identify, with
Ivan it turned out to be the absence of a penis that ultimately signaled
the failure of his otherwise successful performance of masculinity.
By the time the arc resolved, Ivan's queerness was so effectively
disciplined and contained that he embodied the symbolic weight of the
heteronormative while the queer baton was passed to Kit.

Kit, the older, straight woman whose history with men has left her
disappointed but ever romantically hopeful, is intoxicated by Ivan's
chivalrous performance of masculinity, which clearly does the work
of positioning him as more than man enough for her. And, as Janet
McCabe notes in her chapter with Kim Akass on the politics and
pleasures of straight women's desire for female masculinities, there is
a "liberatory vision of sexual promise and romantic possibility" (2006:
150) for Kit, Ivan and, perhaps, the rest of us, in this story, which is
especially condensed into the scene where Ivan serenades Kit with
Leonard Cohen's "I'm Your Man" ("Locked Up," 1:12). Kit is irresistibly
drawn to Ivan despite herself, and her protestations in the face of his
wooing—i.e., that she is a nearly fifty-year-old woman with a lifetime
of heterosexuality—seem a little unconvincing. Kit's attempts to shore

up her increasingly uncertain sexual identity with declarations of heterosexuality arise as a consequence of the disconnect between her libidinal experience of Ivan as man enough and her beliefs about the truth of his sex, which supposedly rule him out as an appropriate object of her desire. I am reminded here of Samuel Chambers' comment that "norms work best when they are never exposed" (2007: 665). Kit's need to articulate her heterosexuality to Ivan seems to do the paradoxical work of weakening our belief in it. Again, I am reminded of Chambers: "Once norms reach the point that they require significant shoring up, then they have already been significantly weakened. This means that reinforcing a norm can never bring it back to full strength, since the very act of reinforcement serves to expose the norm as weaker than it could be" (2007: 665). This is certainly the case with Kit. Rather than being the final word on her sexuality, Kit's declaration ends up being the first word in a potentially queer conversation that goes on quietly in the background over the full six seasons.

If heteronormativity is stabilized on the essentializing/normalizing foundation of the sex/gender/sexual orientation matrix, then significantly shifting any one of these elements at least has the potential to be politically subversive; I limit this claim to potential intentionally. As is obvious with *The L Word* lesbians, simply shifting the objects of their desire to same-sex partners turned out to be no guarantee of political subversion. Where the Lisa storyline primarily engaged this matrix by shifting the relationship between the sexed body and gender identification, the same is also true of the Ivan storyline. But the most interesting subversive work in the Ivan arc turns out to be around sexual orientation and it's Kit's, not Ivan's, that is the most politically interesting. Kit goes from suggesting that sexual orientation and desire finally come to rest on the body of the other—that's the position she implicitly adopts when she says to Ivan "if only you were a man, you'd be the perfect man" ("Limb from Limb," 1:13)—to discovering that perhaps the body is not going to be the truth text of her sexuality after all: perhaps Ivan is indeed man enough for her lifelong heterosexual self. Ivan's performance of female masculinity patently queers sexual-identity categories. However, following the structural lead set by Alice and Lisa, queerness is ultimately sacrificed on essentialist commitments that separate sex from gender and construct the body as the site of the truth of sex. Thus, Ivan's gender performance can be and is construed as a false promise.

The first hint of an interpretive struggle over precisely these issues comes when, in the course of introducing him to Bette, Kit refers to Ivan as "he" and Bette queries the pronoun ("Locked Up," 1:12). Kit is momentarily caught up by Bette's correction and apologizes to Ivan. But Ivan says he's happy either way and we never hear Kit refer to Ivan as she again. A follow-up in the next season repeats this scenario, with Bette even more insistently identifying Ivan's sex as the immutable bedrock of his identity ("Life, Loss, Leaving," 2:1). When Kit repeats the position she took at the card game with Lisa and suggests that perhaps Ivan can self-identify, that is, that he is the one who gets to say whether "he's a man or a woman," Bette proclaims that kind of thinking to be delusional. Once again it seems we have the lesbians waving the flag for the most normative reading of sexual identity possible, although, in this instance, Bette gets support for her position, in a politically reactionary sleight of hand, from Ivan himself.

The romance with Kit is effectively concluded with another interpretive struggle over the place of the body in the gender/desire matrix when Kit walks into Ivan's bedroom while he is showering and sees his strap-on on the dresser. Far less shocked or repulsed than intrigued—shock and repulsion being the normative reactions we might have expected from this moment that is set up as a portentous revelation—as Kim Akass points out, what we actually see is Kit gently run her hand across it in something of a curious caress[5] (Akass and McCabe 2006: 153). When Ivan walks in from the shower, long hair flowing, taping down his breasts, seemingly more feminine than masculine, he sees what Kit has seen and he's the one who is horrified. With the phallus collapsed onto the penis and the dildo again reduced to the status of fake, the circuit of castration closes over Ivan as he pushes Kit out the door shouting for her to leave. If ever there was a heteronormative retreat moment for Kit, a moment where her assertions of heterosexuality were going to mean anything on the terms she herself had set, then this was it. But she doesn't retreat. Instead she stays on the other side of the door trying to reassure Ivan. In this moment, where Kit refuses to let Ivan's embodied femaleness signify as lack, and despite the fact that this is precisely how Ivan experiences himself, there is both a queering and a straightening of the narrative. Ivan's reaction to seeing himself through Kit's eyes ends up confirming Bette's allegation that Ivan's gender performance has been, if not delusion then at least illusion and that beneath it lies the embodied truth—the truth being that in lacking the "real thing," Ivan isn't actually man enough, indeed he's not man at all. Alternatively, in Kit's refusal to see Ivan's female body as lack in relation to his masculine gender identity, i.e., in her refusal to think of this as a deal breaker, she has clearly been moved, if not to a queer understanding of sexual identity, at least in the direction of a considerably less essentialist, less normative one.

Interestingly, while this more or less ends the arc with Ivan it doesn't end the engagement with non-normativity in the stories surrounding Kit. Throughout the third and fourth seasons Kit finds herself in a relationship with Bette and Tina's Manny, the much younger thirty-five-year-old Angus, as well as managing a menopausal pregnancy and a marriage proposal. Perhaps unsurprisingly given the structural proclivity of the show to stage queer stories only to have them disciplined by heteronormative ones, this arc is resolved in the same way that the Lisa/Alice Kit/Ivan ones were: Angus has an affair with a younger white woman—read age, race, and reproductively appropriate—and he and Kit break up. Nonetheless, just to underscore that this isn't the end of Kit's queer cred, her now-established penchant for female masculinities reappears in the fourth season when she attends a bisexual speed dating event and unexpectedly has an erotic encounter with Papi, the Latina equivalent of Shane. Furthermore, in what amounts to an homage to the first-season Ivan arc, in the last season Kit switches it up again, this time with male femininities when she falls for Sunset Boulevard, an African-American cross-dresser. Interestingly, while his version of masculinity out of drag is everything Kit supposedly longs for, it's in drag that she first falls for him.

While the analyses I have offered of gender non-normativity in the first two seasons of *The L Word* don't offer a lot of promise for the place of a truly progressive sexual politics on the series, I want to suggest that they are more than just moments. Taken together they represent a sustained engagement with questions of gender identity, even if it is simultaneously true that the show continually comes down on the side of normativity. But, just as Lisa didn't mark the total disappearance of the gender non-normative characters on the show, so too is Ivan soon replaced. Season three sees the introduction of Moira/Max and, for the first time, there is a more meaningful commitment to developing a storyline of gender non-normativity. Despite being a less than perfect representation of trans issues—this is soapy dramatic television after all—as I noted at the start, the storylines surrounding Max as he transitions from female to male often end up offering a quiet but sustained counter-text to the endlessly normative construction of the lesbians. More importantly, Max's story is a queer story that does not get disciplined into normalcy in quite the same way as those of his predecessors.

Inessential bodies: Recuperating a queer genealogy

If the body was the terrain on which the normative disciplined the queer with the characters of Lisa and Ivan, the same cannot as easily be said of Moira/Max, which is not to say that there aren't continual interpretive tensions surrounding him—there are. In true *L Word* fashion, it's precisely these tensions that often become some of the most cringe-worthy moments that plague the show from the start. Presuming to teach their audience about trans people and issues fares no better than presuming to teach them about lesbians! But, as with the former queer characters, if we graciously suspend disbelief and stay inside the soapy, indeed the increasingly campy *mise-en-scène* of the L·world then, with the introduction of Max, the materiality of the sexed body becomes a far less stable signifier and we are offered a more provocative representation of embodied, gendered subjectivity. From the first episode of season three we are introduced to Max as Moira, Jenny's butch lesbian girlfriend who Jenny's parents mistake for a man; a woman who pees standing up, who describes Jenny going down on her as getting head and who begs her not to leave her with blue balls when they get interrupted ("Lost Weekend," 3:2). Before the question of trans identity is even raised, Moira is revisiting the question of self-identification versus the body that first emerged with Lisa. If we take her at her word, a word not yet encapsulated in self-identifying gender claims but nonetheless gestured towards in the language she uses, then it's a male body she is actively living. I am not proposing here to offer an exhaustive analysis of the character of Moira/Max, nor am I suggesting that everything about this character qualifies as non-normative or progressive. What I do want, however, is to reflect on the ways in which some of the same raw material that was used in the

Ivan/Lisa arcs is recycled with Max but to different political ends. The issue of the dildo/strap-on/pack as not "the real thing" is exemplary.

Soon after Moira/Max arrives back in LA with Jenny in season three, a queer *My Fair Lady* plot emerges in which Moira/Max is given a genderqueer mentor in the form of Billie Blaikie ("Light My Fire," 3:4). Billie is a flamboyant gay party planner who Kit has hired to manage The Planet and who is obviously attracted to Max. At the time they meet, Max is still identifying as Moira, a butch dyke. Billie quickly sees that Moira's life has not exposed her to a world in which the sexual binaries can get shaken up much beyond gender performance and sexual orientation. Billie introduces Moira/Max and Jenny to his friend Tom, an FTM who has transitioned and who sets about inducting Max into the language (top surgery) and practices (testosterone, bilateral mastectomies) of transsexualism ("Light My Fire," 3:4). In no time Moira is gone, and Max is living full time as a dude with taped-down breasts, packing, shooting testosterone and wanting to have sex all the time. Dubious stereotypes of masculinity notwithstanding, all these elements lead to a sexual encounter between Max and Billie that is the first in this queer recuperative trajectory that speaks back to the Ivan/Lisa arc in potentially subversive ways ("Lifesize," 3:6).

Max approaches Billie about his FTM friend Tom at a party one night and they end up alone together in the back room. Billie pats the front of Max's packed jeans with obvious admiring lust and asks him if he's wanting to find out more about how Max can "fully become Max." It's a moment which risks invoking the normative stereotype that for gay men it's all about the cock. However, Billie knows Max is packing so the next scene, which sees him on his knees giving Max a blow job, is a powerful reworking of the scene where Kit walked in on Ivan's disembodied, inert strap-on, his fake penis, lying on the dresser. Indeed, I would argue that this scene is far more provocative than the scene in the next episode where Max actually penetrates Billie. The real/fake distinction potentially operates more subversively in the blow-job scene than it does in the penetration scene precisely because what we see depicted is the increasing desire of both Max and Billie, something that in normative terms seems to conflict with what we think we already know—i.e., that this is not "the real thing" that Billie is going down on. We know that Max is packing, yet what we witness looks like embodied pleasure for both of them. This scene provocatively expands our experience of the representation of embodied desire on the show as it simultaneously subverts the boundary between fake and real. This is anything but Ivan's fake cock we are witnessing here. And at the same time we also witness a provocative queering of sexual identity and sexual orientation that is further compounded by the explanation Max offers when Jenny walks in on them. Max explains that Billie made him feel like "more of a guy; that he wasn't some girl with this thing in her pants" ("Lifesize," 3:6). Was it Max's assumption that Billie possessed the "real thing" that enhanced his own sense of maleness? Was it an implicitly normative evocation of a stereotype that sees gay men as the ultimate signifiers of sexual subjectivity? Is Max exposing an anxiety beneath heteronormativity here: that sexual identity is not in fact mirrored exclusively by differently sexed desire but can include same-sex desire? Or is he inadvertently revealing the way all identities are relational, even at the supposedly immutable level of bodies?[6]

If this scene between Billie and Max goes a long way towards undoing the normative implications of strap-ons as the silicone illusion concealing a deep, dark secret (i.e., the secret of Freudian lack), then a later sex scene between Max and his then-girlfriend Grace at the end of season four reworks the Freudian castration spin that also infused the reading of Ivan. By this point Max is identifying as transsexual; he's on the eve of having top surgery, and he's passing as male in his computer tech job. He's also using his techie skills to work with Alice on turning "OurChart" into a social networking site and he takes Grace on as an intern ("Lacy Lilting Lyrics," 4:9). Having dated transmen in the past, Grace arrives as a knowing insider who immediately picks Max as trans. Eventually Grace seduces him and as part of their lovemaking she says she wants to feel his body ("Literary License to Kill," 4:11). Max responds by saying he's not comfortable with his pre-surgery body, never has been; it's not his body; it will be in a couple of weeks when he gets surgery, but it isn't now. Grace is disinclined to accept Max at his word, but this time it's for all the right queer reasons. Up to now Max has always s/topped his lovers from touching him—all except in the scene just recounted with Billie. But, as with Alice and Lisa, Grace pushes the point, insisting that she is comfortable with his body and leaving us, the audience, with a vertiginous sense of the referent. Which body is Grace comfortable with? Is this Max's female body she is referring to? His male body? Exactly which body are we talking about here? As with Billie, Grace knows Max is anatomically female, that he's got strapped breasts and he's packing, but will she, like Billie, be able to secure his male identity if she exposes the materiality of his body? The potential for this scene to repeat Ivan's castration should be obvious. Moreover, in structural terms it's also a haunting, politically subversive homage to the Alice/Lisa scene. Grace straddles/tops Max and pushes him back in a chair as she removes his jeans and then gently rubs her hand over his bulging packed crotch while asking him if he likes how it feels. Essentialized understandings of the body, including Max's own of himself, are pushed to their limits as we witness his obvious pleasure. Grace slowly slides her hand into Max's boxers and exposes his perfect silicone pack in a move that could have played out as deeply normative, but didn't. Whatever risk there was that Max's body was going to operate as a truth text in the way both Lisa and Ivan's did was counterbalanced by the insistent power of language and relationality to create lived reality. The issue of self-identification that had been heteronormatively contained by the seemingly irreducible materiality of the body was recuperated here via a queer relational linguistic understanding of subjectivity. Perfectly accompanied by trans hip hop artist Katastrophe's "Enough Man" playing in the background, Grace tells Max she wants to suck his cock and she wants him to come in her mouth, and her words, this time, are enough to anchor Max's embodied identity and his embodied experience. Where Lisa's self-identity was sacrificed on the opposition between body and word, Max's is not. In words, Grace creates a queer mirror and while Max looks at her going down on him in a real mirror, the boundaries of sex and gender are significantly destabilized as they both see and live Max as more than enough man—and so do we.

Risking queer

In March 2008 Thomas Beatie made sensational headlines as "the first pregnant man."[7] Beatie was a female-to-male transsexual who had kept his reproductive organs so he could at some point have a child. Having already constructed for Max an ongoing same-sex relationship with Tom Mater, this tale of FTM pregnancy regrettably proved irresistible to *The L Word* producers. In the early part of Tom and Max's relationship, late in season five, we had seen another queer, non-normative shift in Max's sexual identity and indeed in Tom's. In a world of normative sexual binaries, where the assumptions are that whoever is on top stays on top, Max had consistently been penetrative rather than receptive. But in this scene with Tom he was graphically depicted switching it up: in other words, Max was for the first time seen to be taking it[8] ("Liquid Heat," 5:9). When this scene was written Thomas Beatie hadn't made the real-world news and Tom and Max were simply passing as a gay male couple. Rather than being a set-up for another disciplinary castration moment, this time in the form of a future pregnancy, Max's sexual position reversal appeared to be part of an ongoing queering of sexuality that was clearly part of the Tom/ Max storyline.

When it eventually emerged, what the ripped-from-the-headlines FTM pregnancy did enable was one more kick at the normative can where we see repeated again the same structure we have seen so often: queer stories, queer bodies, are made vulnerable to discipline by normative presumptions about the essence of the sexed body. But I want to suggest that despite the controversy surrounding the notorious baby shower scene, which seemed to risk rewriting much of the more progressive work done with this character, it is a mistake to treat this scene as the last word in the Max arc. In contrast to Rebecca Beirne's convincing analysis of the normativity and disciplining at the heart of the Max arc, I want to suggest that actually the last word with Max can be read as a defiant shout out to queer non-normativity and a powerful critique of heteronormativity.

When Jenny throws a Willie Wonka-themed baby shower party for Max towards the end of season six we are ostensibly invited to see him, and by extension, trans subjectivities, positioned somewhere between carnival sideshow and monstrosity. Dressed for the occasion in what amounts to Willie Wonka drag, Max is surrounded by images and dialog that relentlessly draw on the body as the ultimate challenge to his identity. At this time still ambivalent about the pregnancy, the gifts and accompanying dialog from his lesbian cohort seem to highlight his inability to convincingly self-identify—again we see language and embodiment pitted in opposition to each other with the essential body always threatening to have the final word. The scene is saturated in body imagery, from the scatological party game of "chocolate in a diaper" to an exchange in which the women collectively insist that Max must breastfeed—for the sake of bonding and for the baby—despite him clearly saying he has no intention of doing so. But taken as a whole and in context, the scene actually plays against expectations. Max is nearly drowning in gifts and dialog that symbolically attempt to anchor his identity to his straining flesh, and against his continually articulated objections. As each of his friends slip into referring to him variously as a "mother," as "she," and most offensively as a "pregnant lady" Max gets visibly more distressed. At the same time, the women appear utterly blind to Max's gendered particularity as they lose themselves in their essentialist giddiness and excitement. But if the scene is meant to highlight the monstrosity of the pregnant trans body, in reality that's not the monstrosity we witness. On the contrary, audience identification and sympathy is unquestionably and powerfully with Max and it is the violence of the women's insistence on gender normativity and on the body as the site of truth that we experience as monstrous. The scene is a damning indictment of heteronormativity, played out here under the guise of essential maternalism.

Despite the way the baby shower sequence exposes the force and violence of heteronormativity, the scene that immediately follows teases at the possibility of a return to the familiar structure of disciplining queerness. Max is shown naked before a bathroom mirror with the camera panning slowly up his body. The emphasis is again on his embodied femaleness—his swollen belly, his un-taped breasts. Eventually the camera pulls in close on his fully soaped, bearded face and we see him draw the razor down twice before the shot cuts away. Were this to be the last time we saw Max, this would be an unconscionable victory for the disciplining of queer, yet another castration moment in what has been an all too familiar pattern. But it's not. On the contrary, the next time we see him is in the very last episode of the series and it is not with the clean-shaven face and disciplined body we were left to imagine was the consequence of his humiliating experience at the baby shower. What we see instead is both a still-very-pregnant Max and a simultaneous consolidation of his gay male identity. Max isn't clean-shaven at all. On the contrary, he is sporting one of the most recognizable tropes of gay male sexuality—a handlebar mustache! So in the end, then, it is Max's self-identification as a pregnant gay transman that is the last, very queer word in this four-season arc which teetered on the edge, but ultimately resisted succumbing to the same kinds of normative moves that plagued the earlier genderqueer characters in *The L Word*.

Conclusion

I began this chapter with the suggestion that *The L Word* was nowhere more politically edgy, more progressive, perhaps more subversively feminist than when it tackled the issue of sexual identity through overtly gender non-normative characters. I stand by that claim at the same time as I acknowledge that there are those whose version of feminism might not easily accommodate the politics of the kinds of gender-subversive strategies I am highlighting here. In tracing a queer genealogy from the first to the last season I have tried to clear a space for what I don't dispute was a submerged and often marginalized thread. Over the years a significant body of scholarly literature has emerged examining the heteronormative ideologies shaping and constraining the representation of *The L Word* lesbians, and more recently this literature has been enhanced by analyses that also consider the implicit endorsement of neoliberal understandings of sexed subjectivity that saturate every aspect of the *mise-en-scène*.[9] In 2006, when she had only the first two seasons to consider, Merri Lisa Johnson suggested that "conservative and progressive ideologies intertwine and counterbalance each other on *The L Word*" (2006: 116). With four additional seasons, is she still right? Did they really intertwine and counterbalance each other? I think she was being generous, even then. I have suggested here that the relation was more antagonistic than balanced, that the progressive, subversive potential was constantly marginalized and always at risk of being disciplined by the normative. But I am also suggesting that right from the start the most progressive stories in terms of sexual identity, the places where the producers took the most risks—bracketing how well they negotiated those risks—was with the gender non-normative characters.[10] Credit where credit is due—Lisa was admittedly a shaky start. But the Max storyline did allow for a substantive questioning of the kinds of normative values that were simultaneously being affirmed through the main characters. So in taking these marginal arcs seriously we open a space that acknowledges the presence of a critique that was there from the start. In so doing we see the dominant heteronormativity around the core characters revealed to be precisely what it was all along, a ransom paid to get us six seasons of a show focused on lesbians in a media context that presumes it is straight audiences and their desires that pay the bills.[11]

Notes

1 For a recent engagement with these issues see Jennifer Esposito and Bettina Love (2008).

2 Ilene Chaiken clearly retained significant creative control and influence over the show. She wrote thirty-five of seventy-three episodes and directed seven episodes in all. Rose Troche, producer and ultimately executive producer along with Chaiken, also directed twelve episodes and wrote five. While the stable of writers and directors changed over the six seasons, Chaiken is by far the most influential connecting thread, with consistent creative input in either the directing or writing over the entire six seasons.

3 The issues of self-identification and essentialism have also played out in significant ways in race discourses. Season one references these debates through the biracial character of Bette who is continually assumed to be white. In an interesting twist on coming-out stories, Bette rarely comes out as lesbian in season one but instead must continually announce her identity as African-American. See Renshaw and Robinson (2007) for a more extended consideration of the tensions around self-identification and biological essentialism in season one. As an addendum, and with the benefit of four more seasons and hindsight, I now think we were too generous in our characterization of the Lisa/Alice arc.

4 For a very thoughtful engagement with the symbolic significance of the dildo as fake penis see Lorna Wheeler and Lara Raven Wheeler (2006: 107–9).

5 McCabe also describes Kit as confused in this scene and of this I am not convinced.

6 I am indebted to my colleague Dr. Wendy Peters for pointing out that this scene is partially premised on decidedly normative, essentialist undertones. The myths that understand women as notoriously suffering from a lack of desire and lesbians as women who fundamentally reject anatomical penises contrast dramatically with those of gay men who function as the super-signifiers of sexual desire and as those who (like heterosexual women) exclusively desire anatomical penises. Through these myths of sexual desire and orientation anchored in sexed bodies, Max's testosterone-inspired sexual desire allows him to step "up" from lesbians in

order to have his newly elevated sexual needs met. Further, the queerness and effectiveness of the scene rests, in part, on the essentialist presumption that Billie as a gay man exclusively desires the anatomical penis which, through sex with Billie, allows Max to feel like "more of a guy."

7   *The Advocate* ran Beatie's story on its front page in March 2008 and he was quickly taken up by the tabloids and on the talk-show circuit. On February 10, 2010, *The Advocate* posted an announcement that Beatie was expecting his third child.

8   See Wheeler and Wheeler (2006: 99–110) for a very thoughtful analysis of the way sexual positioning both reinforced and challenged gender norms on *The L Word.*

9   For a compelling argument about the privileging of neoliberal values as the core priority in the production of contemporary sexual subjectivities, see Kellie Burns and Cristyn Davies (2009).

10 Taking risks in terms of storyline and characterization cannot be separated from the conditions of production. A show like *The Sopranos* is better positioned to take risks simply because it can take its audience a little more for granted. Even with *Sex and the City* paving the way for a show about women, and porn endlessly paving a way for the appeal of lesbians, *The L Word* was always going to be a riskier, more tenuous venture.

11 In all fairness to the producers they continually commented on these kinds of tensions within the show itself and to do so was to make a political statement. The season two hidden-camera storyline makes this point when Mark, a neophyte documentary maker, places hidden cameras all over Shane and Jenny's house in order to get the "real story" of lesbian lives. Mark is told by his producer that there isn't enough lesbian sex—men want to see lesbian sex! And this commentary was repeated throughout the meta-narrative structure of season five, which tells the story of Jenny's coming-out book, *Lez Girls*, which is being turned into a film. Again, we repeatedly hear the producers of this film demanding changes to the script and even to the appearance of their actors on the basis of what they claim their audience "really wants to see." And of course the audience they are talking about is a presumptively heteronormative, straight one.

12 I owe a debt of gratitude to Michele Kort, Senior Editor at *Ms. Magazine*, who was my inspiration during the writing of this

piece; which is not to say that she would necessarily agree with the analysis; she might not. I would also like to acknowledge Sarah Feige, my exceptional Research Assistant on this project.

5

The Trouble with Shane:
Lesbians and Polygamy

Heidi Schlipphacke

The joke about lesbians is that they are compulsive monogamists: one day after their first date they are renting a U-Haul and worrying about extended feline families. One of the many pleasures of *The L Word* is its playful and conflicted stance towards lesbian monogamy. Shane McCutcheon, one of the most beloved of *The L Word* characters, is an unreformed, incorrigible playgirl throughout the entire series. Like the dashing (male) Shane of the classic Western (*Shane*: USA; George Stevens, 1953), she consistently eroticizes and threatens domestic spaces, entering and departing in a cloud of lust and longing. This chapter will chart the complex engagement with monogamy and its limits in the lesbian world of *The L Word*, beginning with the character of Shane. Famously resistant to the presumed lures of lesbian monogamy, Shane embodies a radically androgynous identity, a woman who loves women yet who refuses to give women what they presumably want: "commitment." However, as I will show here, Shane is not the only character who relishes her polyamorous pursuits. Literally every couple on the show experiences infidelity at some point or other, and this infidelity often occurs with others who are members of the inner circle of lesbians at the core of the show.

In my view, one of the many reasons why *The L Word* resonates so viscerally with lesbians is that it consistently displays the ways in which the seemingly contradictory poles of monogamy and promiscuity (or polyamory) shape lesbian communities. I use all three terms—polygamy, polyamory, and promiscuity—in this chapter, as no one term signifies adequately the unique nature of couplings and cross-couplings in a community of women in which traditional marriage is neither sanctioned nor legalized. These communities (as *The L Word*

shows in an often exaggerated and campy manner) are simultaneously
close-knit and claustrophobic; they represent a mode of kinship that is
non-biological and that consequently does not draw clear lines around
rules of coupling. Relationships slide from friendly to erotic and back:
the seemingly oppositional concepts of polygamy/polyamory and
claustrophobia represent two sides of the same coin in *The L Word*.
Erotic fluidity is tolerated and even nourished to a degree, but the
domesticated relationships within this community as well as within
the larger community itself quickly become claustrophobic. Every
significant character in the series bumps up against this truth, and the
final season (season six) in particular drives home the circular nature
of this close-knit group of lesbian friends and lovers. By season six,
The L Word has offered up both a fantasy and a nightmare model of
lesbian kinship.

Monogamy and promiscuity emerge as the central topics of
concern to *The L Word* women in the beginning of the series. The
pilot opens with the mature and successful lesbian couple, Bette Porter
and Tina Kennard, discussing Tina's cycle as they plan insemination.
The scene is eroticized through their embraces and Bette's declaration,
"Let's make a baby." Fans and critics of the show have pointed out that
this scene mimics heteronormative relationship models,[1] but it also
queers the eros of conception. Here, the spectator believes (if ever so
briefly), is the ideal monogamous lesbian couple. Bette and Tina not
only embody feminine domesticity, but they seem to have retained an
erotic chemistry that is absent from many heterosexual couples trying
to conceive.

The opening scene of the series calls forth clichés about lesbian
domesticity, and jokes about the "lesbian urge to merge" litter the first
episode. At a party at Bette and Tina's house, the friends tell well-worn
jokes about the lack of boundaries that can characterize monogamous
lesbian couples. Prompting a ritualized response, a gay male friend
asks: "What do lesbians bring on a second date?" The lesbian friends
immediately respond: "A moving van!" "A turkey baster!" These
answers are repeated in chorus by the women, underscoring the
truth at the core of the joke while simultaneously poking fun at the
stereotype. Another friend, Alice Pieszecki, asserts that "lesbians think
friendship is another word for foreplay." Already in the first episode,
the stereotype of lesbian monogamy is queered, so to speak. With her
statement, Alice underlines the fluidity of boundaries in the lesbian

cosmos. Friendship between women can quickly lead to a transgression of the traditional taboo on sexual intimacy between friends. Yet the statement also mirrors attempts to domesticate and devalue lesbian relationships in a heteronormative culture. The message is twofold: "Beware of your girlfriends; they could seduce you at any time," and "These girls are just friends, doing those silly things that girls like to do." Relationships between women are simultaneously without boundaries and insignificant. With this statement, Alice highlights the flipside of the "U-Haul" cliché: the taboos in lesbian culture are not clearly defined, and lesbians are therefore not as easily domesticated as the joke suggests.

The "urge to merge" does not always lead to monogamy, as the pilot quickly makes clear. Although Bette and Tina represent in the opening sequence the height of lesbian domesticity and "merging," the stability of their monogamous relationship is called into question minutes into the episode when Bette is late for a couple's therapy session. It is also in the pilot that the bisexual Alice creates the infamous "Chart," a diagram of lesbian promiscuity and incestuous couplings. It is fitting that Alice is the author of this lesbian "family tree"; as a proclaimed bisexual she embodies a fluid mode of sexuality that mirrors the Chart itself. The Chart diagrams the lesbian community in Los Angeles via the sexual encounters of its members, linking them to one another through shared lovers. A mode of kinship is produced here that is seemingly non-hierarchical. Whereas the family tree is vertical, the Chart is horizontal, even three-dimensional in its more elaborate manifestations on Alice's computer screen. There are no fathers and mothers, only incestuous sisters. The Chart offers a fantasy family in which eros is not forbidden and where power is seemingly diffuse. However, what seems to be a utopian world of polyamory at the outset of the series is revealed, by the final season, to be claustrophobic and subject to power dynamics and the observance of taboos.

As illustrated in the Chart, the lesbian world is defined both by multiplication (more lovers) and limits (the same characters return again and again). *The L Word* tells us a great deal about this dialectic that is, to my mind, particular to the lesbian community. Lesbian fans of the show responded enthusiastically to the Chart, creating their own versions online. In her piece on the Chart, Kim Ficera asserts that the two qualities that characterize lesbians best are "bad hair and interrelatedness" (2006: 111). She admits to the embarrassing interconnectedness of lesbians in a world where out lesbians are few and far between, calling the Chart "an excellent example of art imitating life" (2006: 111). It is this quality of interrelatedness that is both liberating and confining. Indeed, the Chart offers an alternative model for kinship, one that is not constructed exclusively around a monogamy/polygamy dichotomy. The recap montage that precedes season two emphasizes this interconnectedness, cutting from shots of couples (those within temporarily monogamous relationships and those simply enjoying erotic encounters) to a picture of the core members of the group. The group image is mirrored in the final sequence of the last episode of the series ("Last Word," 6:8), as individual characters walk towards the camera until they are all connected in a group shot. The first dialog presented in the opening montage of season two is the dialog between Alice and Bette about the Chart:

> Bette: "Why is it so important for you to believe that everyone is sleeping with everyone else?"
> Alice: "Because they are."

And the truth of Alice's statement has already been revealed in the images of coupling that precede this dialog. Indeed, not one couple in the series offers a stable representation of monogamy. It is, in fact, rare for any couple to retain stability for more than an episode or two. Yet the rampant polyamory rarely results in a sustained sense of freedom.

While one could draw certain parallels between lesbian and gay male cultures in this regard, *The L Word* offers up a world of erotic encounters that is particularly lesbian. The "problem" with lesbians, as we all know, is their invisibility. What exactly are they doing? The only significant male character in the first season, Tim, the boyfriend/fiancé and, later, husband/ex-husband of Jenny Schecter, confronts Marina, Jenny's lover, with precisely this question: "What is it you do, you girls? Should I even care? Does it even count?" Of course, no one would ask such a question of gay men; everyone knows that penetration "counts." Hence, while gay male culture is known for its promiscuity, gay men are never accused of "merging." Penises divide. However, *The L Word* avoids presenting a clichéd model of lesbian domesticity by revealing that lesbians are just as promiscuous as gay men. The nature of this promiscuity, however, is less quantifiable and more diffuse, simultaneously more and less expansive.

The lack of boundaries that, for better and for worse, often structures lesbian relationships is represented in *The L Word* spatially by the bathroom and, less frequently, the prison. The bathroom is the space where women seduce and are seduced, and where they cheat on one another. The opening credits of the show depict Shane pulling a woman into the bathroom, and it is clear to what purpose. In particular in the first season, the bathroom at The Planet, the lesbian-friendly café owned by Marina, serves as the site of multiple seductions and transgressions. Once again, what might generally be perceived as the last vestige of privacy in a world that increasingly blurs the lines between public and private becomes precisely a haven for explorations across boundaries. The bathroom in *The L Word* is a liminal, intimate space. Even the walls of the bathroom in The Planet are made of an opaque glass, revealing the shadows of the figures inside. The bathroom is also seemingly unisex (though The Planet is primarily frequented by women). In the first season, as Jenny and Marina begin their affair behind Tim's back, they often retreat to the bathroom for their steamy activities. In episode 1:4 ("Lies, Lies, Lies") Jenny and Marina are kissing in a stall when Tim enters the bathroom and proceeds to pee in the adjoining stall. The scene is shot from a high angle so that the spectator sees all three players: Tim peeing, Marina hiding in the adjoining stall, and Jenny washing her hands in the sink in the common area. The three characters are neither clearly linked nor clearly separated. They rather coexist temporarily in a space without proper boundaries, one that affords a fleeting intimacy and erotic fluidity. While the bathroom creates immediate intimacy independent of a larger context, it is also characteristically claustrophobic. And here is yet another difference between gay and lesbian promiscuity. While the public bathroom has always symbolized the speedy, anonymous commerce of gay sex, the bathrooms of *The L Word* are never anonymous. Everyone always knows everyone else; The Planet is like a lesbian sorority, and the bathroom traffic reflects this level of intimacy. Interestingly, in the final season of the show, Tina and Bette are having their condo renovated, and they are particularly fixated on the renovations for the upstairs bathroom, which is extremely spacious and light. In the final episode, many of the friends spend time in the new bathroom, which was constructed, it seems, to combat the claustrophobia experienced by Bette, Tina, and the community in general.

The complex interplay between intimacy, liminality, and claustrophobia is heightened in a number of scenes in the series that take place in prison cells. In the first season Bette is put in jail in conjunction with protests surrounding the *Provocations* art exhibition that she has curated, and in season five ("LGB Tease," 5:1), the privileged Helena Peabody must serve jail time due to her gambling debts. These scenes cite lesbian pulp fiction from the 1950s in which women in prison invariably engage in erotic activity with other prisoners. These trysts are, like the bathroom scenes in *The L Word*, highly secret yet constantly in danger of being exposed to all. Prison scenes in *The L Word* are often shot from outside the cell in a clichéd representation of entrapment. The spectator sees the bars that confine the prisoners, and the characters are denied all privacy. Yet despite their lack of physical privacy, both Bette and Helena manage to live out their sexual fantasies with another prisoner. The bathroom and the prison stand in for a highly fluid yet entrapping mode of lesbian intimacy and domesticity.

Lesbian domesticity

One of the significant differences between gay men and lesbians is the extent to which domesticity and monogamy shape the world of lesbians despite the less easily defined nature of relationships between women. *The L Word* begins with a utopian scene of lesbian domesticity, but characters repeatedly express feelings of claustrophobia in response to "the merge" throughout the series. It is not only Shane who retreats from every monogamous relationship in which she finds herself (usually within an episode), but even a less promiscuous character like the tennis player Dana Fairbanks recoils when her friend Alice, with whom she enters into a romantic relationship, leaves her little room to breathe. Although she returns to her later, Phyllis, Bette's boss at California Art College (where Bette is a dean), rejects her lover Joyce on similar grounds: lesbian smothering. Shane expresses these feelings in the first scene of the final episode of the series ("Last Word," 6:8). She is being questioned by the police for the murder of Jenny Schecter, her friend and, recently, lover. In response to the question as to whether she killed Jenny, she admits, rather shockingly, to having been tempted, and then segues into a seeming *non sequitur*:

I like my freedom. I do. You know what really starts to piss me
off after a while? When couples always say the word "we." I hate
it. "We think, we may, we might." But "we feel," that's the big one.
Feeling is a solitary emotion. So you may feel like you're falling in
love, and I might feel like I'm being caged.

By the end of the series, most of the characters are disillusioned
about the ideal of lesbian monogamy and the lesbian community.
Yet even Shane flirts with domesticity again and again. In season
four she quasi-adopts her half-brother, Shay, a nine-year-old male
version of herself, when her stepmother abandons him. She not only
becomes a parental figure, but also falls for the mother of one of Shay's
classmates, Paige. The four create a nuclear family of sorts, until
Shane's father returns to take Shay away and Shane experiences the
usual claustrophobia at the thought of cohabitation. In episode 4:12
("Long Time Coming") Shane has sex with Paige while imagining
a 1950s-style nuclear family life with Paige, her son Jared (Jackson
Allan), and Shay. These scenes are shot in a campy style with Shane
playing the working dad in a tie and Paige embodying the role of the
housewife serving breakfast. The montage (cutting between Shane and
Paige making love and the fantasy/nightmare images of domestic bliss)
is shot and acted in a highly ambiguous manner. Is this a fantasy? A
nightmare? The Paige character in the vision is happy; "Dad" Shane
is thoughtful. The 1950s images recall a camp aesthetic of domestic
melodrama, but it is not entirely clear whether this is attractive or
repulsive to Shane. In season three ("Last Dance," 3:11), Shane had
even "proposed" to her girlfriend Carmen and agreed to an elaborate
wedding in Whistler, British Columbia. Thus, for Shane, traditional
domesticity has a pull. She ultimately leaves Carmen at the altar, but
the allure of circumscribed intimacy nevertheless continues to haunt
her in various forms. Like her namesake, Alan Ladd's "Shane" from the
popular Western, Shane is an outsider who nevertheless respects the
"hominess" of others. The film *Shane* begins with Shane's arrival on
the homestead—the space of domesticity (consisting of father, mother,
and child)—and ends after he has preserved the home space through
his courage. After having successfully fought off the ranchers who
threaten this home (a home which he himself has destabilized from the
inside, as the film hints at an erotic connection between Shane and the
wife, Marion), the film ends with his departure as the son Joey yells,

"Mother wants you. I know she does! [...] Shane! Shane! Come back!" Just like Alan Ladd's Shane, Katherine Moennig's Shane both reveres and fears the trappings of domesticity.

Even Pat Califia, the self-proclaimed lesbian non-monogamist (Califia has since become Patrick Califia), admits to the lure of the lesbian home. In "UnMonogamy: Loving Tricks and Tricking Lovers," Califia emphasizes the aloneness of life even during sex: "You are as alone during simultaneous orgasm as you are sitting home while your lover is out on a date" (1984). She ridicules the desire to merge with another and the restrictions of monogamy in general, yet she nevertheless experiences a weakness for the lesbian home:

> I think all gay people feel like runaways or orphans. My lover is the only home I have. I don't belong anywhere else. Nobody wants us to be together—not our families, not the bishop (be he Catholic or Mormon), not our bank, not the President. Not our ex-lovers, at least until they find new relationships, and sometimes not even our friends, who know we would have more time for them if we weren't reading TV Guide and arguing over what to watch tonight. I am stubborn about sticking it out, showing the others they are wrong about us. I take pride in surviving all this hostility. My loyalty is not just to my lover but to the lesbian nature of the relationship. I stay with her and take care of her because that is all I can do to prove that I am still a good woman, a real woman, despite the fact that I will not raise children or keep house for a man. (1984)

Califia wants to insist here on the particularly *lesbian* nature of the home she idealizes, even as she espouses the virtues of polyfidelity. She also points to the resentment under the surface within a lesbian community, where even friends find it difficult to find a place within the intimate world of the lesbian couple.

The model for lesbian domesticity in *The L Word* is initially the Bette/Tina pairing. They are "making a baby," they own a beautiful house, and they finally do have a baby and plan to adopt another. Yet their relationship is fraught with infidelity throughout the series, and the two break up a number of times. At one point, Bette and Tina are even involved in a tryst as lovers behind the back of Bette's monogamous lover, Jodi. Their relationship is defined in terms of domesticity, even when they consistently fail in their attempts at fidelity. Their first meeting is portrayed in a flashback episode ("Looking Back," 1:11) at an art gallery, and the photo framing the encounter pictures the danger and violence of domesticity. It is a photo of the naked back of the lesbian artist herself, Catherine Opie, upon which someone has etched a primitive drawing with a razor blade. The etching depicts a house, a cloud, and two stick figures with skirts holding hands. As Rebecca Beirne puts it, the image reveals the "violence necessary to produce domestication" (2008a: 110). The happy lesbian family is literally cut into the back of the artist, scarring her forever. The fact that Tina and Bette's first meeting is framed by such a violent representation of the lesbian idyll underscores the conflicted nature of their own union, despite the fact that it is viewed as ideal by the other members of the community.

Lesbian kinship

Despite the use of a wide variety of clichés about lesbians,[2] *The L Word* comments on lesbian kinship models in highly astute ways. Alice's "Chart" lays out the ordered disorder of lesbian kinship. As the resident lothario, Shane occupies the middle of the Chart. In Alice's initial draft, almost all roads lead back to Shane. So while the Chart reflects, on the one hand, a horizontal, non-hierarchical and de-centered community, on the other it reveals certain power blocks after all. This notion of power is explored wittily in season four ("Livin' La Vida Loca," 4:2) with the introduction of a new character, "Papi." Through her Chart research, Alice begins to discover erotic links between numerous women and the woman named "Papi." Indeed, Papi is such an accomplished seductress that she is able to lure the heterosexual Kit, Bette's half-sister, into her bed, although the tryst is ultimately unsuccessful. As Alice discovers, Papi destabilizes Shane's center, for she seems to have slept with even more women than Shane herself has. Hence, what initially appears to be a horizontally structured lesbian "family tree" is revealed to contain two power poles. Despite the absence of fathers and paternal lines, power accumulates via multiple trysts. It is certainly no mistake that Shane's main rival for women's desire is named Papi, and Papi openly competes with Shane for women. Papi reminds us that western power is conceived in patriarchal terms and that the "lesbian universe" is a porous construction within the larger heteronormative frame.

Papi is a playful nod to the inevitability of power dynamics, yet her sexual exploits nevertheless resemble Shane's as she seduces women of all types. Throughout the show's six seasons Shane's trysts and encounters cross racial, class, and age lines. In "Look Out, Here They Come!" (5:2) Shane has been hired to style hair for a wedding. Within the space of a few hours, she manages to have sex not only with the bride, but also with a bridesmaid and the mother of the bride. Shane is not the active seducer in these trysts; rather, she is actively sought after by all three women, who view her as an escape outlet for their own sense of heterosexual claustrophobia. Of course, the joke here is that these women are ultimately blind to the particularly claustrophobic nature of the lesbian world about which Shane complains so bitterly in the final episode. This slapstick narrative not only reveals the sometimes exhaustive nature of polyamory but also brings to the fore the question of taboos within the world of the lesbian Chart, as Shane is desired by various women within the same biological family.

Despite the erotic fluidity of the Chart, certain barriers do exist. While visiting her daughter, Alice's mother writes herself into the Chart, having kissed Shane at a party. The inclusion of her mother within the interconnected world of the Chart is highly disturbing to Alice, reminding us that certain taboos structure the community after all. For Alice, Shane's kiss with her mother is taboo. Another example of coupling that is perceived as crossing taboo lines both by other *L Word* characters and fans of the show is the romantic/sexual relationship between Shane and Jenny. Having been "best friends" since the second season, these two friends become sexually and romantically involved in the final season, and the response on the part of their friends is not positive. By the final season of the show, Jenny has made herself unlikable to most of the other main characters through her narcissistic and often thoughtless behavior, yet this doesn't seem to be the primary reason why the others are disturbed. Although *The L Word* characters constantly become involved with a wide variety of sexual partners (including stalkers and men), the liaison between Jenny and Shane generates the most hysteria in *The L Word* universe. The community members react somewhat negatively to Tina's involvement with a man, to Jenny's involvement with a transitioning female-to-male lover, or to Helena's reconnection with the woman who falsely sued her for sexual harassment, but these reactions are usually tempered within a single episode. The shocked and disturbed response to the Jenny/

Shane affair shapes the entire final season. Here, it seems, Shane has hit upon a taboo within the fluid kinship model of the Chart. And fans respond in a similarly disturbed manner to what is perceived as an especially incestuous coupling within an already incestuous world. For example, one discussion on *The L Word* wiki of the Showtime site is entitled, "Shane and Jenny: A Forbidden Love." Here, fans argue that this friendship is too "close" to become a love affair, suggesting that some sort of incest taboo should have been observed in this instance. As "knightsofstjoan2004" writes,

> It was completely wrong for Shane and Jenny to become lovers. Jenny's love for Shane is a forbidden love and falling in love with her was a huge mistake. For this reason Jenny was dead wrong to think that Shane has broken her heart and the truth is that Jenny's heart is not meant for Shane and Shane's heart is not meant for Jenny. All of us should agree that their hearts don't belong to each other.[3]

What is so "forbidden" about Jenny's love for Shane? Why do a number of fans as well as Shane's friends (Jenny has no more friends by the end of the series) feel that this relationship is "too close," using terms reminiscent of the traditional incest taboo? Here, it seems, the fluid world of lesbian polyamory has bumped up against a wall. Everything is allowed except *that.* Yet where, exactly, is the incest located in a kinship structure in which almost none of the members are related by blood? Is one working here with a system of exogamy, in which members marry outside of the clan, or of endogamy, in which members marry primarily within the clan in order to preserve power structures? Of course, no traditional kinship model will map neatly onto the lesbian Chart for the obvious reason that marriage is prohibited to lesbians in most parts of the US, and even in those states where it is allowed, it cannot be said to function in any way parallel to traditional marriage. Nevertheless, the fact that certain power differentials structure the community and that certain pairings are perceived by most members as taboo suggests that, despite the fluidity of erotic attachments, *The L Word* world partially resembles more traditional kinship models.

For Claude Lévi-Strauss, the incest taboo is, formally speaking, an organizational tool: "Considered as a prohibition, the prohibition of incest merely affirms, in a field vital to the group's survival, the pre-eminence of the social over the natural, the collective over the individual, organization over the arbitrary" (1969: 45). Lévi-Strauss points out that the incest taboo is not necessary for natural reasons; rather, it could be seen as an arbitrary marker that intends to produce a sense of order. Within clans, *"A person cannot do just what he pleases. The positive aspect of the prohibition is to initiate organization"* (1969: 43).

Incest indicates coupling between two people who are too close biologically, too similar. As I have already pointed out, lesbian relationships are often viewed along these lines, as "incestuous," revealing an excess of *sameness*. At the outset, *The L Word* seemingly represents a system of lesbian endogamy, one in which same chooses same and, as revealed in the Chart, everyone chooses partners from within the clan. However, as quickly becomes apparent, same is not same. If, in the tradition of psychoanalysis, we map the notion of difference exclusively along gender lines, then there would be no variations of sameness and difference within the lesbian community, and certain couplings (such as that between Shane and Jenny or between Shane and Alice's mother) would not be particularly disturbing. But *The L Word* reminds us that difference must be imagined beyond the traditional dictates of a gender binary. Rebecca Beirne argues that lesbian desire based on difference is "effective and productive" whereas lesbian eros resulting from sameness manifests as "unrestrainable desire and beguilement" (2008: 109). But which categories should be used to determine difference and sameness? Beirne sees the relationship between Bette and Candace (the woman with whom Bette has an affair, played by Ion Overman) as an example of sameness, due to race identifications (though Bette is another interesting example of fluid identities: half white, half African-American). In contrast, she sees Bette and Tina's relationship as defined by difference: Bette is dark, Tina is light; Bette is powerful, Tina is initially traditionally feminine. Beirne also suggests that the relationship between Jenny and Marina doesn't work since they are too similar (in coloring and in their interests); Jenny's alter ego fictional character "Sara Schuster" even drowns at sea after sex with Marina (2008: 112). But surely difference and sameness cannot simply be mapped along racial or gender lines. The relationship between the African-American Tasha and the white Alice illustrates the pitfalls of a racially based model for difference. At a crisis point in their relationship Tasha becomes highly attracted to Jamie, an Asian-American friend. Yet difference and sameness and, for that matter, desire, do not neatly follow white/non-white lines. There are multiple variations of non-whiteness: African-American and Asian-American are not the same. In fact, at the end of the series Tasha returns to Alice, drawn by the complex manifestations of sameness and difference in their relationship.

Thinking difference through gender difference usually leads us to the butch/femme distinction, but even here *The L Word* confounds. Not only do the Bette/Candace and Jenny/Marina pairings quickly go sour; none of the relationships on the show functions well for the duration. Following the logic of gender difference as butch/femme performances, how does the Shane/Jenny coupling, arguably the least successful pairing of the show, represent too much sameness? Shane is a soft butch, and Jenny is an over-the-top femme, almost to the point of caricature. So the issue here is not gender identity. Rather, fans objected to best friends becoming lovers, a relationship that can easily produce an excess of intimacy. Another problem with best friends coupling is that it potentially disrupts the system of fluid lesbian polyamory; if we all simply couple for life with our best friend, then wouldn't this close off connections within the lesbian community even more? Within an already small and often claustrophobic world, polyamory provides a minimal sense of movement. If best friends become romantically attached, then the system stagnates and shrinks even more.

When viewed in this light, the "problem" of Shane and Jenny casts a shadow over utopian notions of the potential of queer kinship models. In *Undoing Gender* Judith Butler asks whether monogamy always already implies heterosexual power structures, arguing that when kinship bonds are formed outside of biological ties, sexuality becomes cut off from kinship, allowing for the "durable tie to be thought outside of the conjugal frame" and thus opening "kinship to a set of community ties that are irreducible to family" (2004: 127). This is the sense of the Chart and of the lesbian community as a whole. David Schneider argues that the prevalence of diaspora and queer communities reveals that kinship is "a kind of *doing*, one that does not reflect a prior structure but that can only be understood as enacted practice" (Butler 2004: 123). This contemporary mode of kinship would then not follow a given model but would rather enact the "assemblage of significations as it takes place" (Butler 2004: 126), a community in process. Schneider points to international adoption as well as to donor insemination as examples of kinship modes that are constructed spontaneously. Indeed, communities are often created around sperm donors in a complex conflation of biological and non-traditional familial ties.

The L Word has an interesting take on these issues, one that contains within it some pessimism as to the utopian potential of lesbian kinship structures. In the first season Tina becomes pregnant through a sperm donation from an artist acquaintance named Marcus. Tina eventually loses this baby, but before the miscarriage she has a hostile encounter ("Losing It," 1:6) with Marcus's new girlfriend, Lei Ling. They happen to meet in the doctor's office, and Marcus and Tina naively talk about the successful insemination. Marcus's girlfriend is horrified, and runs screaming after Tina that the child does not "belong" to Tina: "Our kids will be family!" This woman then proceeds to harass Tina by calling her repeatedly on the phone and threatening her. The issue here is the ownership of Marcus's sperm and, as a consequence, of the child. Where one would hope for a kind of community in which kinship could be spontaneously "assembled" outside of prior models for family and community, as David Schneider suggests, the encounters between Tina and Marcus's girlfriend reveal precisely the dominance of traditional family models.

In her critique of "compulsory monogamy" within the lesbian community, Celeste West asks: "Can we freely express the sexual energy that naturally exists between people and maintain the historic hierarchy of relationship/ownership?" (1996: 40).[4] For West, lesbian "polyfidelity" calls into question the capitalist ideology of the individual and property. *The L Word* imagines such an alternative universe while also remaining aware of the pitfalls of utopian thinking. Judith Butler asks whether kinship must always be thought in heterosexual terms, whether monogamy always implies heterosexuality, and whether kinship is then always tied to the question of property. Clearly, certain de-linkages are forged within lesbian communities, but *The L Word* astutely shows that the world of the Chart is always already embedded within an entrenched heteronormative system. In the final episode of the series ("Last Word," 6:8), Jenny tells Shane: "You are my family. You will get everything when I die." Here, she has delinked family and biology while nevertheless retaining the capitalist system of property and inheritance.

Chart fatigue: The final season

Jenny's revival of a capitalist kinship structure early in the final episode of the series reminds the spectator of the myriad ways in which *The L Word* offers an alternative kinship model that repeatedly encounters dead ends. As the series progresses, a structure of both multiplication and circularity emerges. Already in the first season, certain doublings stand out: one of the women whom Tina dates after breaking up with Bette looks uncannily like Bette; Jenny writes stories about Sarah Schuster, who is less an alter ego than an exact replica of Jenny. In season four Jenny publishes a novel and a short story (in *The New Yorker*) that retells the lives of *The L Word* community members. In season five Jenny's script based on the book and the short story is made into a film, *Lez Girls*. A major part of this season depicts the *Lez Girls* film set that is populated not only by the actresses who play *The L Word* characters but also by the original characters themselves. Bette, Tina, Shane, and Jenny are constantly colliding with the actresses who play Bette, Tina, Shane, and Jenny. In a more outrageous representation of the Sarah Schuster doubling, Jenny even falls in love with "herself," so to speak, in the form of the actress, Niki Stevens, who plays her character in the film. The pinnacle of this mode of doubling and excess arrives when Jenny hosts a party ("Lookin' at You, Kid," 5:5) for the actors and the individuals upon whom their characters are based. The uncanny doublings underscore the ways in which the polyamorous lesbian community has a tendency to expand in a manner that ultimately serves to circumscribe an already claustrophobically intimate community. Here we verge on parody; lesbian "sameness" manifests in absurd ways.

The circularity and claustrophobia that is the flipside of lesbian polyamory colors the final episode of the series. "Last Word" is an often dark reflection on the vicissitudes of the Chart. The season commences with the death of Jenny Schecter in Bette and Tina's pool. Hence, the circumscribed nature of the community is mirrored in the narrative structure; Jenny's new desires were born in the first episode of the series, as she observed Shane having sex in the same pool in which she dies. Similarly, in "Last Word" we see Shane returning home after a night out, stopping to admire the "happy couple" Bette and Tina in a scene that almost exactly duplicates one from the first episode of the series in which Bette and Tina sit on the front steps of their house after having made love. But this circularity points to claustrophobia, as "Last Word" begins with Shane's frustrated complaint to the police about the oppressive nature of "we." This scene is followed by Jenny and Shane's video take for a video present for Bette and Tina, who are moving to New York. Jenny articulates feelings both for herself and Shane, and announces that "we" (Shane and Jenny) will become the new Bette and Tina in their absence. By moving away, then, Tina and Bette have not made a space for a new constellation of lesbians. Rather, Jenny imagines that the given structure will simply shift to make way for a new dominant lesbian couple. Since this scene was preceded by Shane's uncharacteristically cranky complaints about the intimacy needs of others, we are forced to view it in a particularly cynical manner.

All scenarios within the final episode are colored by this kind of cynicism. In fact, Katherine Moennig has admitted that she was not happy with the direction of season six for this reason. Jenny's narcissistic claim that she and Shane will become the new Bette and Tina is followed by a scene in which Tasha and Jamie admit to Alice that they are attracted to one another. What had begun as an eroticized triangle in which all three women felt included deteriorates into a traditional betrayal narrative in which one lover is excluded from the group. Alice has ordered Tasha to sleep with Jamie and then tell her what she wants. In talking to Shane about the situation, Alice points to the excess of sameness, as she perceives it, between Tasha and Jamie: "Eventually they should just stop having sex because they are so the same they could just masturbate. It would be the same thing." Alice mouths here an oversimplified version of the critique of homosexuality as excess sameness. The queen of liminality, of the fluid eroticism of the Chart, emerges in the end as a grouchy defender of boundaries and difference.

The frustrated rejection of the status quo that is articulated both by Shane and by Alice in "Last Word" is echoed by Bette in a conversation with Kit about their community. Bette complains about the claustrophobic nature of their world with an uncharacteristic vitriol reminiscent of Shane's shocking confessions about her frustrations with her friends and lovers at the beginning of the episode. When Kit asks Bette how she feels about leaving LA, she says,

> I am so ready to get out of here. I am so tired of everyone being all up in everyone else's business. I want to go to New York because

I think it would be a good move for us. However, I am happy to be getting out of this little incestuous hotbed of lesbian inter-fucking connectedness.

Here we have the dystopic side of the Chart laid out to the viewer at the moment when she is already feeling premature nostalgia at the loss of the show. What might have been imagined as expansion is revealed as simply mirroring and claustrophobia. The "little incestuous hotbed of lesbian inter-fucking connectedness" is likewise mocked by Peggy Peabody, the rich mother of Helena, who responds to the news that Bette and Tina will move to New York with an invitation: "I want to throw you a party in New York. I have a big house in New York – five floors – so there would be room for all your exes." Despite its ever-expanding nature, the lesbian community can be domesticated and contained within a house. Peggy's joke echoes the laments of Shane, Bette, and Alice: if there is always a house big enough to hold the clan together, then how can one escape?

Despite the cynical tone of the final episode of the series, expressions of claustrophobia are countered by positive assertions about the connectedness of the community. Bette's outburst of frustration with the incestuous lesbian world is followed by an abrupt cut to Kit in the police station, assuring the police that "you will never find a group of people who love one another more and who look after one another as lovingly as these friends do." And when the police enter the party near the end of the episode, Tina tells them, "We are a very tight-knit group," and Shane adds, "Yes, we take care of each other." The final scene of the show depicts the friends arriving at the police station, walking towards a camera located in the vicinity of the station. The emotional tenor is initially sober, and then, inexplicably, the characters begin to walk towards the camera in a celebratory manner. Given the dark mood of the episode, the slow smiles on the faces of the characters initially suggest conspiracy: do they all know who has killed Jenny? Have they perhaps all conspired to get rid of her? Such a reading is disrupted, however, as Jenny herself appears, walking towards the camera in slow motion, her smile gradually spreading. Here, the group is breaking out of any narrative frame. A light wind blows the hair of the actresses, as they seem to transcend their characters and join together as cast. In a self-conscious citation of the opening sequence of the show, a campy, colorful, celebratory montage accompanying the song "This is the Way We Live," the women on-screen make the unusual move from character to actress playing character. In this way, the narrative expands exponentially, potentially even including the world of the fans. What could seem like a kitschy ending to a dark season is actually, to my mind, a witty engagement with fans of the show. The smiling actresses who seem about to step out of the screen and into our living rooms imply that we are intimately linked to *The L Word* world. Our "little incestuous hotbed of lesbian inter-fucking connectedness" both expands and contracts in concert with *The L Word*, the first and, to date, last TV show that cared to chart our world.

Notes

1   Samuel A. Chambers (2006) argues that the show focuses, in particular in the first season, on mimicking heteronormative relationships: "[...] the first season consistently returns to the clichéd heteronormative narratives that will strike the straight viewer as comforting and familiar."

2   Rebecca Beirne sums up her analysis of representations of lesbians in *The L Word* along these lines: "The series does seem to perform something unique, and I think this is situated in the sheer multiplicity of the clichés activated in *The L Word*. This multiplicity creates an encyclopedia of lesbian cultural representation on the one hand, and on the other it offers a certain productive space for reflection on new forms of representing lesbians on television" (2008: 134).

3   *The L Word* Wiki, http://lwordwiki.sho.com/thread/3033360/Shane+and+Jenny:+A+Forbidden+Love.

4   Merri Lisa Johnson (2006) also cites this passage in her chapter, "L is for 'Long Term': Compulsory Monogamy on *The L Word*," in which she analyzes the issue of monogamy in the series.

"L" is for Looking Again: Art and Representation on *The L Word**

Margaret T. McFadden

From the beginning, the creators of *The L Word* understood that their program would have to confront a difficult problem: how to portray lesbian and bisexual women in ways that did not simply reproduce stereotypes and preconceptions shaped by a sexist and heterosexist mainstream culture. However, the creators also knew that in order to have broad cultural appeal (and thus commercial success), the show would have to conform to certain familiar conventions of television. They resolved this tension in a very clever way, by making both issues central themes of the program throughout its six seasons. That is, the show makes visible and critiques the kinds of stereotypical and objectifying portrayals of women and of queers that are normative in US culture—in both popular cultural forms like Hollywood film and pornography, and high cultural forms like painting, sculpture, art photography, and experimental video—and explores the possibilities for inventing alternative forms or images or redefining existing ones. At the same time, the program also shows viewers how Hollywood works, and critiques the ways of doing business that keep reproducing these stereotypical and false representations of queer women. By moving between these two thematic concerns, *The L Word* presents attentive viewers with a detailed history of the problem of lesbian representation, while simultaneously offering new ways to look at and think about apparently familiar images and narratives. In other words, when we watch *The L Word*, we might not be seeing what we think we're seeing.

This chapter will focus on one aspect of this larger project of *The L Word*: its exploration of the representation of gender and sexuality in contemporary art. The show uses the work of particular contemporary artists known for their engagement with questions of female, lesbian, and/or queer representation to present its critique of a long history of erasure, misrepresentation, and objectification, and to argue for innovative female and queer self-representation as a necessary response to that history. These artists are not constrained by the same kinds of commercial pressures as *The L Word* is, so the show's consistent attention to their (and others') work constitutes a formal device that provides a counter-narrative or alternative to those conventions of representation required by the show's need to appeal to a broad audience; in other words, these artists can do things that the show cannot. In addition, the show has offered numerous story arcs that focus on art, using narrative to explore these same issues and to advance its arguments (Heller 2006; McFadden 2006).

The L Word's concern with the complexities of female and queer representation is marked by its almost obsessive attention to the process of creating representations in contemporary visual culture. We see characters creating pornographic, documentary, and fiction films; music videos; video art; sculpture; television programs; websites; podcasts; and marketing campaigns. In virtually every one of these scenes, we are shown a different example of misrepresentation and misunderstanding of lesbian lives by commercial media producers and consumers (often male) who are locked into conventional ways of seeing. We are also shown the realities of the commercial motives that often drive (or distort) such productions. *The L Word* teaches viewers to see this history of misrepresentation, and to notice exactly how media is used to tell lies. In so doing, of course, it draws viewers' attention to its own status as a constructed (and potentially false) text.

A key formal strategy that the show uses to explore these broad questions of representation is making frequent references to specific works of art that are themselves exploring questions of representation in contemporary culture. One of the main characters in the ensemble is Bette Porter, who is at first the director of an up-and-coming contemporary art museum, and who later becomes the dean of a university art school. Her position as a cutting-edge curator and critic provides *The L Word* with a device by which to show viewers a great deal of visual art. Through Bette's character, the program returns repeatedly to questions about the representation of gender and sexuality in contemporary art and popular culture.

For example, in each episode, the work of different artists appears on-screen. The art on the walls in Bette's office changes quite often, and new works frequently appear in her home. She visits galleries and artists' studios, scenes in which we see the work of both fictional and real artists displayed or being made. At other times, viewers are positioned as members of her audience as Bette lectures on specific pieces to other characters. Several of the featured artists even appear briefly in the show, with their work, which is highlighted and sometimes even discussed by the characters. In addition, season one culminates in an extended story arc, in which Bette and her museum must fight a far-right Christian group that is trying to prevent the opening of a show of challenging and controversial works called *Provocations*. The art works shown in these contexts typically comment on the action or the cultural moment in some way, and often serve to challenge the representations of gender and sexuality that seem to be implicit in the show's casting and character development.

The artists

The L Word focuses on the works of carefully chosen artists, people whose work is well known for its engagement with and challenges to the history of representation of women and queers. The presence of these images enables the program to question its own apparent participation in reproducing mainstream narratives about gender and sexuality.

The L Word raises the question of the relationship between art and pornography in the pilot episode. Given that some audiences are likely to view the show's representation of explicit lesbian sexuality and female nudity as inherently pornographic, it is important for the show to stake out its position from the outset; its defense of the right of artists to explore gender and sexuality in their work is therefore not only a defense of challenging art in a free society, but also, at least implicitly, a defense of the show's right to exist. Including the work of Canadian artist Laurie Papou allows the show to develop this theme.

At a gallery talk at her museum that blends the fictional and the real, Bette introduces Papou, by asking:

How do we draw the line that signifies whether an image reads as pornography? I mean, who gets to say what passes as art and what is obscenity? The debate has been taken up by Laurie Papou, in a series of paintings entitled *A Group of Seven*. Please welcome Laurie. ("Pilot," 1:1)

During this introduction, the camera pans the stage, allowing us to see Papou's large-scale painting *Mutual Reflections* (1991) behind Bette and the artist. Later in the episode, we see Bette and Tina standing before two other Papou paintings, *She wished she had been named Hope, as a reminder*, and *Because faith was not lost in the chaos all around her, she was* (both 2000).

The seven canvases that make up *A Group of Seven*, like the ones we actually see, demonstrate Papou's interest in the question of the representation of women, particularly in the European art tradition (Godley 1989: D1). Each of these works is in dialog with the western canon, and all involve restaging well-known works of art, using Papou and her partner Iain Ross as subjects. Most of the time the models are nude, and posed in a variety of lush, outdoor, Edenic settings. For example, *One* is a direct reference to Botticelli's *Venus and Mars* (1485), while *Two* is inspired by a sixteenth-century painting by Paolo Veronese.

In these restagings, Papou is exploring several different questions. By reversing and revising the power dynamics between men and women in the images, she makes visible how often women in canonical works of art have been objectified or made powerless, and she rejects this convention. In all the paintings, she is taking back the female nude from what it has come to mean, and explicitly rejecting the notion that the unclothed female figure is disempowered in relation to the clothed male. Papou argues, "I'm fed up with the idea that female sexuality is something to be oppressed or hidden ... a nude female figure can still be a powerful figure" (Scott 1997: C5).

At the same time, she reclaims Eden as a space of pleasure and freedom of choice (rather than of sin) and reinvents conventions of representation of relations between men and women, in order to create a new language of gesture and metaphor that evokes, but also revises, the history of stories and images that structure western attitudes towards women and sexuality. Further, she defends the use of painting as a medium that is not outdated or hopelessly tainted by its history of misogynist representation (Scott 1997: C5). Implicitly, *The L Word* is making a similar claim about the possibilities of creating new meanings within familiar forms on commercial television.

These paintings have been described by some conservative critics as pornographic (Barrett 1995: C6; Byfield 1995: 44), making very relevant the question that Bette asks within the narrative: Who gets to define the boundary between art and pornography? Papou, like the producers of *The L Word*, is claiming the right to refuse boundaries drawn by those who wish to suppress the right of women and queers to represent their own experiences, as part of a reactionary political agenda. To feature an artist who is working in a feminist vein to take back the power of the female figure and explicitly re-vision art history and art itself is consistent with what the show is trying to do in the context of television. Like Papou, the show refuses simple-minded notions about female nudity and sexuality, and embraces the representation of an empowered female sexuality that is not defined by patriarchy or the male gaze, but that also does not pretend that the patriarchal history of representation of women doesn't exist or have to be contended with.

Although Papou's work is about the representation of women in general, its exploration of the boundaries between art and pornography is quite relevant to the representation of lesbian women more specifically, because the most familiar and ubiquitous representations of lesbianism in contemporary culture are to be found in pornography aimed at heterosexual males. *The L Word* consistently makes visible the specter of the voyeuristic male (or straight couple) gazing or peeping at lesbian sexuality. For example, this dynamic is exposed in the pilot episode (1:1), when Jenny, newly arrived in Los Angeles, watches two women having sex in the next-door neighbors' pool. Later that evening, she narrates what she saw to her boyfriend Tim to titillate him during a sexual encounter. This scene draws attention to the fact that many viewers' preconceptions about lesbians will have been shaped by a form that has consistently misrepresented and misunderstood them, and that has used scenes of "lesbian" sex as a turn-on for heterosexuals. Further, by having the camera take Jenny's point of view, the scene shows viewers that, through familiar conventions of filming and editing, we are participating in her voyeurism (Wolfe and Roripaugh 2006: 49; Heller 2006: 58–9; Moore 2007: 119–20). For viewers who may not have considered how normalized such representations are in mainstream culture, these scenes serve to make a familiar (and now exposed as voyeuristic) viewing position a very uncomfortable one to occupy.

This theme of the effects of pornographic representation on women is explored in much greater detail in the season two storyline about Mark Wayland, a character who becomes the roommate of Jenny and Shane ("Lynch Pin," 2:4). Mark makes low-budget, *Girls Gone Wild*-style porn videos, but, intrigued by his new friends, he decides to make a serious documentary about lesbian culture. Despite his good intentions, Mark is unable to escape his voyeuristic, objectifying perspective and he resorts to planting hidden cameras all through the house to spy on the women ("Labyrinth," 2:5). At the climax of this story arc, after she has discovered the cameras, which she describes as "rapey," a furious Jenny situates the real harm his voyeurism has done to her in a larger cultural context of male dominance:

> What I want is for you to write "Fuck me" on your chest. Do it! And then walk down the street. Anybody that wants to fuck you, say "Sure, sure." And when they do, you have to say "Thank you very much," and make sure you have a smile on your face, and then, you stupid fucking coward, you'll know what it feels like to be a woman. ("Land Ahoy," 2:10)

The L Word thus constructs a representation of a ubiquitous, prurient, objectifying male gaze and connects it to the violent, real-world patriarchal oppression of women. In this way, the program responds to the concern of some viewers that it would simply exploit the representation of lesbian sexuality to appeal to a straight male audience; indeed, some early critics read the scenes with Tim and Jenny as doing precisely that. But the show includes such familiar scenarios to explore the consequences of the objectifying male gaze and of dehumanizing stereotypes on women, especially lesbian women. In other words, *The L Word* is working on multiple levels to make its argument that viewers must learn to see familiar images and conventions anew; in its narrative, and in the visual art it highlights, the show is teaching viewers the history of representation (and misrepresentation) and inviting us to imagine new possibilities, even in commercial media.

Another artist whose work is featured as part of *The L Word*'s exploration of the complexities of representation is New York-based painter Lisa Yuskavage, whose painting *True Blonde on a Mountaintop* is prominently displayed in Bette and Tina's house in season two. Tina explains to her lawyer that Yuskavage is one of Bette's favorite painters. The lawyer, whom we already know as rather a philistine, asks with distaste, "Jesus! You lived with that?" as they (and we) gaze at the painting ("Lynch Pin," 2:4). The lawyer's initial response is perhaps understandable, as the image depicts a cartoony, larger-than-life woman kneeling on a mountaintop; she wears only a beaded thong, which she is reaching into with her left hand as she looks down at her own body. At first glance, the painting might seem to reproduce the pornographic objectification of women so common in contemporary culture and in art history, and thus be an odd choice for the show.

By her own account, Yuskavage is centrally concerned with the representation of women, both in art history and in popular culture (including pornography), and in the relationships between all these different media. She noticed, for example, that *Penthouse* photographers often used models posed and lit classically, and she began to use their photos as inspirations for her work. This influence is manifest most clearly in the cover of the exhibition catalog for a 2001 show at the Institute of Contemporary Art in Philadelphia, in which the artist's name has been superimposed in pink *Penthouse*-font letters over a detail from Yuskavage's painting *Day*, raising the question of the relationship between these different forms of representation (Yuskavage and Siegel 2000). The catalog cover draws our attention to the extent to which our view of the world has been shaped by the omnipresent pornographic imagery in our visual culture. Its goals are therefore parallel to those of *The L Word*, which seeks to explore the same issues.

Yuskavage's rather grotesque female figures are open to interpretation, of course, but many critics see her as lampooning the ridiculously hyperbolic female forms apparently prescribed by straight male pornographic fantasies. The women are typically nude or half-dressed, and they have exaggerated body parts, blurry faces, turned-up noses, and strike familiar, submissive poses. But at the same time, Yuskavage is exploring the complicated effects of these stereotypical, objectifying images on women. Many of her female figures are involved in some form of self-examination. They're looking at themselves, often with a certain puzzlement. Perhaps they comment on the extent to which the female gaze (and women's self-conceptions) have been shaped by the male gaze and representations of women made by and for men. Reflecting on the complexity of these images, critic Roberta Smith asks:

> Do her figures exaggerate or ridicule and deflect the male gaze? Do they perpetuate the stereotypes that assault women every day or illuminate some of the more private and at times darker corners of the female psyche, including those moments of searing self-reproach when a woman appraises her appearance and finds it wanting? (2001: E53)

In a similar vein, critic Marcia Hall argues that Yuskavage's art comments on our culture in complicated and paradoxical ways:

> It is about the gaze, but, more, it comments upon the culture that consumes such images. She critiques the girls, but at the same time, she is deeply responsive to the women burdened with sexual attributes that may be all the world chooses to see about her. ... She celebrates the sexuality of her babes at the same time that she lampoons their ubiquity in American visual culture, as if to say it is not their physicality that is vulgar, but the use made of them by male and female alike. (2000: 23)

In addition to drawing on the ubiquity of pornographic imagery in our culture, Yuskavage also draws on the history of western art. For example, by the artist's own account, the painting *Day* noted above was influenced by her memory of a Degas monotype, *Nude Woman Standing in a Bathtub* (1880–1885), as well by a 1970s *Penthouse* photo. She wants all these layers of meaning and influence to coexist in her work, as they do in our experience of the world (Siegel 2000: 19–20). But to those who would read her as perpetuating the stereotypes that assault women every day, Yuskavage is adamant that she is creating not a real person, but "a constructed pictorial object" (Gould 2000: 11). She explains, "I only let things happen in paintings that can only really happen in painting. They touch on the real world, but they are not the same as the real world" (Siegel 2000: 20).

In this, she is, arguably, doing much the same thing as the producers of *The L Word*, who are creating a "densely layered" fiction that invites us to see the "real world" anew, but that also, like Yuskavage's paintings, runs the risk of being understood simply as reproducing stereotypes and courting a prurient and exploitative male gaze. Both the paintings and the television show ask viewers to consider the effects of the histories of representation of gender and sexuality on all of us, but particularly on women. And both challenge the expectation that what they are doing is straightforwardly documenting or reflecting some external reality.

Part of the power of Yuskavage's work is that while the figures may be grotesque, they are so beautifully painted that they are very hard simply to dismiss. Critic Katy Siegel captures the complicated responses that Yuskavage's paintings generate when she writes: "By this time, years after feminism's lessons, we know we're not supposed to respond erotically to such images, that it is degrading or, at the very least, banal. Still, the women are seductively beautiful, and so is the painting style; they are hard to resist" (Siegel 2000: 19). This insight might apply equally well to both the paintings and the program; despite three decades of powerful feminist analysis and critique, what we respond to visually has still been shaped by a patriarchal and objectifying visual tradition. The need to create new or alternative representations of gender and sexuality to contest and/or replace those that have been so dominant is another issue taken up by *The L Word* and the artists whose work the show highlights. The difficulty of doing this, given the long history of objectifying and disempowering images of female figures and the current repressive political climate, is made legible by the show's narrative. In this historical moment, those who try to make visible an empowered female or queer gender expression or sexuality run the risk of being attacked as pornographers or promoters of "depraved" ideas, rather than as artists making visible what has been largely repressed from view.

Further, the show opens the possibility that while it may indeed be understood as complicit with Hollywood expectations that most of the cast members are conventionally attractive, fashionable, and "femme" in self-presentation, this does not necessarily mean that the program is simply reproducing sexist and objectifying images designed to appeal to heterosexual male audiences. Contextualized differently, such non-stereotypical images of lesbians, who certainly act as well as appear, can be understood as inviting female or lesbian gazes that offer very different forms of visual pleasure to different audiences. In other words, like Yuskavage, whose work acknowledges and interrogates familiar popular representations of women and the complicated and conflicted pleasures viewers take in those images, *The L Word* can be understood to be encouraging viewers to interpret apparently familiar images in new ways. The show makes visible the contradictions inherent in its location on cable television, while simultaneously disrupting or reframing our familiar ways of seeing.

The L Word also features two other artists whose work is certainly in dialog with art history, but who also present much more overtly queer gender and sexual expressions than Papou or Yuskavage. In a presentation to her museum board about the *Provocations* exhibition, Bette highlights a work called *The Flagellation*, by gay male artist Delmas Howe ("Longing," 1:3). The painting is also prominently displayed during the opening of the exhibition in the final episode of season one, and depicts a group of men in an abandoned warehouse, engaged in various S/M practices. This painting is part of a series of twelve large-scale paintings called *Stations of the Cross: A Gay Passion*, which Howe made, partly in response to the Christian right's attacks on gay communities. The paintings connect the suffering and devastation that AIDS caused in the gay male community in the 1980s and 90s with the history of images of suffering in religious art of the past. Howe's painting is based on Caravaggio's *Flagellation of the Christ*, and celebrates the world of diverse gay male sexual expression in the 1960s and 70s, the years before AIDS.

Including this work serves several functions. It connects gay male and lesbian art; it makes visible and celebrates a marginalized sexual minority; and its implicit critique of the hatefulness of the Christian right is a theme that the show highlights powerfully in season one. Also, featuring the work so prominently forces the viewer to evaluate the painting; the discomfort it might cause some viewers is reflected in the reactions of Bette's conservative board members, who exchange horrified glances at the thought of displaying this work instead of a show of impressionists.

The other artist who is featured most often on the show is the photographer Catherine Opie, whose work is well known in many queer communities. Like Papou, she appears in an episode, and many of her works are shown on-screen in seasons one and two. We first see Opie in a flashback that tells the story of Bette and Tina's first meeting, at an art opening at Bette's gallery; Opie is present and her portraits are on the walls. We also see Opie later, at an artist dinner held at the gallery; once again, her work is on display ("Looking Back," 1:11). What we see here are portraits of people who are often invisible outside their sub-cultural communities: cross-dressers, dominatrixes, transpeople of all sorts, drag kings and queens, and other body manipulators, all of whom Opie represents as people who are "worthy subjects for artistic contemplation" and whom she treats with a respect and dignity that dominant cultures typically refuse them. The sitters take traditional studio portrait poses, in front of formal, elegant backdrops. Like other artists featured on the show, Opie's work is strongly influenced by art history, most directly by the paintings of Hans Holbein. Indeed, Opie has explained that she is "constantly looking at the history of photography and art as a source of inspiration" (Reilly 2001: 87). Her portraits engage that history, but also seek to revise it; she has noted that "with all my work, it's also about creating a different language within a language that's already been created" (Nys Dambrot 2006).

Further, Maura Reilly (2001: 88) has argued that Opie's portraits "manage to disrupt the traditional subject–object dialog, insofar as the sitter's intense glance back at the viewer somehow disallows objectification, as well as any pathologization." Arguably, we might see the photographs' refusal of the objectifying gaze as parallel to, or part of, *The L Word*'s attempt to draw our attention to and refuse voyeuristic straight or male gazes.

At the *Provocations* opening ("Limb from Limb," 1:13), we get a long time to look at one of Opies's best-known and most powerful images: her 1993 *Self-portrait* (Opie 2008: 71). She had a friend carve a drawing into her bare back, and the cuts are dripping blood. The drawing is of a happy family of two smiling female stick figures holding hands in front of a tiny house, under a bright sun. This image is compelling, as the obvious pain (and perhaps the pleasure) the sitter must be experiencing is vividly present, and that complex conjunction of pain and pleasure is connected by the drawing to the complicated mix of joys and struggles that so often accompany queer experience in American society. It also makes visible the cutting and piercing practices that are part of S/M culture, and invites us to think about how altering the body is a vital part of constructing one's identity. About Opie's portraits, critic Catherine Lord has argued:

These are not photographs of sexual practices, but of costumes, markings, and alterations to the body that announce the practices of sexual minorities, pictures that encode the clues to such practices within the codes of studio portraiture. These are portraits of mutable flesh, not fixed social identity. Indeed, the point is not somehow to reveal an essence embodied in flesh, but to suggest that flesh itself is used to invent identity. (Hammond 2000: 153)

The presence of such portraits offers a counter-narrative to essentialist notions that might seem to be implicit in *The L Word*'s presentation of lesbian or queer identity.

In 1992, Opie did a series of fourteen photographs called *Being and Having*, which were portraits of lesbian friends sporting false mustaches and beards (Opie 2008: 44–9). She describes her sitters as "heavily pierced and tattooed lesbians from the alternative club scene who are into challenging the typical image of lesbians. … They don't want to be men or to pass as men all the time. They just want to borrow male fantasies and play with them" (Hammond 2000: 150).

The sitters glare out at the viewer from these larger-than-life prints, but if we look closely, we see past the artifice—the webbing of the mustaches, drips of glue—little details that emphasize the constructedness of the gender performance. Opie explained that these images "were all taken with a 4x5 camera so the detail of the false is emphasized. It is the disruptiveness and falseness of the images which explores the extent of the invisibility of the lesbian community and queer culture" (Hammond 2000: 152). But it is not only lesbian invisibility that Opie is challenging, as she notes that in these photographs she also "wanted to play with our expectations of realism in photographic portraits to confront the viewers with their preconceptions about lesbians and lesbian sexuality" (Smith 1991: 83).

In seasons two through six, three of these images are seen every week as part of the opening credit sequence for the show, and they are visually quite prominent. What's significant about their presentation in this context is that they are preceded by images of the main characters dressing and making up to go out to an art exhibition, and the falseness of feminine masquerade and the constructedness and fluidity of gender and sexuality is thus emphasized by the juxtaposition of having the characters, in their high femme finery, looking at Opie's images of constructed masculinity. (They also look at other photographs of women in these sequences.) These contrasting images invite us to ask what exactly are the referents of "this" and "we" in the theme song's repeated lyric that "This is the way / it's the way that we live." In this context, the photographs do exactly what Opie hopes they will. She says about her subjects: "I see this scene as expanding lesbian visibility and showing how lesbian sexuality is heterogeneous and complex. ... That is the aim of these photographs, to represent this hidden subculture and challenge the narrowly defined representations of our sexuality" (Smith 1991: 83).

The photographs also implicitly make visible the whiteness and wealth of the show's West Hollywood *mise-en-scène*, as Opie notes that her sitters (several of whom are people of color) are borrowing their masculine images from working-class Latino gang styles that she defines as specific to Los Angeles. Including them reminds us that the elite West Hollywood world of the show is but one of many communities within a very diverse city.

Both Opie and Howe connect the show's representations of lesbians to a larger and much more complex queer community. The images of their work that we see serve several narrative and visual functions. First, they make very clear that lesbian and queer communities are much more diverse than the conventionally attractive, gender-normative, and wealthy characters would suggest. They also call into question the implicit essentialism that undergirds the show's representation of subjects identifiable as "lesbians," offering—if only briefly—a vision of the instability and variety that might be contained by the term. And by mapping these artists (and others) all together, the show is able to make its point through accumulating these critical and alternative visions as part of the show's *mise-en-scène*.

By highlighting artists whose work makes visible the ways that representations of gender and sexuality have shaped our understandings of ourselves and the world, and who are explicitly challenging and redefining the conventions that have historically had so much power, *The L Word* invites viewers to think about whether the show is doing precisely the same things. That is, *The L Word* shows us that the process of making art in capitalism is constrained by viewer expectations that have been constructed by a long history of misrepresentation and misunderstanding. But even while acknowledging its own participation in commercial culture, and the possibility that it will be misread as conforming to familiar expectations, the show draws attention to its own status as a fiction and suggests that viewers cannot take for granted that we know what we are seeing. It invites us, indeed it teaches us, to look differently.

The problem of making art in capitalism

By season four, *The L Word*'s engagement with the problem of lesbian representation in capitalist contexts had turned into parody. The most overtly comic examples of *The L Word*'s self-conscious attention to its own location in a web of economic and political conflicts emerged that season. In the course of a long story arc, the sexily androgynous Shane is invited to model for a Hugo Boss underwear advertising campaign. Initially she declines, but when her younger brother Shay breaks his arm and needs expensive medical care she can't afford, she reluctantly takes the job, and is soon horrified to find her image plastered on a giant billboard on Sunset Boulevard ("Layup," 4:4). Of course, this whole story arc constitutes one long product placement for Hugo Boss, but at the same time the show also draws our attention to its participation in capitalist media structures and overtly rejects their misrepresentations of women and queers. For example, in episode 4:7 ("Lesson Number One"), Helena's need to pay a gambling debt she can't afford creates an opportunity for the group to have a conversation about how each of them has had to compromise her principles at some time for economic reasons. Shane admits that doing the ad "felt pretty whorish," and the whole conversation provides another small reminder of the show's location within a capitalist system that requires it to compromise with the expectations of the people paying the bills.

On the night when Shane loses custody of her brother, and therefore no longer needs the money from the Boss ads, she calls her best friend Alice, who arrives immediately to offer support to her distraught friend. They sit under the billboard and commiserate over beers, and while the action shows us the power of the bond between these women, it also shows them working together to challenge misrepresentation. Alice has come armed with many cans of spray paint, and, in a comic scene, they vandalize the billboard. Shane's image is rendered unrecognizable as the figure is transformed into a long-haired, bearded male with a giant ejaculating penis, and the legend, "You're looking very Shane today," is rewritten as "You're looking like shit today" ("Lacy Lilting Lyrics," 4:9). *The L Word* has presumably been well paid by Hugo Boss to advertise their clothing, but then has overtly mocked the sort of people who organize such forms of advertising and publicity. We have already been shown Shane's obvious discomfort with the manipulative processes of being photographed and of making public appearances, and when one of her public relations handlers shrills enthusiastically, "Don't you want to just die?" it is clear that Shane's answer is "Yes" ("Luck Be a Lady," 4:6). The show participates in a now-familiar form of advertising, and then makes visible and parodies its own participation, thereby drawing attention to its own complicity, and to the problem of representation more generally.

The particular form that this scene takes also connects the show to a longer feminist artistic and political history. Alice and Shane's handiwork is very reminiscent of photographs that Jill Posener took of feminist vandalism of sexist advertising billboards in the late 1970s and early 1980s; these photos once circulated widely in the form of postcards sold in feminist bookstores and other alternative venues (Posener 1982). By evoking this longer history of resistance to misrepresentation, *The L Word* situates its more postmodern critical strategies in a tradition of feminist analysis and action. So within this larger story arc that reminds viewers that Hollywood does not know how to tell these stories truthfully, we also see an overt, mocking rejection of the very capitalist economic structures that make the show possible. In other words, this entire storyline explores the contradictions of trying to tell alternative stories within commercial mass media. Indeed, during the last three seasons, the difficulty of creating alternative images within the Hollywood system is traced in great detail, as production of the film based on Jenny's book, *Lez Girls*, becomes an increasingly significant story arc. Here again, viewers are taken behind the scenes to see many aspects of how movies are produced, and are shown the constant struggle of Tina and Jenny to maintain what Tina calls "the integrity of the project" within a fundamentally corrupt system ("Lesson Number One," 4:7). It is tempting to read this whole storyline as an allegory for the reality that *The L Word*'s creators encountered during many years of working in Hollywood.

The problem is presented vividly in episode 4:9 ("Lacy Lilting Lyrics"), as Tina and Jenny seek a director for the movie. They interview three well-known straight male film directors: Garry Marshall, John Stockwell, and Lawrence Bender. Each encounter both makes fun of that director's actual history of representing women, and presents him as completely unable to imagine how to tell a lesbian story in other than a sexist and heterosexist way. But when they find a lesbian director, who does know how to direct the film, Jenny schemes with the film's wealthy backer to maneuver her off the project and take control herself. The system enables Jenny, who has no experience with screenwriting or directing, to gain immense power, through a manipulative alliance with a powerful man. Subsequently, in one of *The L Word*'s many homages to film history, Jenny is pushed out of the director's chair by the unscrupulous and ambitious Adele Channing, whose climb to the top closely parallels the plot of the camp classic *All About Eve* ("Lunar Cycle," 5:11). These developments make visible the conflict between artists and producers who want to create alternative images of lesbians, and a Hollywood studio system run by sexist and homophobic men who care only about making money; these executives make decisions that directly undermine the aspirations of the filmmakers, and make it impossible for them to do the work they were hired to do. (At the same time, it also indicts lesbians who will sell out to advance their own careers.)

The problem of who controls lesbian representation in commercial media contexts is staged again in the final episode of season five, as the characters attend the wrap party for *Lez Girls* ("Loyal and True," 5:12). Jenny has crashed the party, and when given a chance to speak to the cast and crew, she makes clear what's at issue, saying, "I know that the movie is out of my hands now, and I hope that those people entrusted with this responsibility will honor it." They won't, because their interest is explicitly in selling tickets to people in "flyover country," not in changing representations.

At the end of the episode, Tina learns that Adele has agreed to the distributor's wish to change the ending of the story and have "Jesse" return to her heterosexual relationship with "Jim." Tina is furious, and names the issue directly: "This is bullshit! We worked really hard on a movie that we believed in, and the marketing people just come along and change the whole ending? The guy gets the girl, the end? This is the movie that was supposed to change all that." Adele argues, "Look, Tina, if the movie is too gay, it's going to alienate audiences." Tina retorts, "Too gay!? It's a movie about lesbians!" Tina's objection is lost on the studio boss and the financial backer, who respond idiotically that the movie is still "chock-full" of lesbians and that only one character changes; Aaron shrugs, "It's not that big a deal." When the rest of the group hears about the change to the ending, they are incredulous. Alice asks, "You're not going to let them get away with it, are you?" but Tina's powerlessness is clear. As usual, Kit comments astutely on the action: "I'm telling you that it's The Man that does this crazy shit!"

But it isn't entirely the Man. Tina demands of Adele, "How do you live with yourself?" but Adele just smiles calmly, secure in the new three-picture deal that her complicity with the bosses has earned her.

This plot development might seem to be pessimistic about the possibility of making alternative images of lesbians within the Hollywood system. But early in season six, we learn that the original negative of the film has been stolen from the lab, so no copy of the film is available for release, and an investment of many millions of dollars is apparently lost ("LMFAO," 6:3). It's not until the final episode of that season that Shane discovers the film reels hidden in Jenny's attic; Jenny has stolen her film back from those who would misrepresent lesbian lives ("Last Word," 6:8). And as the entire series ends, and Tina prepares to move to New York for a great new job, we have no reason to believe that she and Shane will ever reveal what they have discovered. But even if they did return the movie, we are given to understand that, except for the changed ending, the film does have some "integrity," and does offer an alternative to the formulaic Hollywood representations of lesbians.

In this way, *The L Word* implicitly makes an argument that while creators cannot easily reach a broad audience outside of the structures of capitalism, the possibility of telling new stories in new ways does exist, and that every queer story that is created and gains a broad audience contributes to destabilizing and transforming mainstream images and assumptions and thus also contributes to changing the world. The victories may be only partial, but they are real, and they create spaces for more stories and more possibilities for transforming the world.

Notes

* Margaret T. McFadden's "'L' is for Looking Again: Art and Representation on *The L Word*" was first published in *Feminist Media Studies* 10.4 (2010) as "'L' is For Looking Again." It is reprinted here by permission of Taylor & Francis Ltd; http://www.tandf.co.uk/journals.

PART 3

Lineage

Trashy, Trivial, and Testimonial:
From Pulp Novels to *The L Word*

Marnie Pratt

> [T]hese novels played a multi-layered role in lesbian culture,
> existing as description, as witness, as evidence, as connection, as
> representation and, of course, as pleasure.
>
> Walters (1989: 86)

The above quote from Suzanna Danuta Walters exemplifies the work
of scholars who have recently attempted to recover, interrogate,
and recontextualize the significance of lesbian pulp fiction novels
of the 1950s and 60s. This has been an arduous task for several
reasons, not the least of which is that, until the late 1980s, many
individuals, including researchers, regarded lesbian pulp fiction as
having little use value to queer histories or politics (Keller 2005:
387). Fortunately, scholars such as Walters persevered, and, as a
result, many thought-provoking personal testimonies and legacies
have been uncovered.

However, such scholarship not only provides new ways to reflect upon
cultural productions of the past; it also aids in a deeper understanding
of those of both the present and the future. As the popular adage goes,
"If you want to know your future, you must first know your past."
While referring to lesbian pulp fiction texts specifically, the Walters
quote might just as easily be applied to other cultural phenomena that
have proven critical to communities of queer women, such as early
lesbian publications, women's music of the 1970s, independent queer
films, or a television series like *The L Word*.

Like pulp fiction before it, *The L Word* was significant to its
audiences for a multiplicity of reasons. In fact, the show's viewers
would likely be quick to offer passionate declarations concerning its

own "description, witness, evidence, connection, representation, or pleasure." It is also important to bear in mind, though, that cultural consumption is not always founded upon a purely positive relationship, and the negotiations of meaning or use value are complexly varied. The frequent negative reactions also expressed by both *The L Word* and pulp fiction audiences continually remind us of this.

This chapter will juxtapose the histories of lesbian pulp fiction and *The L Word* in order to draw comparisons and contrasts between the two forms. This approach uncovers that while much has changed both socially and politically from the 1950s to the 2000s, much also remains the same with regards to the consumption of such cultural productions. The deep investment of audience members, regardless of their positive or negative reactions, accounts for one of the most remarkable similarities, and I offer a framework for interrogating this commonality. I argue that Eve Kosofsky Sedgwick's concept of "the closet," when considered in combination with the historical collision of a marginalized group forced into invisibility and a dominant culture increasingly enamored by the visual, creates a uniquely strong yearning for cultural representations on the part of queer individuals. While these representations are not received as consistently accurate or positive, queer individuals remain drawn to and often supportive of their existence. They continue to make use of them through strategies such as what José Esteban Muñoz calls "disidentificatory reception" (Muñoz 1999). Finally, this comparison enables a speculation on how the existing legacies of lesbian pulp fiction may illuminate *The L Word*'s possible role in future queer history books by borrowing Henry Jenkins' model of "collective intelligence" for fan communities. However, I contend that *The L Word*'s viewers have created a collective intelligence of not only the series itself but also queer culture as a whole. This kind of engaged spectatorship is highly valuable for a minority group's historical documentation, community creation, and even, as Muñoz points out, politics.

Before embarking further, however, I would like to first add a note about methodology. While the information in this chapter on lesbian pulp fiction is drawn from historical texts and the work of other scholars, the information regarding *The L Word* and its audiences is largely drawn from ethnographic fieldwork conducted by myself between 2004 and 2008. This study included maintaining a presence upon several prominent viewer-run websites and discussion boards related to the series, attending events and viewing parties for the show, and reading numerous online and print reviews by both professional and amateur journalists. This was further complemented by a survey administered online to over 100 individuals in the fall of 2007. Many of the audience quotes within this chapter are drawn from this extensive study. Viewers have been identified by their screen name whenever possible. If none has been given, however, they should be considered an anonymous survey respondent.

A historical backdrop

The mid-twentieth-century pulp fiction publishing boom, enabled by advances in printing technology and the discovery of new distribution outlets, brought out "hack writers of all stripes [who] turned out tales of sex and violence in huge quantity, falling into a variety of sub-genres – teen drug abuse, white slavery, murder mysteries – of which 'lesbian lust' was among the most successful" (Nealon 2000: 747). While Pocket Books led the charge with regards to pulp fiction in general, it was Fawcett Publications' new Gold Medal Books that broke ground by issuing the first and eventually most well-known lesbian pulp fiction books. In 1950, they published Tereska Torres' immensely successful *Women's Barracks*, which sold 2 million copies by 1955 (Seajay 2006: 18). Additional titles quickly followed, including Vin Packer's (a.k.a.: Marijane Meaker) *Spring Fire* (1952), Valerie Taylor's (a.k.a.: Velma Young) *Whisper Their Love* (1957) and *The Girls in 3-B* (1959), and Ann Bannon's *Odd Girl Out* (1957). Bannon's book signaled the beginning of what would eventually become a series of five novels known as *The Beebo Brinker Chronicles*, which contain arguably the most well-known books of the lesbian pulp fiction genre, earning Bannon the title "Queen of Lesbian Pulp Fiction" (Forrest 2005: xviii).

The glory days of lesbian pulp fiction are generally considered to be from 1950 to 1965, during which time both female and male authors produced more than 500 titles (Keller 2005: 388). American McCarthyism, infamous for its promotion of a return to normalcy, conservative values, and anti-homosexual sentiments, formed the backdrop of much of this time period. However, while this era is often stereotyped as being deeply secretive and repressive with regards to non-normative sexuality, in many respects it was quite the opposite. Senator Joe McCarthy's desire to uncover homosexuals in political offices or other positions of influence actually resulted in a proliferation of discourse on the subject. In other words, homosexuality was everywhere and on everyone's mind. Historian Lillian Faderman explains, "since homosexuals were of great interest to the media as sick or subversive, knowledge of homosexuality was more widely disseminated than at any previous time in history" (1991: 160). No doubt, lesbian pulp fiction novels owe some of their enormous success and popularity to this increase in consciousness regarding non-normative sexualities.

However, homosexuals were still considered mentally ill and their sexual activity still criminal. As a result, publishers, who generally envisioned their readers to be heterosexual men seeking tantalizing tales. remained obedient to censorship codes, and homosexual content was only conveyed to readers through suggestive images and specialized language. Titles and taglines often contained such coded words as twilight, odd, strange, shadows, forbidden, or unnatural. Publishers also adhered to a moral code with regards to content by requiring authors to have their queer characters meet "appropriate" endings, including a conversion to heterosexuality, institutionalization, misery, or death.

Despite these seemingly prominent negative aspects, however, lesbian pulp fiction novels connected with queer female readers. "I was thrilled by what I read: that we could support ourselves and make our lives together, and that there were many other women like us," explains Carol Seajay (2006: 18). These texts afforded lesbians an excitingly new and rare mainstream cultural representation. The cheap prices (usually 25–50 cents) and mass distribution also made these cultural productions readily available to women in virtually every corner of the country (Seajay 2006: 18). Perhaps most importantly, however, these women were now discovering that they were neither alone nor abnormal. Bannon elaborates:

> [T]he most important things [readers] learned were that 1) they weren't unique and doomed to lifelong isolation, 2) ... they weren't "abnormal," and 3) there was hope for a happy life. ... Their lives were so insular, their access to information so restricted, that they were convinced they were an isolated mistake of nature. So it was the really important and affirmative message that my books

carried out to the farthest nooks of this nation to people who most
needed to hear it: You have company! You are okay! (Quoted in
Dean 2003)

Queer women also used these texts as a way to identify and connect with
each other. "For millions of lesbians in the 1950s," states *PlanetOut*'s
David Bianco, "buying a pulp novel could be a courageous public act, one
that expressed a desire to explore or claim a lesbian identity in a time
of repression. [Lesbians] circulated them and discussed them, creating
an underground community of lesbian readers" (Bianco 1999).

However, while intensely important to many women during this
time period, they were not consumed uncritically. For example, Bannon
notes that while she enjoys the sentimental kitsch attached to the texts
contemporarily, "at the time, I wanted something dignified" (quoted
in Munger 2005). And writer Joan Nestle affirms, "[O]ur need was
greater than our shame" (quoted in Keller 2005: 404). Unfortunately,
however, women of this time period had few available options when it
came to representations, and thus lesbian pulp fiction novels remained
critical to early queer women's communities. "[Readers'] reluctance
to judge, plus the scarcity of lesbian fiction overall, precluded their
rejection of these books," explains pulp fiction scholar Yvonne Keller
(1999: 4). After all, lesbian pulp fiction was offering a rare glimpse
of lesbians living out their lives with relative normality, which was
something unavailable in other media outlets, such as television.

While references to homosexuality date back even as far as
television's predecessor, radio, the topic was long considered taboo,
relegating it to extremely rare, heavily obscured, and deeply
derogatory moments. In fact, the topic was so reviled within the
public consciousness during the medium's early years that even anti-
gay discussions were sometimes banned from television airwaves
(Capsuto 2000: 3). When queer content was allowed on the small
screen, it was generally reduced to a few character types, such as
the humorous effeminate gay male, villainous murderer, and child
molester, or to certain storylines, such as the case of cross-dressing
and mistaken identity or the tormented soul who meets an unseemly
demise (Capsuto 2000: 48–9).

As the queer rights movement continued to grow throughout the
1970s and 80s, representations on television slowly increased, but it
wasn't until the 1990s that significant changes began to happen. This

decade's representational crowned jewel is of course Ellen Morgan's (Ellen DeGeneres) coming out on ABC's *Ellen*. Queer television historian Steven Capsuto explains this event's significance:

> *Ellen* became the first primetime series with an openly gay leading character and the first American network comedy or drama with a vocal, openly gay star – in a title role, no less. With its voluminous news coverage, DeGeneres's and *Ellen's* coming out rocked American culture, setting off pervasive debates about homosexuality and gay visibility. (2000: 379)

While this moment is undoubtedly groundbreaking, the decade saw numerous important moments related to queer representations on television, including two male characters having a discussion in bed on *Thirtysomething*, a kiss between two women on *LA Law*, and a lesbian wedding on *Friends*. Additionally, gay and lesbian characters began appearing on other popular shows, such as *ER*, *Buffy the Vampire Slayer*, and *Roseanne*.

The L Word, which debuted in January of 2004, developed on the foundations of this 1990s queer television explosion and was similarly hailed as groundbreaking television. While it was obviously not the first show to have lesbian characters, relationships, or even affection, it was considered unique because the majority of its large cast was queer women, and their lives, relationships, and social or political issues were the focus of the series. Additionally, the placement of the series on the premium cable network Showtime allowed it to depict these characters' lives in a more forthright, if not occasionally explicit, way. Similarly to the lesbian pulp fiction before it, queer women passionately consumed *The L Word*'s new mainstream representations. Running for a total of six seasons, it reached out to millions of viewers (Cole 2006) and became the most quickly renewed series in Showtime's history (Rosenduft 2005: 23). *The L Word*'s success was also felt in the second market of DVD sales, which according to the show's creator, Ilene Chaiken, were "through the roof," and a plethora of affiliated products (quoted in Stockwell 2006: 48).

The viewer communities of cyberspace are perhaps even more emblematic of this consumption. One of the show's earliest reviews already noted that "[e]nthusiastic fans trade show secrets and leak spoilers or plotlines through weblogs, unofficial websites, and gossip circles" (Rosenduft 2005: 19). In fact, online audience communities began appearing before the pilot episode even aired. The most notable of these were l-word.com and thelwordonline.com. During the show's run, the former had over 30,000 members and around 150,000 visitors per month (Jacky 2005) and the latter averaged around 11,000 visitors a day. By the series' conclusion, thelwordonline.com had registered over 17 million hits (Sitemeter.com). The series also had a handful of official sites created by Showtime, such as *The L Word*'s Sho.com microsite, a devoted "island" within Second Life, and the short-lived social networking site, OurChart.com.[1]

Regardless of the venue, though, *The L Word* had rapidly developed a significant and engaged following, many of whom frequently proclaimed their deep appreciation of the series. According to one viewer on a website message board, "[a]s someone who grew up in the 60's, I've just got to say, watching this show each week is becoming almost a spiritual experience for me. Needless to say, I didn't see any lesbian role models on TV when I was growing up. ... [I]t almost brings a tear to this middle-aged dyke's eye" (Tenderwolf 2004). Another poster echoed a similar sentiment, but added references to support for coming out and community building: "[t]he show has also given me an enormous amount of courage to sometime (soon hopefully) come out; I'm no longer denying what I am. I can thank the show for that and along with the show ... this message board and the people who use it" (Malou 2005).

However, it would be highly erroneous to assume *The L Word* was simply consumed uncritically with little reflection. The show was in fact frequently critiqued from a variety of angles. Some viewers simply wrote off the series entirely by labeling it "an enormous waste of time," while others were more specific in their criticism, "[t]he writing is horrible, the characters [are] often very one dimensional/caricatures of themselves, and the storylines are even worse, often playing to what is trendy rather than what is more often real."[2] The major focus of criticism, however, was centered upon arguments of damaging representations, especially with regards to those individuals further marginalized within the larger queer community. For example, one poster discusses the show's lack of diverse racial images by stating, "I love Bette [played by Jennifer Beals] and the fact that her presence has forced some discussions about biraciality. But I crave more than that and wish there were more opportunities for diversity outside of some faces in a crowd every once in a while ..." (Arkaycee 2005). Another audience member addresses the way the series dealt with issues of transgender identities by stating,

> Max [played by Daniela Sea] is a sorry portrayal of an FTM. Very similar to my problems with Ivan Aycock [played by Kelly Lynch], they still can't seem to get it right. While I like that they are trying to bring this very real subject to life through a show that touches so many viewers, I really think they defeated the purpose with Max. (YouAreSoAnalog 2006)

Both *The L Word* and lesbian pulp fiction caused consumption to be complicated for their respective queer audiences. These cultural productions were on one hand thrilling and even life-saving, but on the other, they offered up a significant amount of disappointment. This is just one of several noteworthy comparisons.

Lesbian pulp fiction versus *The L Word*

Prior to comparing the cultural texts themselves, it is valuable to consider the socio-political contexts from which both these icons of lesbian culture arise, and at least initially, these seem strikingly different. After all, lesbian pulp fiction came about during the conservative 1950s, which is the era of the happy housewife mythology, post-World War II's return to traditional family values, censorship and surveillance, and as already mentioned, McCarthyism. Additionally, it was not only socially unacceptable to be queer, but it was also, in fact, a crime. As Faderman asserts, this was "perhaps the worst time in history for women to love women" (1991: 157). Queer men and women lived daily with this distressing reality. "According to the American Psychological Society, I was sick. According to the law, I was a criminal," recalls author Katherine Forrest (2005: x). Conversely, *The L Word* developed on the shoulders of all that came after this cultural moment, such as the Stonewall Riots, lesbian-feminism, the battles of Harvey Milk, Queer Nation, New Queer Cinema, and the aforementioned 1990s queer television boom. Such shifts seem to imply only contrasts between these historical backdrops; however, some useful similarities can be drawn as well.

While McCarthyism is long over, the citizens of the United States live with new administrative bodies that limit their rights, while arguing these limitations represent a dominant public opinion and desire for safety. Some scholars have already drawn comparisons between McCarthy's communism and the contemporary War on Terror. "Then, as now, fear of a foreign enemy and an unfamiliar ideology was deployed to bully the American people into abandoning customary standards of civil liberties, academic freedom and common sense. There are, of course, important differences between the two historical periods. But the similarities are nonetheless striking," argues Joel Beinin (2004: 102). While homosexuals are not the explicit targets of the current obsession with surveillance and safety, the similar culture of fear has certainly led to a climate in which the curtailment of rights and freedoms is considered acceptable.

Additionally, the first decade of the new millennium has witnessed queer communities struggle on several other fronts. Many state laws still fail to include adequate anti-discrimination or anti-hate crime laws. On the grounds of protecting traditional family values, queer individuals have been vehemently denied the right to marriage and adoption through both federal and state laws or constitutional amendments. And until 2011, the military continued to rely on its "Don't Ask, Don't Tell" policy regarding the rights of homosexuals to serve in the military. While of course these issues do not hold quite the same severity as being considered insane or criminal, they do illustrate similar climates of discrimination, which in both cases have resulted in frustration and a desire for connection or escape.

Lesbian pulp fiction and *The L Word* are not only grounded within similar cultural climates, but are also the result of opportunities made available by technological advances. Changes in printing and distribution processes of the publishing industry allowed for the niche of pulp fiction, while *The L Word* was made possible by the development of serial programming on premium cable networks. Both of these technological shifts also enabled these cultural texts to tell their stories in specific ways. *The L Word* was able to present its frank discussions and depictions of lesbian sexuality because it was featured on a subscription-based channel, which falls outside of the regulations imposed upon other television programming, and while pulp fiction was to some extent limited by the restrictions of censors, it did not come under nearly the level of scrutiny as that faced by other media industries of the time period, most notably television or film (Taylor 2003: xi). The Hays Code closely regulated the motion picture industry, and television was strictly monitored by the code of the National Association of Radio and Television Broadcasters. Therefore, both pulp fiction and *The L Word* were able to distribute content considered inappropriate within other mainstream formats of their respective time periods.

However, these media formats also highlight a striking difference between the consumption of lesbian pulp fiction and *The L Word*. Whereas the former was widely available to its audience because of an inexpensive price and wide distribution, the latter's viewers were limited by the same aspects. Access to cable television and premium channels, such as Showtime, is not universal. Both require subscription fees, which can be costly. Then again, other developments in technology helped maintain *The L Word*'s accessibility and lessen its price tag. Audiences unable to shell out the money for a cable television and premium network package may have found purchasing or renting DVD sets affordable. Not to mention that, during the series run, the Internet was filled with pirated videos posted by viewers on sites like youtube.com. In fact, it was quite common to find a copy of an episode online within an hour or two of its initial airing. Communities of lesbians also worked together to lessen costs by holding *The L Word* viewing parties at homes and local social venues. Such practices allowed for one paid subscription to reach, in some cases, hundreds of viewers, significantly expanding the show's accessibility.

Another important point of comparison between the two forms lies within their approaches to marketing. Lesbian pulp largely made itself recognizable to readers through lurid cover art with sexy tag lines, but as Bianco points out "the cover art of pulp novels always depicted ultra-feminine women, [but] the 'real' lesbians in the stories were often tomboys or 'bad girls' who seduced innocent straight women" (Bianco 1999). *The L Word* also boasted ad campaigns each season with images of the cast in sexy poses and clever tag lines to entice its audiences, such as "The Definitive New Sex in the City," "Same Sex, Different City," "L Hath No Fury," and "Hot as L." Such marketing campaigns consistently depicted all members of the cast in a feminine manner; however, within the confines of the series some of these characters were more non-traditional or androgynous in their gender presentation. One such androgynous character, Shane McCutcheon, can be read as one of

Bianco's "real" lesbians. She attracts nearly every peripheral character, whether straight or gay, sleeps with most of them, breaks numerous hearts, and is perceived and discussed as infamously desirable.

Both of these cultural productions were also aware of their heterosexual male audiences when it came to marketing. As previously mentioned, lesbian pulp was openly marketed to straight men, and in fact it was only marginally aware of its lesbian constituency. As author Meaker explains, "[*Spring Fire*] was not aimed at any lesbian market, because there wasn't any that we knew about" (quoted in Keller 2005: 390). What was an open marketing campaign on the part of pulp publishers became a quiet acknowledgment for *The L Word*. Although not completely indifferent towards this audience, statements were issued more sparingly. For example, in one interview Chaiken states, "It [straight men watching the show] doesn't bother me at all. It's a fact of life. It's amusing and interesting and intriguing. … But it's a facet of life" (Topor). Interestingly, however, the only requirement Chaiken has conceded as being placed upon her and her crew by Showtime was related to this straight male audience. Leading up to the second season, Showtime requested they include a straight male character "for the straight male audience to have a guy they could relate to" (Fonseca 2005: 41). Of course, what is perhaps most intriguing regarding the scenario is how this request was fulfilled by *The L Word*'s production team.

Season two did include a straight male character named Mark Wayland, but Mark ends up clearly being one of the show's villainous characters. He enters the story as a roommate for Jenny (Mia Kirshner) and Shane and quickly becomes despicable when he installs cameras to spy on and record the lives of his lesbian roommates. When the truth comes out, he makes the argument that he is attempting to make a serious documentary, and the narrative does seem to indicate that Mark may have reached some sort of epiphany regarding his original opinions of lesbians. However, this has come too late, and he is punished for his voyeurism by losing his job, his friends, and his home.

In these scenes, the character given to the straight male audience for identification ironically becomes an excessive caricature of why that viewer might come to *The L Word* in the first place. While Keller asserts that lesbian authors of pulp fiction did attempt to subvert some of the homophobic nature of the genre, a subversion of this stature would have been virtually impossible for these writers (Keller 1999:

5–6). *The L Word*'s ability to blatantly challenge Showtime's request in this manner is certainly a result of its socio-political moment.

Thus far, the comparisons made illustrate that while on some level many things have changed when it comes to queer politics, representations, and social existence, much also unfortunately remains the same. This is perhaps most striking, however, when examining the ways in which audiences consumed and made use of these two phenomena. As has already been discussed, lesbian pulp fiction was virtually the only representation available to queer women at the time, and its unique nature fulfilled a dire need for many of them. "I needed them the way I needed food and shelter for my survival," states Donna Allegra (quoted in Keller 2005: 385). These women were finally able to see beyond their isolation and witness cultural representations of themselves within a mainstream context, and this fostered a deep investment in the novels. "In large numbers, we were speaking to an audience of women who were starved for connections with others, who thought they were uniquely alone with emotions they couldn't explain and couldn't find mirrored in their own worlds," explains Bannon. "In our way, we held up that mirror – not always a perfect reflection, alas, but often a comforting one" (quoted in Zimet 1999: 14). Moreover, these cultural representations provided the strength to assert their newly recognized existence by reaching out and forming communities. "They also sometimes conveyed a sense of lesbian culture, and sometimes helped lesbians find others like themselves," confirms Libby Smith (quoted in Walters 1989: 86).

It seems only logical to assume that the use value found within *The L Word* would be quite different. After all, it was by no means an oasis of lesbian representation in a vast wasteland of invisibility. By its debut, a more socially accepting culture and an increased accessibility to media forms resulted in a greater array of available images, many of which depicted lesbians as happy, well adjusted, and fully enmeshed within the larger culture. However, *The L Word* was still the first television series to focus almost entirely on queer women's lives and issues, and while the overall climate had changed since the 1950s, by no means were its queer viewers living without discrimination and oppression. Not to mention that its location within the medium of television placed it more boldly within mainstream culture than other available representations, such as independent films or literature. These scenarios combined to create a significant devotion on the part of audiences and caused the series to function for viewers in much the same way as lesbian pulp fiction did fifty years before.

The L Word's audiences frequently referred to the series using such terms as "favorite," "addictive," "important," "groundbreaking," or "transformative." Others connected with the show because it offered a way to help negotiate their own difficult situations, such as a viewer who stated, "Whenever I feel sad of my situation I keep watching *The L Word* and somehow it makes my heart feel light. ... I may never be outed, but this show makes me feel welcome [in] the world" (Stillinside 2007). And just like pulp fiction readers, many audience members of *The L Word* referred to the series as helping them make connections and build community. "*The L Word* and these [viewer networking] sites have expanded the community and its ability to network," confirmed one viewer. Connection and community-building were exceptionally critical for some viewers, who were able to find support and understand their own identities because of the series. "Without this show, I probably wouldn't have realized that I like women" (ilovebette 2006), states one individual, and another explains, "*The L Word* has definitely helped me feel much better about myself and my sexuality" (lilWannaB3_ROcK$t@R 2005).

Furthermore, a significant number of viewers saw the series as contributing to visibility politics, a critical tactic of the larger queer socio-political movement. "I think [visibility] is very important because it places a marginalized group into the mainstream popular culture," states one viewer. "Anytime we ... can get exposure on a broader scale like this, I believe it helps normalize us in a world that fears what they do not understand or have not experienced." Another individual echoes a similar sentiment, "It's great for lesbians because it encourages acceptance from straight people who watch it, and it's important to see gay relationship issues dealt with. We are not alone."[2]

Such narratives of visibility, support, community, and escape are not far removed from those found among the readers of lesbian pulp fiction, which leads to an interrogation of this trend. How is it that cheap novels and a soap opera can rise to the level of helping individuals get through their day or even save their lives? I contend that the answer is found by contemplating several important historical moments in conjunction with "the closet."

In *Epistemology of the Closet*, Eve Kosofsky Sedgwick discusses the unique nature of marginalization and oppression for queer individuals.

She describes the closet as ever-present for this population and explains that, "vibrantly resonant as the image of the closet is for many modern oppressions, it is indicative for homophobia in a way it cannot be for other oppressions. Racism, for instance, is based on a stigma that is visible in all but exceptional cases ... so are the oppressions based on gender, age, size, [and] physical handicap" (1990: 75). Thus, certain markers related to aspects of skin tone, physical ability, gender, or age may cause the oppression of some marginalized groups; however, at the same time, these traits also render the individuals of these groups visible. In other words, they constitute them as existing in that identity. For queer individuals, who are haunted daily by the closet and hiding an often important aspect of their identity, invisibility becomes central to their oppression. As a result, the investment in representations may be high for all marginalized groups, but for queer individuals it is closely linked with the ability to exist at all.

Moreover, it is useful to contextualize this oppression through invisibility within a larger historical framework. A number of prominent scholars have argued that homosexuality was not enabled as an identity category within the United States until around the turn of the twentieth century when sexologists of the medical industry began discussing homosexual individuals, as opposed to homosexual behavior. For example, Michel Foucault discusses this cultural shift in *The History of Sexuality*:

> We must not forget that the psychological, psychiatric, medical category of homosexuality was constituted from the moment it was characterized. ... Homosexuality appeared as one of the forms of sexuality when it was transposed from the practice of sodomy onto a kind of interior androgyny, a hermaphrodism of the soul. The sodomite had been a temporary aberration; the homosexual was now a species. (Foucault 1990: 43)

This naming of "the homosexual" not only gave society the ability to discuss same-sex behavior as attributable to a specific type of individual, but it also provided an identity to those with same-sex attraction (Faderman 1991: 59).

This historical time frame is also marked by another important cultural shift that remains crucial to understanding the importance of the visual for queer individuals. The same western historical moment marked by the emergence of a gay identity is also characterized by the development of numerous technologies related to visual culture, such as motion pictures and photography's use in advertising. In *Selling Out: The Gay and Lesbian Movement Goes to Market*, Alexandra Chasin explains, "Whereas nineteenth-century advertisements had been informational, almost exclusively composed of words, the rise of photography and then cinematographic technologies enabled a shift to images in the early twentieth century" (2000: 103). Even the book publishing industry was impacted by this shift to the visual.

Alan Powers, author of *Front Cover*, explains, "Consumers, who were growing up in a culture richer in visual images than any before, and were experiencing motion-picture films for the first time, were beginning to take in visual images subliminally as well as to read text for information" (2001: 7). Illustrated book jackets became increasingly more common throughout the early 1900s as their printing became less expensive (Powers 2001: 7). The paperback industry, which has already been discussed, took this emphasis upon exciting cover art even further, and a book's cover image quickly became one of its primary selling tools (Robinson and Davidson 2001: 13). By the time lesbian pulp fiction emerged in the 1950s, cover design had become just as critical to the consumption of books as the stories contained within. "The design of book covers helps to make a book something more than mere "information," something that, even though it may have many thousands of identical siblings, still demands a relationship [with its audience] ..." states Powers (2001: 11). Authors Frank M. Robinson and Lawrence Davidson make a similar case in their book on the art of dime and pulp novels by claiming, "the covers themselves remain ... as important as the stories they illustrated and the magazines they promoted. In one sense we can compare the old covers to the special effects in contemporary movies. They were what grabbed the eye, made you buy the magazine, and stayed with you in your imagination as you read the story" (2001: 13).

When taken together, the dominant culture's new emphasis on visuality emerged virtually simultaneously with an identity group whose existence was strongly obscured. In other words, while the western world became enamored with the new technologies of the visible, queer individuals found it increasingly necessary to make their own identities invisible. Therefore, Sedgwick's theories, taken in conjunction with such historical narratives, present a framework for understanding the unusually strong investments in queer representations when they do emerge.

Nevertheless, it has also been illustrated that both of these cultural forms were not universally praised without criticism. Lesbian pulp fiction readers may have possessed the need Nestle previously described as being "greater than their shame," but they also still recognized the texts as containing "sad moments, ugly moments" (quoted in Walters 1989: 90). One of the most problematic aspects of these texts was the fact that queer characters were often forced into unhappy or deadly situations at the story's conclusion. Katherine Forrest explains, "We despairingly hoped that stories in the original paperbacks would not end badly but realized that in the view of the larger society, "perversion" could have no reward in novels about us, even those we ourselves wrote" (2005: xiv). Perhaps the most virulent statement of critical consumption comes from Allegra, "I look back now and see where those books and their ideas rotted my guts and crippled my moral structure, [but] in nothing and nowhere else in the world I live[d] in could I have seen the possibility of a lesbian happily-ever-after" (quoted in Keller 2005: 386).

The L Word was similarly consumed with significant amounts of criticism. It was condemned for numerous aspects regarding storylines, politics, and cinematic aspects, but by and large the most common critique concerned representations. Just as some viewers found the show to have a positive impact upon visibility, others felt its representations were unrealistic if not damaging. Often the depictions considered most problematic involved a politics of multiple identity categories, such as the intersections of race, gender, or class with sexuality. Some of these criticisms were mild, such as one viewer who described the series as full of "runway models, which ... is not representative of the lesbian community."[2] Meanwhile, others were significantly more scathing, "Showtime should consult with any critical thinking lesbian about diversity, race politics, relationships ... this show REEKS!" (Bigsmooches 2004).

Yet there are still remarkable similarities between the audiences of these two forms, in that, despite the fact that many became frustrated, angry, and even scornful of certain aspects, a significant number remained invested. For example, one of *The L Word*'s viewers posted a lengthy list of complaints about the show to a message board followed by the statement "[n]ow that I am done being negative, I truly enjoy the program" (Apollonia-6 2004). Another individual replicated a similar idea by explaining, "I love the show for the most part, but it has its flaws and a few things that piss me off" (Mflover 2004). This invested, yet critical response to *The L Word* is again very reminiscent of the relationship queer women of the 1950s had with lesbian pulp fiction. Keller confirms, "What were embattled lesbian readers to do, given their strong desire for lesbian representation and the inevitable proximity of voyeurism and homophobia in the only readily available books with lesbian themes? They did the only thing they could – they compromised and turned a blind eye, so to speak, to the homophobic looking relations installed in these texts" (1999: 3). While this statement also makes clear that these readers likely stayed invested more out of a lack of other choices than out of pure enthusiasm, their commitment remained, and they negotiated their conflicting responses to these texts, just like the audiences of *The L Word.*

There is significant existing scholarship within the areas of queer, media, and cultural studies that examines the ways in which queer populations make use of mainstream (generally read as heterosexual) texts; however, the audiences of lesbian pulp fiction and *The L Word* differed from such studies in two critical ways. First, and most simply, lesbian pulp fiction's and *The L Word*'s audiences were consuming already-queer texts. They were not required to perform readings in order to queer content generally assumed to be heterosexual. Second, a large portion of the work done on queer media audiences does not prioritize their queer identity with regards to media consumption. By this I mean that while there are numerous studies examining how audience members negotiate their queer identities with certain mainstream media texts they happen to enjoy or even within the audience communities of those texts, the audiences of this project have largely been drawn to the text as a result of their queer identities. A queer identity is not negotiated because of consumption, but, rather, consumption occurs and is negotiated because of a queer identity. Therefore, I propose José Esteban Muñoz's theory of disidentification, which not only focuses upon queer texts and prioritizes a queer identity but also speculates on the socio-political value of consuming representations.

Muñoz begins by cautioning against the binary understanding of identities as either essentialist or social constructivist, and instead argues that identity is formed where these two perspectives meet. He explains, "This collision is precisely the moment of negotiation when hybrid, racially predicated, and deviantly gendered identities arrive at representation" (1999: 6). In other words, the essential understandings of self clash with the socially constructed representations of that self. Furthermore, such representations will always be homophobic, sexist, racist, etc., because they must exist within the dominant culture, or what Muñoz refers to as the "majoritarian public sphere" (1999: 4). As a result, he envisions a new type of identity politics in which minority subjects must simultaneously identify and disidentify; the self is constructed both in relation to and against cultural representations. Use value then remains accessible within problematic representations when particular aspects are reworked or reconfigured through the performance of disidentificatory reception (1999: 6). Finally, Muñoz posits that this disidentificatory reception enables politics through engagement and avoids the "unproductive turn toward good dog/bad dog criticism" of representations (1999: 9).

I argue that readers of lesbian pulp fiction and viewers of *The L Word* performed disidentificatory spectatorship. Identity/identification was formed during the clash between the audiences' hybrid selves and the socially constructed representational medium that failed to provide consistently satisfying images of those selves. Both texts disappointed because they existed within the dominant culture, which is always already homophobic, racist, sexist, and classist. In other words, the audiences of these two forms are simultaneously drawn to and repulsed by aspects which either complement or conflict with their own positionalities. Visibility and identity validation, however, are preserved through engaging and reconfiguring the homophobic, sexist, racist, transphobic, or classist aspects. By making use of cultural texts in this way, "the minoritarian subject [is offered] a space to situate itself in history and thus seize social agency" (1999: 1). It is through such socio-political value that the legacies of lesbian pulp fiction and *The L Word* begin to emerge.

Imagining the future with the past

The L Word has only just concluded within recent years, and thus it is difficult to imagine what it might leave behind for queer communities of the future. It would be easy to assume that claiming and occupying a queer identity will be different following *The L Word*'s existence; however, determining exactly what form those differences might take is a much more complex task. Lesbian pulp fiction, on the other hand, ended its run of prominence decades ago, and suggesting its contributions is a much more realistic undertaking. By extending this chapter's comparative analysis further, I propose some possibilities for considering the post-*L Word* future through an examination of the post-pulp fiction past.

With regards to the consumption of lesbian pulp fiction, Keller argues that "the largest discourse on lesbianism in US history to date helped to lead to the greatest number of women ever who identified openly as lesbians" (2005: 405). She further advocates that this rise in identity formation should be considered to have had a direct impact upon the birth and growth of the modern-day queer rights movement (2005: 406–7). Others offer correlations analogous to Keller's. "The importance of all our pulp fiction novels cannot possibly be overstated," explains Forrest. "Whatever their negative images or messages, they told us we were not alone. ... And once we found each other, once we began to question the judgments made of us, our civil rights movement was born" (2005: xviii). Even Bannon describes the readers of these books as "the vanguard of what later became a proud and brave social movement ..." (Zimet 1999: 15). Each of these statements makes a case for connecting the awareness brought about by lesbian pulp fiction to the queer rights movement beginning in the following decade. No doubt each of these individuals would concede that other factors played a part in the movement's genesis as well; however, their statements request the recognition of what this often-diminished aspect of culture has offered a marginalized population.

I would add that this is an example of the politics through engagement, which Muñoz suggests is a result of disidentificatory reception. These individuals, empowered by the formation and validation of their identities, were enabled to foster discourse about those identities in relation to the socially constructed images offered to them by the wider culture. "The importance of such public and semipublic enactments of the hybrid self cannot be undervalued in relation to the formation of counterpublics that contest the hegemonic supremacy of the majoritarian public sphere," explains Muñoz. In turn, such interrogation of the relationships between the self and public led to what might be considered more traditional or apparent socio-political action.

The L Word occupied a very different historical moment from that of lesbian pulp fiction. It is no longer considered either a sickness or a crime to be gay, and queer communities, organizations, and even representations are much more readily available today than in 1950. The modern-day queer rights movement discussed by Keller is well established. However, while this study has illustrated that many things have changed, it has also demonstrated that much has not. For example, *The L Word* can be attributed with fostering some of the same types of relationships among its viewers as lesbian pulp fiction did with its readers. Viewing parties, fundraising events, fan conventions, and virtual networking sites were created as a result of the series. Additionally, as has been shown, a number of audience members described the series as having an impact upon their ability to come out, meet others, and even simply feel comfortable within their own skin.

With regards to the virtual spaces specifically, individuals found a space, sometimes unavailable to them elsewhere, to discuss both the show and their own lives. Regardless of the diverse reactions to the series, productive dialogs occurred within such locations. In *Convergence Culture,* fandom scholar Henry Jenkins refers to such groups as "knowledge communities" and their discourse as creating "collective intelligence" (2006: 27). He explains, "[k]nowledge communities form around mutual intellectual interests; their members work together to forge new knowledge often in the realm where no traditional expertise exists; the pursuit of and assessment of knowledge [collective intelligence] is at once communal and adversarial" (2006: 20).

For Jenkins, such practices within the virtual world have thus far been generally limited to discussions around aspects of popular culture, such as his examples of *Survivor, Star Wars,* or *Harry Potter;* however, I contend that *The L Word*'s audiences created collective intelligence not only for the series itself, but also of queer culture. In other words, discussions which began as praise or condemnation of the show often extended to address wider issues related to queer existence, such as coming out, homophobia, viable political action, or diversity concerns within the larger queer community. Such autobiographical documentation of a community long forced into silence and invisibility is highly valuable. The collective intelligence of these sites, as well as other forms of engagement brought about by the show, are once again examples of the politics surrounding identity formation and representations discussed by Muñoz.

However, it is also unfortunately true that, at least for the networking sites, the politics is transitory. While many of these networking sites have remained active after the series' conclusion, several, such as thelwordonline.com and l-word.com, have already begun to experience financial difficulties as their advertising revenue filters to new sites believed to have a more significant consumer base. It is likely only a matter of time before their collective intelligence is lost to the server gods. This is disheartening, but it is also useful to remember that if and when this scenario materializes, cyberspace itself will not disappear. Those fostering relationships on these sites or in other venues related to the show will hopefully shift their queer dialogs to new spaces, and herein lies perhaps one of the most exciting legacies of *The L Word*: its audiences. Similar to pulp fiction before it, queer women have been awakened, connected, angered, and inspired over not only a television series, but also their socio-politicized identities. They take the collective intelligence of their interactions with them into new worlds, real and virtual. Just as the scholars of lesbian pulp fiction advocated for the recognition of lesbian pulp fiction's value, the audiences of *The L Word* remind us that there is value in its representational form as well. Is it ideal? Of course not, but these audiences never claimed it was. In fact, its failings are now the fuel for the political fire.

Notes

1   Playing on the old adage that life imitates art, Showtime created OurChart.com as an official real-world networking site tie-in to the show. Within *The L Word*'s narrative, "The Chart" is laboriously created by the character Alice (played by Leisha Hailey). Introduced to viewers already within season one, the Chart is a diagram displayed on Alice's apartment wall that illustrates all the romantic or sexual connections between people within their community. By season four, this wall diagram evolved into the website OurChart.com, which was an expansion of Alice's radio show. The networking site included written, video, and discussion formats that addressed aspects related to the lives of queer women in their community. Showtime's OurChart was essentially the

same type of site. In fact, when Alice's "OurChart" was displayed on-screen during a season five episode, screen shots of the real "OurChart" (including screen caps and profiles of real users) were visible. The site shut down during the show's final season.

2 The quoted statements in this paragraph are taken from the online survey conducted in the fall of 2007, as discussed in the introduction.

From the Bottom to West Hollywood: Finding Community in *Sula* and *The L Word*

Winnie McCroy

Whether it is found in a pool hall in a small Ohio town, or in the smoky haze of a gay disco in West Hollywood, finding and preserving a sense of community binds minority groups together. Communities on the fringe protect what is theirs fiercely, defending it against interlopers, uniting against a common enemy. Sometimes, this enemy comes in the form of an outsider. But just as often, the enemy walks among us, a scapegoat for the evil we seek to repress—much like the golem of Jewish folklore. The downfall of the golem is its creator's hubris; made to do its master's bidding, it inevitably becomes a monster, indiscriminately destroying both good and evil. And, like Percy Shelley wrote in the introduction of the second edition of *Frankenstein*, we are all responsible for this monster.

In looking at the communities presented in the literary works of Toni Morrison, specifically her novel *Sula*, and the Showtime television series *The L Word*, one can see how both minority groups— the African-American and lesbian communities, respectively—deal with evil by creating a scapegoat or golem to assume it. In *Sula*, it is the namesake character's disregard for traditionally feminine social conventions that unites the African-American community of the Bottom in their hatred of her. In *The L Word*, it is the formerly straight interloper Jenny Schecter who fulfills this role. When comparing the two works, it is interesting to note the parallels between how both women function within their communities—with callousness, sexual licentiousness, and mindless cruelty—and how both narratives end with a watery grave.

Although the townsfolk of the Bottom meet their demise as a result of their own actions, it remains uncertain as to what exactly happens to Jenny Schecter. What we do know is that after six seasons of Showtime's runaway pulp lesbian hit, *The L Word*, the high-drama high jinks of a close-knit group of lesbian friends living in the gay ghetto of West Hollywood, California, comes to a close exactly where it began—with Jenny Schecter and Bette and Tina's swimming pool.

Some viewers speculate that either bad romance or backlash from a betrayed community is to blame for Jenny's death. Is the murderer Niki, the jilted lover? Is it Tina, angry over discovering Jenny had indeed stolen the original reels for the film, *Lez Girls*? Could Jenny have simply fallen over that missing stair railing, bumped her head, and plunged into the pool? Is it an accident—or could it have been a conspiracy? Is it possible that after six years of watching Jenny Schecter morph from an emotionally damaged straight woman to the embodiment of every negative lesbian stereotype imaginable (and several heretofore unimagined) that the larger lesbian community finally comes together to put her, and ourselves, out of her misery? Who kills Jenny Schecter? We all do. But in doing her in, we also seal our own fate, as the death of Jenny effectively brings to an end the lives of the women of *The L Word*.

In the fall of 2003, several months before the show first debuted, I attended *The L Word* opening party in Times Square, where I discovered that the "lesbians" were a bit too Hollywood for my taste. I asked actress Katherine Moennig, who played the bad-boy Casanova character Shane, why there were no "real-looking" lesbians on the show. She countered, "It's TV, not reality, and sex sells. It doesn't try to represent the reality of every lesbian, just this group of friends." In a *New York Blade* op-ed titled "L is for Invisible," published later that month, I voiced concern that "a look into the fake lives of a bunch of ersatz lesbians probably isn't going to be the least bit real or insightful or educational to the problems real lesbians face. I'll hold my breath waiting for storylines dealing with affordable health care, domestic partnerships, and having children" (McCroy 2003).

Despite my early critique, I admit ungrudgingly that I did not have to hold my breath for long. For although *The L Word* did represent the limited lesbian reality of a small group of friends living in an (already disparate) gay ghetto, throughout the years producer Ilene Chaiken did a remarkably good job of presenting a full range of storylines dealing with the trials and tribulations of lesbian life. The op-ed was cited in numerous articles, including Eve Kosofsky Sedgwick's "*The L Word*: Novelty in Normalcy," in which the author similarly lauds Chaiken's groundbreaking efforts, but also points out how pandering to a heterosexual audience is manifested in the pilot. The newcomer Jenny first confronts her own sexuality after "watching two young women strip and plunge into a backyard pool, romping amorously in a scene that would not be out of place in soft-core girl-on-girl pornography aimed at heterosexual men or couples" (Sedgwick 2004: B10). If the audience does include the occasional "Joe Sixpack tuning in for a quick thrill" (McCroy 2003), the show unquestionably succeeds in providing the mass culture with a visible depiction of the lesbian community, even if that visibility is based on an elitist representation of Hollywood glamour, consumer-palatable lesbian sex, and somewhat heavy-handed morality tales.

Storylines run the gamut from serious to outlandish. Among them are the trials faced by Dana, a gay athlete coming out and dealing with the media repercussions, and later dying of breast cancer. Feisty bisexual Alice takes on media censorship and gay teen suicide in her on-air stance for gay rights. Gay parenting (and lesbian bed death) is the lesson we learn from the saccharine family life of "Mama B" and "Mama T" and their thankfully avoided custody battle. Tanya tackles the heavy issue of gays in the military with her battle against "Don't Ask, Don't Tell," and her deployment to Iraq. Chaiken takes a heartbreaking look at the perilous lot of gay foster parents when Shane's half-brother Shay comes to live with her, and is later taken back by his father. She even visits the issue of coming out late in life with Cybill Shepherd's character, Phyllis Kroll, who says, "once you finally figure it out, who you are, it's impossible—it's deadly—to deny it" ("Literary License to Kill," 4:11). Mercifully, Chaiken allows "Heads Will Roll" Kroll to find love with Jane Lynch's pitch-perfect lawyer/lesbian silver fox character Joyce Wischnia (is there a scene written that this woman can't steal?).

Throughout the seasons, Chaiken also introduces transgender plotlines, first somewhat comically, through Kit's relationship with drag king Ivan Aycock, and then more seriously, through the character of Max, who is ostracized at the workplace, in the community, and by his family, who call him a freak and tell him he is unwelcome at his own mother's funeral. After the high-profile pregnancy story of transman

Thomas Beatie hit *Oprah*, Chaiken even wrote in a pregnancy—and a gay male lover—for Max. Chaiken presents a complete spectrum of lesbian characters, including secretly married gays like Marina, rich-bitch lesbos like Helena Peabody and her extortionist trick Dylan, lady-killers Shane and Papi, sassy Latina lesbian Carmen, Dana's fame-fucker girlfriend, a controlling nightclub owner, a few saucy bisexuals of both genders, a straight male drag queen, and a deaf lesbian hell-bent on pushing the boundaries of controversial artistic expression.

Every lady was a lesson, and each loveable despite her faults. All but Jenny. As Kera Bolonik of *The New York Times* wrote,

> Jenny-bashing became a spectator sport almost from the moment she arrived in Season 1—a state of affairs the show's creator, Ilene Chaiken, still finds shocking: "People read into the character that she was a manipulator, self-absorbed, a troublemaker who put other people in service of her own neurotic agenda. I think people react so strongly because she is just a mess in the way that so many people are." (Bolonik 2009: 11)

Is Chaiken right? Does the lesbian community tolerate this trouble-maker because we see something of ourselves in her? Or could it be that we need lesbians like Jenny because, when placing our lives next to hers, things don't seem so bad?

As Sedgwick notes, it all begins in the pilot episode, when Jenny spies on Shane and her lover canoodling in Bette and Tina's swimming pool. The character's lives are transmitted to the viewer voyeuristically through this wide-eyed *ingénue*, and as she observes this close-knit group of Hollywood lesbians, she sets about to become like them. But despite Jenny's proximity to and involvement with these women, she is never truly one of them. From a literary point of view, she is little more than a McGuffin: an object around which the plot revolves, but about which the audience doesn't much care.

But to return to the comparison I suggest at the outset of this chapter, although *The L Word* is campy television fare and the novel *Sula* is widely recognized for the classic beauty of Morrison's writing, the character of Jenny Schecter functions in the same way as Morrison's character Sula. Throughout Morrison's novel, Sula acts as the negative force that brings the town together. Her liberated sexuality and indifference to social convention unites the town against the evil they perceive her to be, and when she dies, she takes the best of them with her.

Another comparison can be drawn here between Jenny Schecter's newfound lesbianism and Sula's liberated take on sexuality, via Barbara Smith's frequently cited essay, "Toward a Black Feminist Criticism." Smith notes that Sula's presence in the community functions in much the same way as that of a lesbian, reading that in the opening paragraph of the Radicalesbians 1970 essay, "The Woman-Identified Woman":

> What is a lesbian? A lesbian is the rage of all women condensed to the point of explosion. She is the woman who, often beginning at an extremely early age, acts in accordance with her inner compulsion to be a more complete and freer human being than her society— perhaps then, but certainly later—cares to allow her. These needs and actions, over a period of years, bring her into painful conflict with people, situations, the accepted ways of thinking, feeling and behaving, until she is in a state of continual war with everything around her, and usually with herself. She may not be fully conscious of the political implications of what for her began as personal necessity, but on some level she has not been able to accept the limitations and oppression laid on her by the most basic role of her society—the female role. (1981: 9)

Under this rubric, Smith argues, Morrison's novel *Sula* works as a lesbian novel, "not only because of the passionate friendship between Sula and Nel but because of Morrison's consistently critical stance towards the heterosexual institutions of male–female relationships, marriage, and the family. Consciously or not, Morrison's work poses both lesbian and feminist questions about Black women's autonomy and their impact upon each other's lives." As Smith notes, "Sula and Nel find each other in 1922 when each of them is twelve, on the brink of puberty and the discovery of boys. Even as awakening sexuality 'clotted their dreams,' each girl desires 'a someone' obviously female with whom to share her feelings" (1981: 7).

As Jenny did, Sula comes to an understanding of her sexuality by watching it from a distance; the easy pairings of her mother and neighborhood men in the pantry taught her that "sex was pleasant and frequent, but otherwise unremarkable" (Morrison 1992: 44). But unlike her grandmother Eva, who charmed men, or her mother Hannah, who "rubbed no edges, made no demands, made the man feel as though he were complete and wonderful just as he was" (43), Sula uses men for pleasure, and discards them after one turn. With the exception of her feelings for her lover Ajax, which presage her downfall, Sula's only truly intimate moments come with her friend Nel, the person with whom she shares the sexual exploration of adolescence.

Apart from her relationship with Nel, Sula shows feeling for no one in Medallion's Black neighborhood of the Bottom. Although just a child when she witnesses her mother, Hannah, burn to death in her front yard, even her grandmother knows that "Sula had watched Hannah burn not because she was paralyzed, but because she was interested" (Morrison 1992: 78). On the day of Nel's wedding, Sula leaves the Bottom. She returns years later to the scorn of her grandmother and the townsfolk, to discover that, as Smith notes, "Self-definition is a dangerous activity for any woman to engage in, especially a Black one, and it expectedly earns Sula pariah status in Medallion" (1981: 9).

As Morrison writes, "The conviction of Sula's evil changed them in accountable yet mysterious ways. Once the source of their personal misfortune was identified, they had leave to protect and love one another. They began to cherish their husbands and wives, protect their children, repair their homes and in general band together against the devil in their midst" (1992: 117–18). At this point, Sula functions as a scapegoat or golem, created to unite the townsfolk of the Bottom in hatred of her. Jenny Schecter similarly functions as a televisual golem, created by Chaiken's on-screen lesbian community to absorb all of our most negative traits. Like a skilled mimic, Jenny brings to life every deplorable stereotype with which lesbians are saddled.

Forwarding a theory that Jenny is not to be taken seriously as a character, critic Grace Fannie writes, "Jenny, in a nutshell, is us exaggerated to ridiculous proportions … She is basically an unfiltered Freudian id who gets to say whatever is on her mind and still maintain her friendships because, hey, she's just Crazy Jenny" (2009). To wit, Jenny does seem to function on a primal level from the beginning, as she leaves her lover Tim for a married woman, Marina, and mangles her way through legions of surprisingly caring lovers. She leaves Robin when the woman expresses interest in a long-term relationship, she steals Carmen away from Shane, she brings tranny boi Max back to LA then lambasts him for becoming "the enemy," she fucks and then fucks over Niki. Even in the final season, when Jenny is dating Shane—a woman who can't say no—she seeks to control and change this churlish Casanova, going as far as to move all of Shane's belongings into her room in a forced push for intimacy.

Both Sula and Jenny also betray their best friends by sleeping with their partners. Nel is almost irreparably damaged when she walks in on Sula and her husband Jude "down on all fours naked, not touching except their lips right down on the floor … on all fours like (uh huh, go on, say it) like dogs" (Morrison 1992: 105). Jenny similarly betrays her roommate and future lover Shane, who catches her and her former fiancée Carmen fucking in the bathroom. Neither Sula nor Jenny is apologetic, as neither believes they are doing anything wrong. Throughout the seasons of *The L Word*, Jenny exhibits countless examples of this id-driven malevolence. She seeks revenge on Stacy Merkin, a hapless magazine writer who dares to write that Jenny's central thesis linking her childhood sexual abuse as both a cause and excuse for her deceitful adult behavior was "both insulting and dangerous to those myriad women who have suffered at the hands of predatory men" ("Livin' La Vida Loca," 4:2). After screaming obscenities at the woman's house in the middle of the night à la *A Streetcar Named Desire*, Jenny targets Stacy's veterinarian girlfriend, Lindsay. She adopts an older dog, makes up a sob story, and has the vet put the animal to death.

In the final season of *The L Word*, Stacy reappears to interview Kate, the producer for *Lez Girls*, and confronts Jenny about the ghastly incident. Shocked, Kate asks Jenny, "Do you prey on people whose lives are already falling apart, or do you actually take a more aggressive role in creating their grief and destruction?" ("Long Time Coming," 4:12).

The answer, of course, is both. Jenny shamelessly mines the lives of her so-called friends to create her much-touted book, and then denies any resemblance, although the characters' names and situations are nearly identical to those of her friends. When Tina tries to help Jenny revise her script, she blows her off to buy a Pomeranian, then shows up uninvited to a script meeting, where she levels charges at her friend's integrity, curses her out, then smiles innocently as her pedigree puppy urinates on the conference room table.

Excluding lesbian drama, the only thing Jenny ever creates is her maligned doppelganger/personal assistant Adele, whom she feeds on a diet of tyranny and abuse, and who ends up assuming the very life that Jenny is soon to exit via death.

Despite all of her negative behaviors, Jenny herself is never really evil or good, per se. By never acknowledging that any of her actions are wrong or bad, she neuters their malice—and her culpability. As would a golem, Jenny simply does the bidding of her masters, in this case by providing high drama and reinforcing lesbian stereotypes. After six seasons, everyone in West Hollywood (and nearly the entire viewing audience) wants to kill Jenny Schecter. But at the end, no one does. We never actually see the murderer or the death, we all just sort of will Jenny out of existence. And in the final episode, Chaiken's technique of telling the story via flashbacks (courtesy of police interrogation) further distances us from this crime.

For all intents and purposes, Jenny is a caricature of a lesbian. Without a moral center, she is unable to accept the onus of her deplorable acts. And just as the folks in the Bottom never directly confront Sula for functioning outside of social convention, the tight-knit group of lesbians tolerates Jenny's behavior, and continues to invite her to join their activities. These women seem to rely upon her malice to make their own lives seem richer. Jenny's casual cruelties unite her community against her. Her blackmailing of Bette over compromising (but ultimately innocent) footage of her and the blonde bombshell Kelly only strengthens Bette's bond to Tina. Her callous comments to a pregnant Max make him more determined than ever to deal with motherhood on his own terms. And, as revealed in the final episode, Jenny's attempt to hide Molly's letter loses her Shane's love forever.

For all Jenny's loud declarations about what it means to be a lesbian, it is her innate outsider status, her inability to truly share in the joy of being part of a lesbian community, which leads to Jenny's revilement among those very same women. By the end of the series, nearly everyone voices the wish that Jenny were dead. Even mild-mannered Tina vows, "I'm going to put her out of her fucking misery!" ("Last Word," 6:8).

Much like Sula, Jenny is the evil within, and the community of lesbians deals with her how they always have coped with bigotry and oppression: through the collective strength of tradition and community identity. For Sula, the end comes when she displays typical female behavior for the first time. She falls in love with Ajax and, just as Jenny did with Shane, her attempts to tame and change her lover drive him away. Sula does not even realize until much later that she knows nothing about this man. Reading the name "Albert Jacks" on his driver's license, she is left with a slipping feeling, and realizes that, "When for the first time in her life she had lain in bed with a man and said his name involuntarily or said it truly meaning him, the name she was screaming and saying was not his at all" (Morrison 1992: 136).

Sula is dying, and Nel comes to visit her, and to speak her peace. "You laying there in that bed without a dime or a friend to your name having done all the dirt you did in this town and you still expect folks to love you?" Nel asks (Morrison 1992: 145). But Sula doesn't care about the love of her community. At the moment of her death, her only regret is that she can't share with her friend Nel the sensations of going "down, down until she met a rain scent and would know the water was near, and she would curl into its heavy softness and it would envelop her, carry her, and wash her tired flesh always. Always. Who said that? She tried hard to think. Who was it that had promised her a sleep of water always?" (Morrison 1992: 149).

Although Jenny also finds her end in a "sleep of water always," because her death remains a mystery we can only speculate on whether she craves or expects the love of the community she inserts herself into and systematically betrays. But after six seasons of watching Jenny epitomize every negative lesbian stereotype, most viewers agree on one thing: Jenny Schecter must die. In the final episode, Jenny herself acknowledges this fact when she says, "I can see that my friends don't want to be around me anymore, that they want me to shut the fuck up and go away. I just want to do the right thing" ("Last Word," 6:8).

Women unconnected to the community—those for whom Jenny's drama-laden acts signify what it means to be a lesbian—mourn her death, but lesbians in the mainstream go so far as to claim they did it, some even purchasing "I Killed Jenny Schecter" T-shirts (available on zazzle.com). But no one person killed Jenny Schecter—we all had a hand, and what's more, we all wore a red dress to the funeral and danced on her grave. What we fail to see was how her death is linked to our own.

Gina Abelkop of Jewcy.com makes a valid point when she writes that "Jenny was made to die because her transgressions were made to seem entirely unforgivable and two dimensional" (2009). Abelkop also posts the comments of a friend, who notes:

> We squirm because we identify with her, even if we hate her. It's like the writers dreamed up a cast of stereotypes and then decided to

riddle one of them (the sexually confused one) with every single one of the hangups anyone in the community might experience. It may make her storylines difficult to watch, but I'll take sympathetic discomfort over sex scenes designed to appeal to the hetero male gaze anyday.

Jenny's final act of compiling a video of the characters bidding farewell to Bette and Tina before they move to New York is in essence the cast's final farewell to us, the viewers. Jenny saves the last word for herself, saying, "You guys changed my life, and I'm never going to forget you" ("Last Word," 6:8).

Unfortunately, just as the townsfolk of the Bottom discover, the lesbian community soon realizes that the absence of evil leaves a vacuum to be filled; that "The tension was gone and so was the reason for the effort they had made. Without her mockery, affection for others sank into flaccid disrepair" (Morrison 1992: 153). Women stopped coddling their men, daughters complained bitterly about taking care of their mothers-in-law, and the compassion that Sula's evil had inspired left Medallion. So when Shadrack comes ringing his bell on National Suicide Day, instead of hiding, the townsfolk laugh. The vacuum left by Sula's death prompts them to follow him down New River Road to the mouth of the tunnel that Blacks were never permitted to work on, where it grows into anger over years of opportunities denied them. They begin to destroy the tunnel, to kill what they were for so long forbidden to build. The bracing walls fall, and, as Morrison writes, a lot of them died there, sucked into the chamber of water and ice. Not too many more years pass before everything else about the Bottom is dead as well, the community turning from a "real place" to "just separate houses with separate televisions and separate telephones and less and less dropping by" (166).

Like the death of Sula, destroying Jenny does not come without consequences. Life as we know it—or at least as the characters of *The L Word* know it—comes to a close with her death. Jenny's watery grave is also ours, just as Sula's death foreshadows the sucking into oblivion of the townsfolk into the tunnel they are never permitted to build. Yet without *The L Word*, the lesbian community may never have had the opportunity to cohesively become a visible presence. And without Sula's death, Nel may have never realized that life goes on, that what she was missing wasn't her husband Jude, but the sense of community she found with her childhood friend.

Nicholas Fonseca of Popwatch aptly notes that, in some ways, who killed Jenny has been moot from the start, when he asks, "Years from now, will it even matter how the show went out in its final hour?" He observes that it was the other sixty-nine episodes that made *The L Word* a TV milestone, "its impact expand[ing] far beyond its barrier-busting stories." In this piece, Fonseca also refers to comments made by Chaiken that if her next show, "The Farm," airs, it would be Alice Pieszecki who takes the fall for Jenny's death, despite her own admittance that, "I don't know that she actually killed Jenny" (2003).

At this point, talk of "The Farm" is as dead in the water as Jenny. But is it mere coincidence that Chaiken thought to pin the death of the lesbian stereotype on the show's only actual out lesbian cast member? And is it a simply a lark that Lucy Lawless (a.k.a. Xena, Warrior Princess: the quintessential stereotype of camp lesbian TV fare) plays the police detective investigating the case?

Although lesbians both real and imaginary wish for Jenny's death, her absence signals an end to a safe space we had created, a space in which lesbian lives and visibility thrive. It is up to us now to avoid the fate of the townsfolk in Morrison's *Sula*. If there is a parting message, it is that we must not let our anger over the many years we were forbidden to build our own tunnel to the mainland suck us down into a watery grave.

9

"No Limits" Entertainment: All-consuming Transgressions in Showtime's *The L Word*

Deborah E. R. Hanan

On its face, *The L Word* was a serialized drama centered on a tight group of economically solvent, decidedly urban, normatively attractive same-sex friends, their loves, sexual lives, and personal interactions. Although touted as groundbreaking for its homocentric, sexually transgressive female focus, even a modest perusal of English-language media history reveals that this is not an entirely new or original premise. In fact, from the beginning, Showtime emphasized the show's televisual genealogy by linking it in gay and lesbian print media campaigns with what some had called its "older brother" *Queer as Folk* (2000–2005).[1] In its attempts to attract more mainstream audiences, the network also likened it to another highly successful premium cable series by using the tagline "Same Sex, Different City"—a transparent move to capture HBO viewers cut loose after *Sex and the City* concluded its final season. While it is notable that *The L Word*'s focus on lesbian-centric narratives helped expand premium cable's already established heritage as cultural provocateur, what is truly "groundbreaking" about this series was how its creators used female transgression to circulate and demonstrate the application of an alternative ideology founded in queer theory and the politics of deconstruction. By portraying (and potentially catering to) queerly transgressive and culturally unrecognized consumers through a product that presented identity as highly unstable and situationally contingent, the series worked to both reinforce and undermine contemporary cable network strategies centered on niche marketing models.

Queerly familiar: Transgressive female sexuality and gender-bending in mass-distributed media

Although marketed as "groundbreaking," *The L Word* was not the first media product to center its narrative around transgressive female sexuality and gender alterity. In fact, these are storytelling devices that can be traced back to the cultural dynamism of the Roaring '20s and the releases of novels like Virginia Woolf's *Orlando* (1928) and Radclyffe Hall's *The Well of Loneliness* (1928). While Hall's semi-autobiographical portrayal of female gender variance met with more notoriety and less financial success than Woolf's fantastical narrative, *The Well of Loneliness*, its subsequent foreign and domestic legal battles over content, and its marketing within lesbian pulp and sexual "inversion" literature, insured its otherwise obscure author a secure seat in literary history. Similarly, throughout the history of cinema, filmmakers have incorporated female sexual and gender transgression to attract mainstream audiences, as exemplified in Marlene Dietrich's portrayal of a gender-bending, sexually provocative cabaret singer in *Morocco* (dir. Josef von Sternberg, 1930), and Greta Garbo's gender-variant Swedish monarch in *Queen Christina* (dir. Rouben Mamoulian, 1933).

Produced by and distributed through major publishing houses and film studios for mainstream consumption, *Orlando*, *The Well of Loneliness*, *Morocco*, and *Queen Christina* not only illustrate media industries' historic willingness to exploit transgressive female sexuality and gender-bending for profit; they also reveal that for-profit media played a role in circulating the maxim "gender as performance"—a central axiom of late twentieth-century queer theory and ideology. While gender-bending dispositions and sexual tensions between female characters often played out in ways that were more implicit than explicit, the prevalence of these themes in mass-distributed media history suggests that some awareness of gender-variant or "third gender" identification has continued to persist in the western world even if the English lexicon has failed to account for them since the late 1800s.[2]

One of the more lucrative devices used to explore female transgression in mass-distributed media products has been character cross-dressing. Commonly used for comic relief, the cross-dressed female character has typically been presented in association with gender play and the discovery of secrets, both of which have traditionally translated into economic profits by offering what Russo (1987: 14) has identified as "maximum fantasy appeal to men." Through this lens, female cross-dressed characters function to tantalize heterosexual male audiences with the possibility of an accidental kiss between two women, without constructing either character as lesbian or gender variant. Thus, when integrated into popular mainstream products as gender play (as opposed to gender alterity), character cross-dressing potentially captured leisure dollars that might have otherwise been lost to the "blue movie" and adult book industries.

However, *The L Word*'s incorporation of cross-dressed characters was anything but gender play meant to excite heterosexual males—a task that was already fulfilled rather handily by the show's more normatively constructed lesbians. Instead, cross-dressing was used to reflect the possibility of an alternative ontology—an alternative way of experiencing sex, sexual, and gender identity in indeterminable locales not accounted for in binary logics and configurations. As such, Showtime and *The L Word*'s creative team were able to surpass the standard goal of satisfying and attracting known niche and mainstream audiences, and introduce subplots and characters that could attract emerging minority markets that other networks had yet to identify and harvest. Fulfilling this ambition while maintaining the interest of more normatively identified viewers required integrating alternative ways of being that could both challenge and maintain the logic of a bifurcated framework for sex, gender, and sexuality.

Noting the potential inconsistencies the show encountered in straddling these two disparate positions, Wheeler and Wheeler (2006: 100) have suggested that *The L Word* did not begin to push the ideological envelope until it had already developed a strong and loyal following among lesbian, gay, bisexual, and LGBT-friendly cable viewers in 2005. From their perspective, it was not until the end of the second season that the series shifted markedly towards queer ideology, arguing that "*The L Word* alternately normalizes and differentiates the lesbian, shifting from a theoretical perspective steeped in 1980s identity politics [in the first season] to a more inclusive and current queer approach towards the end of the second season." However, while the central axioms of queer ideology enjoyed a more explicit and heightened role after Moira transitioned to Max in season three, central principles associated with queer ideology were woven into the series from its inception, manifesting most prominently (but not exclusively) in the construction of one of the show's most popular characters, Shane McCutcheon.

As Heidi Schlipphacke also argues in this volume, Shane constantly transgressed her position as the show's seriously damaged stalwart female by slipping into various incarnations as a hyper-predatory, male-identified, cross-dressing female, or an androgynous "other" capable of attracting all sexes, genders, and persuasions. In fact, gender fluidity was instrumental in developing and distinguishing this character during the first season. This was illustrated most explicitly in the sixth episode ("Losing It," 1:6) when a flashback reveals that Shane used to disguise herself as a male prostitute, servicing gay men in exchange for money and drugs. Moennig's previous television roles also coded this character as transgressive. Before joining *The L Word*, Moennig was cast as the cross-dressing, male-identified Jacqueline "Jake" Pratt on the WB Network teen drama *Young Americans* (2000). Later, in 2003, she played Cheryl Avery, a male-to-female pre-op transsexual in *Law and Order: Special Victims Unit*. Early in her career, Moennig also had the distinction of almost landing the role of murdered transgender Brandon Teena in the Oscar-winning film *Boys Don't Cry* (dir. Kimberly Peirce, 1999).

During the first two seasons, Shane and drag king Ivan Aycock were the show's primary vehicles for explorations of gender fluidity. They also functioned as theatrical foils for its more assimilating characters—females whose fixations on domesticity, children, the comforts of consumerism, and other bourgeois pursuits posed little threat to the dominant order. However, some scholars and critics have argued that the centrality of *The L Word*'s other, more normative characters undermined any claims the show might have had on being "groundbreaking" or contestational. Summarizing a common critique frequently levied at the series during its first two seasons, Samuel Chambers (2006: 82) argued that, "*The L Word* – despite (and perhaps because of) its central cast of characters – often serve[d] to perpetuate, preserve and sustain the normativity of heterosexuality. In short, one might best describe the show aporetically: *The L Word* is a heteronormative show about homosexuals."

While Chambers' rather bleak assessment may have been an accurate "first read" of one tine in the show's multi-pronged politics, it discounted *The L Word*'s recurring emphasis on trangressive sex, sexual, and gender identity among females, and the persistent appearance of queer ideological axioms in the show's storylines, dialog, and character constructions. First identified in Sedgwick's clarifying manifesto "Axiomatic" (1999: 321–39), these foundational principles serve to illuminate sex, gender, and sexual identities that have yet to be sufficiently theorized, discussed or accounted for in contemporary western identity discourse.[3] However, these axioms were explicitly embedded in *The L Word* and made salient not only in the characters of Shane and Ivan, but also in the construction of Alice's lesbian-identified male lover Lisa, and most fully realized in the corporeally and ontologically fluid character Moira/Max.[4]

In the first two seasons, these four characters and their relationships made it clear that the current taxonomies western culture relies upon to render a gendered, sexed, or sexual soul have been woefully inadequate and highly misleading. This challenge to normative subject positions was demonstrated most prominently in Moira's lesbian (then Max's straight) relationship with Jenny; Max's queer relationships with Billie Blaikie and Grace; and his gay relationship with Tom Mater.[5] Also, even though Max decided not to fully complete female-to-male surgical reassignment, he still persisted in claiming a "gay male" relationship with Tom, and Tom remained attracted to Max despite his corporeally unresolved status. These identity complications potentially left audiences to ponder how they could adequately reference Max, Tom, or their relationship using the currently available labels of "man," "woman," "male," "female," "gay," "lesbian," "bisexual," and "straight." Perhaps more significantly, the construction of these characters and their relationships potentially inspired some audiences to consider how adequate or inadequate their own identifications might be, at the same time that they were being targeted by a network interested in profiting from identifiable minority niches.

While some may have received the show as merely another "girl-on-girl" sexploitation text for the yet unculled market of lesbian and bi-curious female audiences, *The L Word*'s "new" media spaces (e.g. official website, fansites, OurChart.com and its now-defunct territories in Second Life) revealed resistance among the show's creators and actors (as well as some fans) to decode the show as just another heteronormative text about lesbians. In fact, on the network's official website for the show, some cast members drove *The L Word*'s more ideologically contestational messages home by openly discussing their personal identities and relationships in terms that were fluid and/or unnamed. For example, on the interactive quiz page "Who on *The L Word* is Gay?" the show's official online wiki claimed that actress Mia Kirshner's real-world identity resided "in the gray zone," citing a *New York Times* review in which she reportedly stated that, "[*The L Word*] shouldn't be considered a gay show, because it's beyond that." When pressed to respond more directly about her own identity, she remarked, "gender is of no consequence to me."[6] On the quiz's Daniela Sea page, it was reported that she once described herself to AfterEllen.com as someone whose own identity lies somewhere along "the queer spectrum," adding that she doesn't "believe gender is just binary," and while she may "sometimes politically identify as a lesbian," she also feels "like there are people all along the spectrum" and her identity is more "open-ended."[7] Whether or not Kirschner's or Sea's comments were motivated by professional considerations or personal convictions does not obscure the importance of these actors publicly declining to identify themselves within the binary when they were actively involved with the show. In discussing certain cast members' refusals to declare a particular sexual or gender identity, some online fans responded to Kirschner and Sea's lead by revealing their own ambivalence in identifying within the man/woman and gay/straight divides.

"No Limits entertainment": Showtime, branding, and niche markets

While *The L Word*'s creative team might have been driven by a combination of financial success, creative satisfaction, and personal or political convictions, it would be inaccurate and misleading to suggest that Showtime's explorations into transgressive content were fueled by anything more than the pursuit of potential revenue that could be mined from untapped or not yet financially exhausted niche markets. Additionally, in the 1990s, aggressive gay and lesbian consumer campaigns helped promote the perception that white, middle-class, gay and lesbian consumers were both loyal minority audiences and viable new markets ripe for harvest and worthy of programmers' attentions.[8] Therefore, it was not entirely unexpected that Showtime would actively pursue these niche audiences by developing sexually provocative gay and lesbian-friendly programs like *Queer as Folk* and *The L Word*, and also creating an immersive transmedia experience replete with what Catherine Johnson (2007: 15) has identified as "diegetic and pseudo-diegetic" merchandise (i.e. products that directly and indirectly reference a program's fictional world).

From a branding perspective, *The L Word* undoubtedly pushed premium cable's erotic envelope; and therefore helped to justify Showtime's claim of being the "No Limits" and "Daring to be Different" network. However, in order for these claims to stimulate continued growth and maintenance of its subscriber base, the network also needed to employ what Henry Jenkins (2006) has termed "affective economic" strategies—marketing tactics that could activate viewer attachment to the network through emotional, interactive, and personal investment in authenticating the connection viewers have with its programs. When *The L Word* first debuted in 2004, affective economics had already revealed itself to be the operating logic behind the promise of niche media and micro-market—a logic that threatened to overshadow long-established models of economic growth based on mass consumption, brand fortification, and appeals to consumers' rational decision-making. In an effort to induce greater viewer engagement and investment in its programming, Showtime applied this logic by occupying nearly every inch of terrain associated with viewers' discretionary spending and media leisure activities. In the case of *The L Word*, this included creating an *L Word* presence in multiple online platforms, giving audiences an opportunity to influence show content through a "fanisode" competition that "kept fans engaged between seasons" (Mayberry 2006), and producing merchandise that affiliated viewers with the show and its more provocative themes and characters.

Under the direction of the television industry's first openly gay entertainment president, Robert Greenblatt, Showtime's rebranding strategy also involved producing "aggressive non-mainstream, daredevil programming" featuring sexually complicated and emotionally challenging characters and plotlines (Goodman 2011). Nonetheless, Showtime was not the only cable network to court marginalized sex, gender, and sexual communities in the US. In addition to gay on-demand and niche cable networks like Here!, MTV-subsidiary Logo, and the short-lived Q television network, the popular NBC-affiliated cable channel Bravo implicitly set out to redefine itself as "THE" channel for GLBT-friendly comedy and reality television. With unsubscribed access to over 75 million homes in the US, Bravo made a huge cultural splash with its "breakout hit" *Queer Eye for the Straight Guy* (2003–2007), and sustained its GLBT-friendly reputation with other reality programs featuring "out" gay, lesbian, bisexual, and trans-identified hosts and contestants on shows like *Boy Meets Boy* (2003), *Project Runway* (2004–2009),[9] *Top Chef* (2006–present), *Work Out* (2006–2008), *Top Design* (2007–present), *Flipping Out* (2007–present), *Tabatha's Salon Makeover* (2008–present), *The Real Housewives* franchise (2006–present), and *Watch What Happens Live* (2006–present). With GLBT audiences increasingly identifying Bravo as their favorite cable television network (Faulkner, Fedrizzi, and Garber 2006: 22), Showtime executives understood that if they were to compete successfully for these target audiences they would have to attempt something that hadn't been done before. As *San Francisco Chronicle* reporter Tim Goodman (2004) observed about the series and its network, this drama would need to go "boldly where other series have only flirted" if Showtime's assertion of "No Limits" entertainment were to be taken up by audiences as anything other than a meaningless branding maneuver. Whether or not the concern was to authenticate the network's daring marketing claims, Showtime did boldly agree to push boundaries with *The L Word*, an ongoing development that reached its maximum narrative potential in the character Moira/Max.

"Lipstick lesbians" and the "Max" factor

It was at the end of season two, when Moira was first introduced, that I first became interested in examining *The L Word* as a site in which the alternative worldview embedded in queer theory was being inextricably linked with economic participation. Originally constructed as a working-class, flannel-wearing Midwestern dyke, Moira was one of the few masculine female characters to join the series' otherwise hyper-feminized line-up. As an out-of place interloper in the fantastically constructed urban lesbian Mecca of West Hollywood, California, Moira was pejoratively marked by her awkward, blue-collar masculinity and lack of economic viability—qualities that placed her in stark contrast to Jenny's unapologetically bourgeois, excessively confident "lipstick lesbian" social circle.

Contradistinctions between Moira and the show's main characters (Jenny, Bette, Tina, Alice, Dana, and Shane) became conspicuously evident in the third episode of season three ("Lobsters," 3:3). In this episode, Moira's failure to successfully navigate one of the group's erudite gatherings at a swanky West Hollywood restaurant demonstrates for viewers the kind of uncomfortable collisions that can occur when working-class palates and pocketbooks meet bourgeois menus. Soon after Jenny and Moira arrive at the restaurant—Jenny in an evening dress and Moira notably underdressed in a cut-off flannel shirt hanging out over a plain white T-shirt and jeans—the twosome peruse a menu featuring $42–52 entrées that include Velouté of Butternut Pumpkin, Roasted Mulloway, and Assiette of Glenloth Rabbit. Ordering "merely a salad and side of fries," Moira's cheery demeanor begins to falter when she is unable to engage with the atmosphere or table conversation. Leaving the table to wash her hands, Moira overhears two women snickering about her appearance in the bathroom. When she returns and her salad arrives, she looks around to compare her sparse presentation of undersea grass and Jerusalem artichoke shavings to her tablemate's full lobster dinners. Seemingly unphased by Moira's discomfort, several at the table draw attention to her paltry meal by offering her lobster scraps from their own dinners.

Repeatedly refusing what seems like condescending charity, Moira asks Jenny to find another ride home and she departs (with Jenny following behind). After they leave, the others speculate on why Jenny would ever date a "stone butch" like Moira. Only Shane bothers to directly question this assessment of Moira's identity. After Carmen points out to Shane that even Moira refers to herself and Shane as "us butches," Bette explains that this is because Moira "comes from a place where, you know, you have to define yourself as either/or. It's probably just the only language she has to describe herself." As everyone else continues to speculate on Moira's presumed "role playing," Shane gets increasingly perturbed, finally asserting, "You know, what difference does it make whether someone is butch or femme? Let's just leave labels alone and let people be who they are" ("Lobsters," 3:3). This scene marked a turning point in the show, in which the weekly titillation of "girl-on-girl action" began to cede ground to more substantive considerations of class differences, consumption, and freeing oneself from dominant conceptions of identity.

Not surprisingly, the line that confirmed the association between where Moira "comes from" and how she identifies was initially voiced by the affluent, Yale-educated Bette, whose upper-class status and corporeal transgression as a biracial character were inexorably tied, especially when juxtaposed with her less affluent, less educated and not biracial half-sister Kit. Bette's possibly well-meaning but condescending remark concerning Moira's limited identity vocabulary is just one of the show's numerous dialogic and visual assaults on non-urban and/or economically marginalized populations. Framed as largely irrelevant to the urban consumer discourse woven throughout much of the dialog, these populations were often characterized as unable to fully comprehend or experience fluid identity because they lacked the financial and cultural capital to do so.

While Shane's libertine and overtly male-coded behavior and dress did not prevent her from moving comfortably among the supercilious females who anchored the show's narrative, Moira was socially marginalized by most in the group because of her crude, working-class affect. Although gender variance informed the constructions of both Shane and Moira, these characters' queer natures were distinguishable on two levels. First, unlike Shane, Moira's early failure to find employment reflected an inability to "pass" as economically viable or as a cultural trendsetter worthy of support. Second, Shane's sexual and gender transgressions were acceptable because Shane never overtly rejected or aggressively critiqued (as Moira did) the unrestrained consumerism that united most of the other characters in the series. The text constructed Moira as an under-educated female with non-consuming values, and made it clear that she would never be able to fully comprehend the meaningfulness of a fluid identity and break free from binary identification until she understood the deep linkages between economic participation and transgression.

Moira's awareness of these linkages began to unfold in the following season. The more Moira/Max explored the terrain of female masculinity and then sexual and gender transgression, the more financial abundance and independence this character attained. After transitioning to Max and assuming a male identity, ~~he~~ landed a well-paying job with a technology firm; then left the company to strike out on ~~his~~ own as a digital media entrepreneur (a self-employed webmaster of Alice's "new" technology undertaking: thechart.com). In the process, Moira/Max traversed a journey that far exceeded the parameters of class difference and butch-lesbian identification—one that bled deep into the radical terrain of contesting western ideology. By the fourth episode of the third season, socializing with a new group of decidedly non-normative friends, Moira/Max took steps beyond the known; exploring gender, sex, and sexuality in profound and transformative ways ("Light My Fire," 3:4). It was during this period that Jenny and Moira met Billie Blaikie, a male genderqueer whose character construction defied dominant culture's bifurcated system of identification. Billie's polysexual attractions and relations with gay males and female genderqueers (e.g. Moira/Max) didn't just upend the dimorphic logic sustaining hetero-, homo- and bi-sexuality; for many viewers it provided the much-needed confirmation that Showtime truly was the "No Limits" network and that *The L Word* was indeed "groundbreaking."

In season three, shortly after meeting Billie, Moira adopted the male personae Max and began taking hormones in preparation for sex-reassignment surgery. Bypassing more orthodox healthcare channels, Billie helped Max procure black market testosterone injections, while Jenny organized an event at The Planet to raise money for ~~his~~ sex-reassignment surgery. However, in the midst of Moira's transition to Max, Jenny discovered that the testosterone injections radically altered ~~her/his~~ personality and made Max a more volatile and aggressively sexist partner. Initially constructed as bisexual, Jenny was repelled by this transformation, a reaction that led to the couple's breakup and Jenny's eventual identification as a lesbian solely attracted to women-identified females.

Rejected, curious, vulnerable, and not surgically reassigned, the dildo-accessorized Max has sex with Billie in the back office at The Planet. In what is arguably the most queerly transgressive moment in television history, Billie performed oral sex on the prosthetically enhanced Max, an event that forced the other characters to wrestle with how best to refer to this hormonally altered but not surgically reassigned male-identified female. Occurring "backstage" at The Planet—sullying the primary locale where *The L Word*'s more normative spectacles of vapid consumer discourse, "acceptable" lesbianism, and bio-determinist debates transpired—the scene served to underscore the dramaturgic roles that queer theory and its transgressive ideology played in developing this entertainment media product and all of its "new" media progeny.

Harvesting transgressive pleasures and "new" markets

Both by conscious design and circumstance, ideological analysis of this show's content and its ancillary and associated "new" media channels reveals that, over time, the franchise became increasingly transgressive on three levels. First, the show maintained several non-dimorphic characters in recurring roles. *The L Word*'s depiction of these characters' sexual practices and erotic relationships transgressed previous media marketing strategies of simply indulging heterosexual male fantasies involving "girl-on-girl action" or pandering to a loyal minority consumer market. Instead, English-language audiences were placed in the position of voyeuristically experiencing a variety of sex, gender, and sexual identities and relationships, experiences that demanded these audiences at least consider what lies beyond western binary formulations. In addition, the series transgressed genre conventions by integrating gender-variant people into the more mundane landscape of the soap opera drama—a move that exceeded the parameters of science fiction and fantasy genres in which these characters typically appear. In so doing, gender and sexually fluid characters were rendered in compassionate ways that humanized (rather than exceptionalized) their lives. Endowed by their positions as perpetual outsiders, these characters served as *The L Word*'s Greek Chorus that critiqued, tempered, and drew attention to the sometimes thoughtless and cruel actions of the show's occasionally vindictive woman-identified females.

Second, as the show progressed, storylines delved deep into the psychology and lives of sex, sexual, and gender variants, portraying the unnamed outsider as one that is empowered only after it rejects labels and embraces difference. By resisting full surgical reassignment but still performing male, Max was able to land a well-paying job with the same technology firm that originally rejected his alter ego Moira. After outing himself to his employers, he quits and becomes a "new" media entreprenuer. It is through this professional transformation that he meets and enters into a relationship with Grace, who inspires him to reject the restrictive landscape of the binary and reconsider the necessity of sex-reassignment surgery. Through Grace, Max discovers that sex, sexual, and gender identity are not anatomically dependent, and (in true cliffhanger fashion) the fourth season concludes with Max questioning whether or not to remain physically intact as a male-identified female gender variant. While Max's role in the narrative arc noticeably receded in seasons five and six, this character remained a polyamorous, male-identified female gender variant through the end of the series, further challenging normative culture with ~~his~~ unexpected pregnancy and struggles with identification and parenthood.

Before the series concluded, I had the opportunity to ask the show's producer/creator Ilene Chaiken if there had been any pressure from the network or the show's lesbian fanbase to eliminate or alter Max's provocative development by rendering this character back into the logic of the binary through sex reassignment. Chaiken insisted that the creative team was intent on keeping the identity of this character ambiguous, stating that as far as she was concerned, "Max's identity will never fully be resolved"—an objective that the team did in fact fulfill.[10]

The third and final way that *The L Word* franchise became more transgressive developed in the "new" media spaces the series inspired and incessantly cross-promoted: the network's official *L Word* site (http:// www.sho.com/site/lword/home.do), the show's social networking site (OurChart.com), and its virtual properties in Second Life. These interactive spaces also exemplified some of the more prominent ways in which the show's creators forged links between economic exchange and transgressive sex, sexuality, and gender identity. Throughout the life of the franchise, the network promoted both a deconstructed view of personal identity and a reconstructed forging of affinity through brand identification by featuring a panoply of boundary-busting products on the show's official website.[11] During season four, on the heels of the show's explorations of gender and sexual fluidity, several *L Word*/Showtime-branded products directly conflated the show's more transgressive themes with Showtime's "No Limits" brand.[12] According to network executives, this ancillary revenue stream and the show's saturation of "new" media spaces were key to Showtime's overall branding strategies—a calculation that took into account the important role that "new" media could play in extending the franchise's longevity and increasing the network's subscriber base. Commenting on "new" media's relevance to increasing the network's share of the US cable market, Showtime CEO Matt Blank stated in the spring of 2006 that "a lot of this technology [has leveled] the playing field for Showtime, which has been restricted by our distribution environment in terms of the number of homes that can get us and can access us at a reasonable price" (Steinert-Threlkeld 2006). However, while network executives may have perceived that web-based media was another platform for solely delivering content and attracting larger audiences, these sites gave *The L Word* a life of its own. With "authoring" placed in the "prosuming" hands of fans and users of these commercial media sites (e.g. in the forms of user-generated fan-fic, commentary, and social networking), not only was the franchise extended; it entered the non-corporeal, fluid world of Internet discourse—a journey that all but guaranteed that gender and sexual deconstruction would continue to circulate in relation to *The L Word* narrative long past the show's concluding season in 2009.

One of the more popular "new" media spaces associated with the series was OurChart.com. Based on "The Chart," a leitmotif that helped propel the storyline since the show's inception, OurChart.com became a main portal through which *L Word* audiences could easily violate and defy the once bound and clearly defined spaces of television, "new" media, and real life. Founded on Milgrim's social capital theory (a.k.a. six degrees of separation) and Shane's bounteous sex life, the Chart visually graphed how all lesbians in *The L Word* are connected to one another through sexual trysts and friendships. However, in season four the show's creators enacted an ingenious maneuver of hyper-hyperreality, moving the Chart online (both on the Internet and in the series) so that audiences could add their own histories to this fictional graph, and thereby merge the imaginary world of *The L Word*'s characters with their real-world relationships. When OurChart.com launched, the online advertising sales department framed this cross-platform marketing strategy in words and phrases that were political and liberating in tone:

We were first introduced to Alice's chart of hookups in season one … Since then, it's been the connecting thread throughout all of the relationships on the show. Whether or not the characters have slept together, they're all together on Alice's wall. The underlying friendships in the group are the real foundation of all these connections, and that's where OurChart comes in. Until now, there's never been a central meeting place just for us—lesbians, dykes, queer girls, gay women, high femmes, butches, drag kings, bois, transwomen and transmen—however we define ourselves.

However, as emancipating as the above declaration sounded, since it appeared on a page specifically designed to generate more advertising sales, the underlying message was that liberation for those who remained recalcitrantly unidentified necessitated some kind of economic participation. This social networking site was replete not only with advertisements featuring Showtime programs, commercial CDs, live concerts, film festivals, etc., but also with solicitations for non-Showtime advertisers interested in reaching this "broad, desirable target market" of OurChart users. Notably, in an era of niche marketing and target advertising, the "desirable target market," while (perhaps) politically linked, was uncharacteristically nonspecific. As the blurb declared, its users constituted a random assortment of sex, sexual, and gender minorities, as well as "however we define ourselves" populations. Thus, advertisers were asked to consider not only already identified GLBT niches as "desirable" consumers, but also the show's more fluidly identified fanbase as a potential source of revenue.

Shortly after OurChart.com went live online, the network announced that the show would be "the first cable television series to go virtual with the launch of *The L Word* in Second Life."[13] Second Life (SL) is a simulated online world that allows its members (citizen residents or "netizens") to create personalized 3-D avatars and interact freely in a fairly unregulated environment. As an SL netizen, users exchange real-world currency for Linden dollars, which then allows them to purchase virtual property, products, services, and experiences (e.g. islands, anatomical features, clothing, food, beverages, furniture, vehicles, concerts, films, etc.). In 2007, the year that *The L Word* became a presence in this simulated world, SL reportedly had 3.5 million "residents" who had spent an average of $50–60 per week within this virtual space. As a result of Linden's reported estimates of netizen spending, many real-world companies like IBM, American Airlines, Dell, General Motors, and Showtime quickly moved to establish an SL presence (Cain 2007).

When I first began this study in 2007, I visited the short-lived L Word in Second Life and discovered that the degree to which its users could actually enact or demonstrate transgression was directly connected to economic exchange, and to a user's ability to invest in a variety of visual codes (e.g. unusual or customized "skins," appendages, clothing, and accessories) available to defy dominant frameworks defining gender, sex, sexual, ethnic, "racial," generational, and marital identification. As I "walked" about the main corridors of L Word island, I was able to observe some of the "dating" and interactions that occurred in this "Grid" environment—encounters that always involved some kind of consumer transaction, whether it be for dining, drinking, and entrance fees, or purchasing clothing, accessories, or erotica. During my virtual excursion, I also "met" a handful of netizens whose avatar forms were complexly accessorized in ways that made it difficult to describe their identities within the dominant conceptual frameworks of female/male or woman/man. What I discovered in the visits to L Word island, as well as OurChart.com and the show's official blog and fan websites, was that all the "new" media activities and interactions solely occurred within the context of consumer-rich environments. Still, despite the influx of corporate interest that had initially migrated to "The Grid" and L Word island, this site tied a substantial amount of its commercial activities to identity building, adult entertainment, and virtual dating. In so doing, the franchise had grown to include a place in cyberspace where boundaries could safely and routinely be transgressed and where L Word netizens could experience an alternative way of making meaning of the world and their place in it.

Concluding remarks

Nadia Guidotto (2006: 2) has argued that when it comes to media representation of marginalized sex, sexual, and gender communities, "the capitalist economy actually stifles diversity and minority interests." She has questioned whether the only liberation that can come from the kind of niche marketing cultivated by Showtime and other networks is the liberation of dollars from the wallets of minority interests. Others, including John Campbell (2005: 677–8), have voiced similar concerns, suggesting that while "recognition in the marketplace constitutes one form of political advancement," it also reinforces the ideology that recognition is inextricably tied to purchasing power.

My intent here has been to consider the degrees to which truly transgressive ideological content emerged out of a cultural product otherwise saturated with normative pleasures, dominant encodings, and economic interests. I wanted to consider whether, as D'Acci

(2004: 384) has suggested, television is simply creating more citizen consumers or if it is in fact "contributing to the formation of new types of human beings—ones less forged by all the conventional binaries (male/female, white/black, rich/poor, young/old, etc.)." While most Showtime executives may know very little about queer theory or couldn't care less if its transgressive ideology circulates in the culture, both of these constructs—as they appeared in *The L Word*—served at least two masters: the capitalist pursuits of a competitive network, and those unnamed others whose collective desire is to be acknowledged by the culture.

Notes

1   This Showtime Original series was a North American adaptation (US/Canadian joint venture) of the British Channel 4 television series of the same name, which originally aired in the UK from 1999–2000.

2   English-language terms denoting female gender variance (e.g. "tommy" and "sapphist") disappeared from the popular lexicon when dimorphic schemas of gender, sex, and sexuality began circulating in German, British and US medical and psychiatric journals ca. 1890. For a fuller account of these vernacular transformations, see Serena Nanda (2000) and Randolph Trumbach (1994).

3   In "Axiomatic," Sedgwick postulates six self-evident truths from which a theory of sexed, gendered, and sexual difference could progress and be made relevant as a political project: 1) "People are different from each other"; 2) "The study of sexuality is not coextensive with the study of gender; correspondingly anti-homophobic enquiry is not coextensive with feminist enquiry. But we can't know in advance how they will be different"; 3) "There can't be a prior decision about how far it will make sense to conceptualize lesbian and gay male identities together. Or separately"; 4) "The immemorial, seemingly ritualized debates of nature versus nurture take place against a very unstable background of tacit assumptions and fantasies about nature and nurture"; 5) "The historical search for a Great Paradigm Shift may obscure the present conditions of sexual identity"; and 6) "The paths of allo-identification are likely to be strange and recalcitrant. So are the paths of auto-identification."

4 Alice's lesbian-identified male lover Lisa was introduced in season one's fourth episode, and appeared three more times before Alice dropped her for a "less complicated" lover. Sea's character was initially introduced as Moira in season two before adopting the identity of Max in season three.

5 Moira entered into her relationship with Jenny in season two and then, after transitioning to Max, entered ~~his~~ relationship with Billie and Grace in season three, and Tom in season four. Here I use the Derridian or deconstructive method of striking through certain pronouns (e.g. ~~he~~, ~~she~~, ~~her~~, ~~his~~) and placing them *sous rature* or "under erasure" to indicate their inadequate yet necessary function in identifying how non-dimorphic characters present themselves within the binary.

6 Showtime Networks Inc., "The L-Word Wiki: Who on *The L Word* is Gay?" Question 5. Available at http://lwordwiki.sho.com/page/5c, accessed June 8, 2011.

7 Showtime Networks Inc., "The L-Word Wiki: Who on *The L Word* is Gay?" Question 10. Available at http://lwordwiki.sho.com/page/10c, accessed June 8, 2011.

8 For a fuller detailing of the development and results of these campaigns, see Faulkner, Fedrizzi, and Garber (2006); Guidotto (2006); and Hennessy (1995).

9 Still in production, Bravo lost its number one hit show *Project Runway* in April 2008 when the show's producers decided to join rival cable network Lifetime.

10 This exchange occurred in February 2007 during a Q&A sponsored by University of Southern California's School of Cinematic Arts (Los Angeles, California).

11 Products included but were not limited to clothing, jewelry, bags, belts and other accessories, kitsch memorabilia, and housewares, ranging in price from $20 to $165.

12 Among these types of products were T-shirts that featured declarations like "Don't classify me" and female "boi" briefs bearing the "SHO" bug logo.

13 Showtime Networks Inc., "Announcements: Showtime Networks and Electric Sheep to Launch *The L Word* in Second Life," January 22, 2007.

PART 4

Legacy

Imagining Queer Community in *The L Word*

Cristyn Davies and Kellie Burns

Many queer viewers will identify with the tension between the pleasure of consuming *The L Word* and critiquing character and plot development. Viewing lesbian characters at the forefront of a television series—"talking, laughing, loving, breathing, fighting, fucking, crying, drinking, writing, winning, losing, cheating, kissing, thinking, dreaming"—shifted lesbian representation on television from the periphery to the center. Elsewhere we have argued that *The L Word* marks a significant moment in television history because it foregrounds lesbian and queer lives, and offers important political commentary on a range of issues related to queer living (Burns and Davies 2009). However, this content is mediated within a serial narrative and setting that idealize and normalize elite and exclusive consumptive practices. Many viewers disidentified with the homogeneity and relatively narrow depictions of lesbian life in the series in spite of the pleasure attached to consuming the program.

In this chapter, we focus on the ways in which race, ethnicity, and parenthood are produced and consumed within a program that prioritizes elite consumer lifestyles. Desire for the queer viewer is not only constructed through the recognition of viewing queer lives at the forefront of a television series, but is also assembled through practices of consumption, defined by neoliberal governmental regimes. A shift from mass marketing to more specialized targeting of consumers enabled through neoliberal deregulatory policy regimes and open global markets has enabled companies and organizations to promote consumption of their products and services. This is undertaken through carefully crafted political rhetoric that appeals to consumers' political and ethical beliefs and values, such as embracing diversity and difference.[1] The increasingly neoliberal policies and practices that define contemporary broadcast and network cultures shape television programming and content. Neoliberalism not only organizes technologies of televisual delivery, it also produces ideals and norms of sexual citizenship, so that difference is made consumable rather than politically challenging (Burns and Davies 2009; Davies 2012).

Screening neoliberal cosmopolitan communities

Televisual culture has shifted from the traditional broadcast era, which relied on the dispersal of information from a central source, to the post-broadcast era characterized by more fragmented and fluid network structures consumed across multiple platforms. The rise of cable television and niche marketing principles has repositioned individuals or certain groups as viable niche markets. Programming no longer has to satisfy the interests and demands of a mass audience, but can instead address niche audiences. While these industrial changes have created opportunities for television with queer content, this increased visibility does not necessarily reflect political equality, but rather signals opportunities for networks to market queer content to niche consumers. Queer citizens are targeted consumers, cosmopolitan citizens who are invested in certain consumptive and lifestyle practices and bound to neoliberal practices of self-management.

Cosmopolitan queer living is associated with sensibilities and tastes that are seen as exemplarily diverse, stylish, inclusive, and therefore readily consumable by mainstream audiences. The aesthetic and cultural tastes that validate queer subjects as a respectable niche audience or group of consumers, also position them to be consumed. Global cosmopolitanism encompasses cultural and consumer practices, including being open and able to interact with a variety of different world cultures, and the acquisition of cultural capital by becoming increasingly worldly, cultured, and diverse. Within televisual culture, diversity and difference have been carefully managed and marketed. For example, while *Queer Eye for a Straight Guy* embraced difference in terms of the sexual orientation of the "fab five," the erasure of differences in makeover subjects, especially with regard to socio-economic class and masculinity, was demonstrated in the master narrative used by Bravo in their series.[2] In this American reality program, five gay men were positioned as cosmopolitan consumers premised on the stereotype that they have superior taste in fashion, cuisine, interior design, culture, and everyday living. The "fab five" transformed the outward appearance, skills, and taste of heterosexual men beyond the confines of cosmopolitan Manhattan. The aim of the makeover was to produce an idealized form of heterosexual masculinity. In doing so, makeover subjects' individual differences were erased to produce a singularized understanding of masculinity valorizing metrosexual modes of consumption. The aesthetic and cultural tastes of the "fab five" were used to validate gay men as expert sexual citizens who possess a set of skills and attributes that, when taken up, make them a more attractive package deal. In a way not dissimilar to *Queer Eye*, the cosmopolitan lifestyles and self-management practiced by *The L Word* characters produces an idealized model of lesbian identity that overlooks the complexity of difference.

The L Word is set against the backdrop of trendy West Hollywood and depicts a lesbian community that has easy access to cultural resources and social mobility. The characters are model neoliberal consumers and cosmopolitan citizens invested in consumption and the projects of self-management and self-enterprise. Individually, each character upholds the neoliberal project in which hard work and maximizing personal choices increases status and opportunity. Perhaps the most notable examples are Jenny Schecter's geographic and career development, firstly from the Midwest to West Hollywood, and secondly from struggling writer, to published novelist, to screenwriter; Tina Kennard's seamless transition from social worker to film industry executive; Bette Porter's career trajectory from art curator in a public gallery to dean of a prestigious university; and Shane McCutcheon's success as hairdresser to the stars after a life of bad foster care experiences, sex work, and homelessness.

Queer community on *The L Word* is also defined through elite consumer lifestyles. Throughout season one, community is constructed over coffee, food, and gossip at The Planet café (a business owned and run by Marina Ferrer in the first season and purchased by Kit Porter in season two), but also through the characters' shared appreciation of high culture, including everything from designer clothing, to hair, cars, real estate, expensive restaurants, and fine art. In season two, the power of the pink economy and the appeal of identity-based consumption are emphasized through sponsors' support of Dana Fairbanks' coming out. In season three the heteronormative economies of parenting (Bette and Tina) and marriage (Shane and Carmen) are central season plotlines. In season four, Helena Peabody's struggle to acclimatize from a life funded by her family fortune to being self-sufficient finds her involved in gambling and a fraught relationship, rather than applying for standard employment. In seasons four and five, the cultural and class differences of Eva "Papi" Torres and Tasha Williams are made consumable by the key characters (and the audience) to extend their profiles as urban cosmopolites. Finally, in season six the struggle to maintain community despite the normalizing practices of the money-driven film industry functions as a type of queer dénouement, where the central characters in the text (and the audience) are forced to reflect on repercussions of trading increased visibility and access to "identity-based consumption" (Chasin 2000) for "real" equality and recognition.

While it is pleasurable for audiences to consume queer living within an elite cosmopolitan milieu, screening queer characters within this context can be mistaken for a shift in social attitudes towards queer citizens achieving equality and rights. The liberal dictum of equality and citizenship rights is mediated through the marketplace, wherein purchasing power and consumption have come to symbolize a new generation of queer politics, marginalizing the need for other types of political action (Davies 2008b; 2012). Access to and visibility within the televisual economy often results in normalized and sanitized representations of queer living, which overlook inequalities. For television with queer content, this means that historically marginalized sexual citizens—but also ethnic minority groups, the working class, and women—are transformed into niche markets consumable by viewers.

Consuming diversity

After the *The L Word*'s first season, critics commented on the program's lack of political engagement and its failure to reflect "real" lesbian lives, especially issues of class and racial differences within queer communities (Burns and Davies 2009). In response, the series' writers diversified the scope of lesbian representations on offer in succeeding seasons (Sedgwick 2006). The series positions the viewer to consume this diversity through the perspective of the already-established key characters, who are primarily white, middle-class, and upwardly mobile. The exceptions included Bette Porter and her on-screen half-sister Kate "Kit" Porter. Bette is an affluent and Ivy-League-educated (she was an art history major at Yale) lesbian of African-American and Caucasian heritage, while Kit, who shares the same father as Bette, is a recovering alcoholic with ties to the music industry. Socio-economic and class differences between the sisters are clear, and both women are positioned within the series as differently entrepreneurial. Lesbian and queer citizenship and constructions of community in the program are otherwise primarily white, such that representations that challenge racial, ethnic, class, gender, and ability are always defined against norms established through the key characters.

Across the six seasons, the series introduces "difference" (from the white, middle-class, able-bodied lesbian subject) through the characters of Bette, Kit, Carmen, Papi, Jodi, Moira/Max, Tasha, and Jamie, and provides pseudo-political commentaries on interracial relationships and same-sex and transgendered parenting, among other political hot topics. In season two, the series' writers introduce Carmen de la Pica Morales, the Latina DJ from East LA Season three addresses transphobia within and outside the lesbian community through the character of Moira/Max Sweeny, a female-to-male transgender character from the Midwest. In season four, three new characters diversify *The L Word* community—Papi Torres, *The L Word*'s Latina Casanova; Tasha Williams, an African-American captain in the US National Guard, on leave from a tour in Iraq; and Jodi Lerner, a deaf visual artist. In seasons four and five, the surveillance and silencing of gays and lesbians in the military is explored through Tasha's character. In season six, Jamie Chen, a vegetarian counselor at the Los Angeles Gay and Lesbian Youth Center, is introduced to further develop the program's ethnic diversity. All of these characters offer an opportunity to imagine lesbian life beyond the confines of The Planet and the chic, trendy façade of West Hollywood. Difference interrupts the ubiquity of white, middle-class, able-bodied lesbian lives.

However, when this difference is mediated within an idealized cosmopolitan televisual landscape, it serves to solidify the white middle-class lesbian as the idealized norm. Papi and Tasha are key examples of the limits of representing racial and ethnic diversity within a cosmopolitan framework. Despite their integration into the everyday comings and goings at The Planet, both characters occupy an outsider status because they are the only suburban, working-class lesbians amid an otherwise middle- and upper-middle-class social set. Alice is determined to meet the sexually infamous lesbian known only as "Papi" ("Daddy" in Spanish) who has managed to infiltrate her online social network and sexual mapping tool, "The Chart." As a cosmopolitan *flâneur*, Alice visits the foreign clubs and streets of East LA and finally meets Papi who is working as a limousine driver. Alice's eroticization of Papi's ethnic, class, and geographic difference upholds the stereotype of the Latina/Latino other (Rodríguez 1997). Throughout season four, Papi is allowed little character development other than through her performance of sexual consumption. This sexual consumption is positioned against Shane's, who effortlessly attracts women. *The L Word* writers frame the first meeting between Papi and Shane as a pastiche of a standoff from Sergio Leone's 1966 Italian epic spaghetti Western, *The Good, the Bad and the Ugly*.[3] While Shane remains indifferent to Papi's arrival on her turf, Papi's antagonism and competitiveness with Shane is framed through the characters' racial and ethnic difference. Papi endeavors to be a more powerful and successful sexual consumer than the "little white girl" Shane, whom she refers to as "Vanilla Spice." While Papi's sexual consumption exceeds Shane's, Papi is required to put much more labor into her sexual and gendered performance. The series positions Papi as the aspirational neoliberal subject whose sexual prowess functions as a skill for improved social status and class mobility. In contrast, Shane does not require the same level of self-work, as she easily seems to gain access to women and resources.

Throughout the series, diversity and difference are frequently depicted from a normative middle-class, white, and able-bodied perspective. During Alice's podcast interview with Papi focused on the best places to meet girls, Papi reveals that Sunday pick-up basketball at West Hollywood Park is a prime location for meeting "all different kinds of girls" ("Layup," 4:4). Papi challenges Alice and her friends to a basketball match, which acts as a mode of engaging class, race, and ethnic difference. Papi warns Alice that her team will "whip [their] asses all the way back to Rodeo Drive, where [they] can go shopping, which is the only sport" they can play. Situated in Beverly Hills, Rodeo Drive is a shopping district known for designer label and haute couture fashion. Sporting ability and shopping are set up against one another, the former representing working-class competitiveness, and the latter, elite bourgeois lifestyles. Alice has to assemble her team through manipulative means, given that her friends are disinterested in sporting competition, and builds team spirit through the politics of consumption. In their team-shopping trip to purchase Puma leisure shoes, rather than basketball footwear, Helena questions, "When did trainers get this expensive? I mean really!" Having been cut off by her mother from the family estate, her comment signals her newly disenfranchised position, and her prior disinterest in cost. Kit's desire for consumption is depicted through her determination to squeeze into trainers that are a size too small for her, signifying her willingness to conform to the norms of a petite feminine bodily ideal. Alice's team also dons purple matching uniform tank tops, featuring their surnames and a player number, signaling once again their easy access to resources. They are called the "bourgie ass girls," based on an insult leveled by Papi to Alice about her friends' bourgeois social status and capitalist practices. Revealing her capacity to turn the slur on its head, Alice explains the politics and power of re-signification—that is, using Papi's slur to empower rather than offend her team members. The match scene is initially set in slow motion and sepia tones, with Papi's team composed primarily of Black and Latina butch women, who warm up exhibiting their athletic skill, while Alice's team show up speaking on mobile phones, wearing designer sunglasses, and not having trained for the game. Just as the sporty lesbian works to pass within normative sporting cultures, the "bourgie asses" attempt to pass with very little success as "authentic" or legitimate sporty lesbians.

Before the match begins, Tina arrives to participate, but is shafted by Jenny, who makes a disparaging comment about Tina's newfound heterosexual privilege. This is ironic given that the series has positioned Jenny and Alice as formerly in relationships with men. Kit's interjection that "it depends what color of heterosexual you are that gets you all them privileges" serves as a reminder of the ways in which sexual identity is mediated by the politics of race and cultural background. Kit's comment calls attention to the marginalization of race as a category within both heterosexual and queer cultures, which is a critique that has been made of western feminism and lesbian, gay, and queer political movements (hooks 1992; Lorde 1996; Muñoz 1999). Over her shoulder, Papi dismisses the preoccupation with lesbian sexual identity politics, inviting Tina to play with her team, making it known that she doesn't care with whom Tina sleeps. Kit is invested in providing a critique of race to their friendship circle, and Bette is committed to making visible to her opponents her African-American heritage, especially to Papi who perpetually reads Bette's cultural background through her elevated socio-economic and class status. Throughout the match, Papi offers a critique of white privilege; however, she does so through different tactics and strategies. Her racial slurs are mobilized as a critique of socio-economic class and the politics of consumption—Shane is renamed "Shame," Bette is "Rodeo Drive" and "Brown Barbie," and Helena is "the British bombshell"—that calls attention to the "bourgie asses" class privilege.

In a fascinating reversal of the lesbian sporting stereotype, the "bourgie asses" are positioned like the gay male stereotype functioning in *Queer Eye*, wherein gay men serve as experts in the feminine pursuits of shopping, style, and grooming. The "bourgie asses" are largely incompetent on the court: Kit leaves the court with sore feet because her shoes are too tight; Jenny drinks a latte and travels with the ball as she commands others to step out of her way; and Alice screams wildly in an effort to scare her opponents off. It is Helena's "hail Mary shot," perfected in an earlier scene with socks in a laundry basket in Alice's one-bedroom apartment, which earns the team their only basket. While the winner is never resolved, the "bourgie asses" debrief about their performance over coffee at The Planet, revealing their disinvestment in sporting culture other than as a means to pick up women and to maintain social power. The key characters in the series are invested in the neoliberal pursuits of self-management, transformation, and capital accumulation, not in developing their basketball game—a sport stereotypically associated with working-class and poor communities within a North American context (Ladson-Billings 1998).

In seasons four through to six, Alice is intrigued by and attracted to Tasha's difference. Tasha's character raises significant issues about the place and experiences of lesbians in the US Armed Forces and the "Don't Ask, Don't Tell" policy.[4] The policy, crafted by Colin Powell, went against Bill Clinton's campaigning for presidency and his promise that all citizens regardless of sexual orientation should have the right to openly serve in the Armed Forces.[5] Tasha's patriotism clashes with Alice's white bourgeois disapproval of the US's involvement in the invasion of and war in Iraq. Alice's reticence to understand Tasha's silence about her sexuality and their relationship demonstrates her attachment to a politics of visibility and pride. Conversely, Tasha's willingness to adhere to the "Don't Ask, Don't Tell" policy illustrates her precarious position of employment.

After being spotted publicly by other military officers, Tasha is investigated for homosexual misconduct. Captain Beech, a senior colleague of Tasha's, is assigned to be the legal representative in the case mounted against her. Beech is initially highly antagonistic concerning Tasha's efforts to defend herself. The investigation plot, central to season four, culminates in Captain Beech's visit to Alice's apartment. Marking a major turning point in the season, Captain Beech is convinced by his wife to rethink his position and offer his support. Alice's feminine gender performance, which positions her in the likeness of Beech's wife, makes him more amenable to Tasha's situation (Davies 2008a). Tasha's understated and patriotic gender performance provides a point of identification for Beech. Given their butch-femme dynamic, Alice and Tasha's relationship is understood by Beech through conventional heterosexual relations. Beech's authoritative heterosexual, white male gaze rearticulates Tasha and Alice as intelligible and acceptable sexual citizens (Halberstam 1998). The gender performance of the women, their conventional attractiveness, and their careful handling of class and racial/ethnic differences allow Beech to sympathize with Tasha's circumstances.

While season four addresses the discriminatory measures of the US Armed Forces, the program's attempt to problematize this discrimination is mediated alongside the ideals and values of neoliberalism and cosmopolitanism. Tasha and Alice are legitimized as acceptable lesbians and patriotic citizens because their gender performance is understood within the norms of heterosexual, consumer lifestyles. Significantly, Beech's character development is enhanced through his support of Tasha and taking up the cause of "the Other." This adoption of cosmopolitan values, and his engagement with difference and diversity, is performed without compromising his own core values: family, nation, and patriotism.

In season six, Alice is committed to transforming Tasha into a more worldly, cosmopolitan, urban lesbian. At the beginning of the season, the couple are experiencing relationship difficulties, which call attention to their cultural and class differences. After Tasha is discharged from the US Armed Forces, she comments to Alice: "We have nothing in common; it was exciting and hot to you when I was a soldier, but we have nothing in common" ("Long Night's Journey into Day," 6:1). Tasha's statement foreshadows the couple's demise—the beginnings of which are played out when, after an argument, Alice follows Tasha back to her home, shared with Papi. Alice picks up Papi's doll, which is dressed in traditional costume, and sarcastically comments, "Hmmm, beautiful." When Tasha disapproves of Alice's comment, she retorts: "You have to admit it's a little tacky." Alice's racist disapproval of the doll reflects her white middle-class taste and style, positioning her to consume cultural difference with an air of superiority. Tasha's response, that the doll reflects Papi's culture, prompts Alice's defensiveness: "I'm not saying *you* would buy this; you don't have these [dolls]." Alice's comment reconstitutes Tasha as a cosmopolitan lesbian expected to share her white, bourgeois tastes. Constantly aware throughout their relationship of Alice's socio-cultural mobility, Tasha observes that Alice has become a snob, and that she wasn't like this when they met. They resolve to sort out their relationship "differences" through therapy, a technology of self-transformation that Tasha is not so keen to undertake. In convincing Tasha to attend therapy, Alice solidifies her position as an agent of transformation and continues her plight to make-over Tasha as an appropriately middle-class, neoliberal, cosmopolitan lesbian who has more in common with her and her friends.

In season six, episode two, Alice and Tasha sit at The Planet with friends. Alice criticizes Tasha for eating too fast, and when Tasha stands up to remove crumbs from her new suit, Tina compliments her on how amazing she looks. Positioning herself as having superior style, taste, and cultural capital, Alice blurts out that *she* dressed Tasha, and that Tasha had refused to wear Alice's first suggestion because it made Tasha "look like a girl." Tasha's understated, reserved performance of masculinity that initially attracted Alice now gets in the way of cosmopolitan civilian life in which traditionally coded feminine attributes (shopping and gossiping) in this queer community seem to be most valued (Davies 2008a). For Alice, looking good is equated with Tasha assimilating into her cosmopolitan social set and acquiring certain class traits for social mobility.

Consumer experiences with or of "the Other" produce the queer cosmopolite as worldly, more tolerant, more eclectic, and are used to enhance cultural capital (Burns 2012a; Burns and Davies 2009; Duggan 2003). The norms that govern the queer cosmopolitan citizen, represented in *The L Word* by Alice and her community, are produced against the bodies and lives of non-cosmopolitan sexual citizens, here represented by Tasha and Papi. Becoming a queer cosmopolite involves accruing skills and experiences that shape and work on the self; values that Alice attempts to instill in Tasha. Helena Peabody's comment to Tasha as she leaves the café that she "looks like a million dollars" solidifies the ways in which *The L Word* positions its key characters as model cosmopolites in a climate of neoliberalism in which consumption represents access to citizenship and belonging.

Later in series six, Alice and Tasha befriend Jamie Chen—a vegetarian counselor at the Los Angeles Gay and Lesbian Youth Center with grassroots politics and a family background in police work. Although she is conventionally attractive like most cast members of the series, Jamie's grassroots politics contrast with most of Alice's friendship group, whose cosmopolitan consumer practices have come to foreground their political beliefs. These contrasting sets of values and practices are staged most overtly when Alice and Tasha attempt to set up Helena with Jamie—the two characters representing political and socio-cultural polar opposites—with dismal results. Instead, Tasha and Alice develop a crush on Jamie, whose difference is also reflected in her socio-cultural background. It is no coincidence that Melançon, who is Filipino, ends up more attracted to Tasha, who is also feeling marginalized not just because of issues of race and class, but also because of the expectations Alice has of her to be more appropriately cultured and cosmopolitan.

Alice's dance marathon charity event to support Jamie's queer youth center stages the ways in which Alice and her network mobilize private identity-based consumption as a substitute for public activism. The women's highly competitive dance routines and their desire to be publicly celebrated for donating the largest sum of money marks a desire to assimilate with mainstream consumer practices. Jenny's purchase of Niki Stevens for a date with Shane positions her as the ultimate neoliberal cosmopolitan consumer with her ethics and motivations completely askew. Through her purchasing power, Jenny seeks retribution against both Niki and Shane for having defied her trust. It is at the dance marathon that the relationship difficulties between Alice and Tasha culminate in Tasha gaining some clarity around whom she should be with. Tasha's choice—to be with Alice or Jamie—is not just a choice about love, loyalty, and sexual desire, but also between queer cosmopolitan consumer practices and socio-cultural difference marked by grassroots politics.

Cosmopolitan parenting

The neoliberal technologies of self-management, entrepreneurialism, and cosmopolitan consumer lifestyles are also upheld through the series' engagement with issues of pregnancy and parenting. In seasons one and two, Bette and Tina's efforts to "make a baby" are central in defining their lifestyle and relationship. The couple celebrate the economies of parenting and fertility: hosting an insemination party in search of a suitable donor; paying for fertility treatment; attending prenatal classes; planning home renovations; contracting a doula/midwife for home-birthing; investing in early childhood learning; and hiring a nanny. Bette and Tina's decision to have a family is also narrated through a politics of sexual identity that assumes a singular experience of queer parenting and overlooks the complexities of gender, class, and geography. Discourses of queer family in the series fail to contest dominant assumptions and institutions that uphold and sustain heterosexual norms (Duggan 2003).

However, in season six, two additional narratives of pregnancy emerge with the potential to unsettle heteronormative and cosmopolitan constructions of parenting: the first is Max Sweeney, who gets pregnant by his gay male partner, Tom Matar, and the second is Marci, the single mother from Nevada who promises to allow Bette and Tina to adopt her baby in order to "give him a better life." While both of these pregnant bodies fall outside the norms that structure ideas of the pregnant body (Burns 2012b) and family, throughout the season both characters are positioned as cosmopolitan Others who are less well equipped to parent sufficiently. Max's body becomes a project that the key characters in the serial seek to transform, and Marci's body is viewed as a surrogate to their idealized notion of family, while her child is positioned as a commodity.

Since Max's introduction into the series in season two (as Jenny's girlfriend, Moira), both his gender construction and his social class place him on the periphery of the group's imagined queer community. Throughout the series he is positioned to fail in demonstrating the interests, tastes, and culture valued by the other characters. His decision to transition is not widely embraced and his transitioning body acts as a contrast to the highly feminized lipstick lesbian normalized by the other key characters. The transgendered imaginary offered by the series is normalized and very limited, failing to reflect the realities of transgendered bodies and experiences. The introduction of a transgendered character tests the limits of the key characters' "tolerance" for gender diversity and creates a divide between the politics and interests of these women and the politics of transgendered recognition (Halberstam 2012). In the context of the primarily feminine lesbian and queer community depicted in the series, Max is read as an outsider, gender deviant and always peripheral.

The storyline of Max's pregnancy was screened in dialog with the widely publicized story of Thomas Beatie, an American FTM who got pregnant through donor insemination because his wife could not conceive.[6] Beatie's pregnant body was met with public shock, criticism, and confusion for it exceeded bodily gender norms. In an online news article, Margaret Somerville of the McGill Centre for Medicine, Ethics and Law in Montreal, Canada, commented that "It's a very touchy thing, this deconstruction of our biological reality. Where I would do a reversal on this is to say, you've artificially made yourself a man. You're not a man, you're a woman and you're having a baby and you're actually having your own baby" (cited in Hector 2008). Somerville, positioned here as an expert, suggests that gender variance is a "touchy thing" and reasserts gender difference as binary. Her efforts to assert that pregnancy makes Beatie necessarily "a woman" illustrate the ways in which the cultural and symbolic significance of pregnancy can be used to uphold the gender order, and also the ways in which "minority masculinities … destabilize binary gender systems" (Halberstam 1998: 29). Somerville applies a heterosexual set of norms to make Beatie's body intelligible. The struggle by many of *The L Word*'s key characters to engage with Max's pregnancy is mediated through neoliberal discourses of tolerance and transformation, used to stabilize their homonormative lesbian and queer community (Duggan 2003).

Jenny, one of the series' most contradictory characters, represents the normalizing discourses of feminist essentialism and lesbian and gay politics that negate and exclude transgender and intersex citizens. Throughout Max's pregnancy, Jenny is antagonistic and patronizing about his experience of pregnancy and his hesitation to become a parent. She refuses to acknowledge his pregnant body as male and continually comments on the beauty of his *feminine* body. In season six, episode four, Jenny arrives at The Planet and joins Alice, Tasha, Shane, Max, and Tom for lunch. As she enters she asks, "How is the beautiful mother-to-be?" Agitated, Max gives Jenny the finger and Tom, coming to Max's defense, says, "He doesn't like to be referred to as a mother." Jenny, with a bewildered look continues, "I'm simply saying you look beautiful. You have these breasts now. You have these hips and you're curvaceous and you're becoming womanly now. I'm not trying to be insulting I'm just saying you should be proud to be a mother, a beautiful mother." Jenny's justification in erasing Max's gender difference mirrors the series' failure to represent the masculinizing effects of testosterone use for transitioning. Moreover, this failure reflects broader neoliberal industrial imperatives, which must effectively package difference for easy consumption, even within an economic climate of niche marketing. When Max storms away from the table, Jenny shrugs and asks, "Why is *she* so sensitive?" In the scene to follow, Max cries in the bathroom as he contemplates his inability to pass, or to be intelligible as male during the late stages of pregnancy within his very normative lesbian friendship circle.

As noted by Rebecca Beirne and Candace Moore in this volume, the infamous baby shower scene ("Lactose Intolerant," 6:6) in which Jenny hosts a *Charlie and the Chocolate Factory* themed party for Max operates as a moment for the key characters to "shower" him with their values, pedagogies of parenting, and consumptive practices. As though in an effort to be inclusive, Jenny refers to Max as Mom-Dad while the group gathers around for gift giving. As various expensive accessories are rolled out, Bette and Tina enthusiastically explain the details of strollers, birth plans, labor, and episiotomies, with Max getting visibly uncomfortable about the culture of parenting on offer. Parenting in this community only acknowledges and celebrates the female body. Max's anxieties are read by many of the key characters as typical trepidations of immanent motherhood rather than as challenging his gender identity. When Max opens Jenny's gift, a breast pump, she begins to explain how it functions. Max interrupts Jenny and insists that he does not plan to breastfeed. Tina interjects with first-hand advice that breast milk is a must as it is the best sustenance for the infant and provides a wonderful opportunity to bond with your child. Mobilizing the dominant discourse of the selfless mother, Jenny then steps in to advise that while she understands Max identifies as a man, as a parent his responsibility is to put his identity aside and do what is best for the child. Max reasserts his choice, but his efforts to define himself outside the gendered experiences of his lesbian friends and against the dominant discourses of "good parenting" fail.

The scene culminates with an awkward toast by Alice in which she idealizes children growing up in homes with two parents (pointing to Bette and Tina as the model couple), but suggests that Max's experience "as both genders" will make him a parent whose adversity and struggle will provide him with strength. Alice's rearticulation of the idealized neoliberal progress narrative, in which a failed subject reinvents him or herself through various forms of self-work, fills Max with deep anxiety, such that he begins to hyperventilate as if demonstrating further bodily failure. Max pleads with Tina and Bette to adopt his child, but the couple insist that Max's anxiety is "just the hormones" and when Alice offers remedial medication, Jenny interrupts with "She's pregnant! You can't give a pregnant lady drugs!" As the scene closes, Max's male identity and his efforts to reconcile his pregnant body with his transitioning body are violently rearticulated within the norms of gender that organize ideals of family and lesbian and queer community.

In a concurrent narrative in season six, Tina and Bette are trying to adopt a child and are interviewed in Nevada by Marci, a potential birth mother. Over coffee, Tina reports to her friends that she and Bette will travel to Nevada to meet Marci, who is a young single mother "completely okay with [them] being [lesbians]" and notes that the father is African-American, an ideal parentage for their already biracial family. When Bette and Tina arrive in a small town in Nevada with their daughter Angelica, their middle-class, cosmopolitan values and politics are mediated against Marci's suburban, non-cosmopolitan lifestyle and attitudes. Marci explains that she has two other sons, whose fathers are both unknown. The series positions Marci as a stereotypical teenage mother whose children are unplanned rather than planned positive life experiences (Phoenix 1991). Looking around her small and crowded house, Marci situates herself within the limitations ascribed to young motherhood, and sums up her predicament by explaining that she "obviously can't afford to have another one." Bette's reply—"You know, I think it is admirable what you're doing for your family"—attempts to evacuate their class difference through shared feminist values governed by mothers' rights and choices.

Marci's own parents, who arrive home later in this scene, further position Marci as a disempowered young mother. Marci's parents question Bette and Tina's relationship to Angelica, asking which of the women is her mother. Bette and Tina reply in unison, "We both are." Confused, Marci's father presses: "I sure would like to know how that works," to which Bette earnestly clarifies their choice of an African-American donor to ensure that the child looks like both of her mothers. Growing increasingly agitated and confused, Marci's mother asks, "Are you still together with the father?" to which Bette explains, "He was just a donor; I adopted Angelica from birth." Marci's parents press Bette further: "But you're married?" Bette then enters into a monologue about why they are not and how they are waiting for gay marriage to become a federal law. Registering more quickly what Marci's parents are actually asking, Tina quietly interrupts Bette: "I think she's asking if you're married to a man." Marci's parents' failure to register Bette and Tina's lesbian relationship positions them as non-urban, non-cosmopolitan citizens and positions queer living as belonging to urban centers. At the same time, Bette's failure to read Marci's parents' homophobia demonstrates her sheltered, privileged, cosmopolitan existence where engaging with difference is limited, palatable, and consumable.

After Marci's parents ask Bette and Tina to leave, the couple return to their small motel where they continue to appear displaced; their designer pajamas and healthy complexions contrast with the dated, shabby motel decor. Bette reflects that they "dodged a bullet" and that perhaps the family's prejudice—their "way of thinking"—might somehow be in the child's "biological imprint"—something they don't want in their family unit. As Tina reassures Bette that children are constructed through their social environment and that any child would be positively shaped in their care, Marci arrives on her own, announcing her desire to have Bette and Tina adopt her child. Marci's feminist reclamation—"It is my body and my choice"—of her right to choose in matters relating to her body, challenges the stereotype of the disempowered young single mother. The division between cosmopolitan, urban living and rural and suburban existence is further exacerbated through Nevada's state laws prohibiting same-sex adoption. In order to overcome these discriminatory laws, Marci agrees to live with Bette and Tina in the final stages of her pregnancy. With Duffy's "I'm a Dreamer" playing, Bette and Tina wait for Marci to get off an interstate coach in LA, but Marci never arrives. Bette and Tina's desire to extend their family is left unresolved, but the viewer is certainly positioned to empathize with their loss. As the scene draws to a close, Duffy's lyrics lend merit to the neoliberal technologies of resilience and self-management.

Finale

The pleasure of viewing television that foregrounds lesbian life and queer community in an ongoing series is not to be underestimated in the current socio-cultural and political era. Historically, most televisual depictions of lesbian life have been relegated to subplots, desexualized or hyper-sexualized, demonized, faded-out, or simply absent. In this chapter, we have explored how depictions of lesbian and queer lives are mediated through neoliberal and cosmopolitan values and practices that idealize and normalize elite lifestyles and consumption. Diversity and difference are commodified within the series in order to appeal to a broader audience. In particular, we have focused on how these values and practices overlook differences across gender, race, ethnicity, and class. Neoliberal values and practices not only inform the broader television landscape, but also shape narrative and character development, and televisual constructions of queer community. The examples we have used throughout this chapter illustrate the ways in which lesbian and queer characters and their narrative trajectories are constructed through discourses of enterprise, cosmopolitanism, and consumerism that both negate and produce the quality of our viewing pleasure. Investing lesbians with consumer power, *The L Word* produces sexual citizens who purchase their sexual identities while often conceding some of their citizenship rights. The challenge therefore is to ensure that the pleasure we derive in consuming *The L Word* is not bound to a politics of visibility, where success on a mainstream television network functions as evidence of greater social acceptance of sexual difference or greater citizenship rights.

Notes

1   United Colors of Benetton, a global, luxury fashion label based in Treviso, Italy, is an infamous example of a company that embraced politically motivated advertising campaigns based around the politics of diversity and difference as a means of attracting consumption: http://www.benetton.com/.

2   *Queer Eye for the Straight Guy* premiered on the Bravo cable television network on July 15, 2003. The series was created by David Collins and David Metzler, and produced by their production company, Scout Productions.

3   *The Good, the Bad and the Ugly*. Dir. Sergio Leone, United Artists, 1966.

4   The "Don't Ask, Don't Tell" policy was officially known as Pub.L. 103–160 (10 U.S.C. § 654). Unless one of the exceptions from 10 U.S.C. § 654(b) applied, the policy prohibited anyone who "demonstrate(s) a propensity or intent to engage in homosexual acts" from serving in the United States armed forces because apparently it "would create an unacceptable risk to the high standards of morale, good order and discipline, and unit cohesion that are the essence of military capability."

5   "Don't Ask, Don't Tell" was the official United States policy on homosexuals serving in the Armed Forces from December 21, 1993 to September 20, 2011. Under President Barack Obama, a federal appeals court ruling on July 6, 2011 prohibited the continued enforcement of the US military's ban on openly lesbian and gay military personnel.

6   Beatie (2008).

"The D Word"

Candace Moore

In 2005, Dasha Snyder produced a brazen parody of *The L Word* entitled *The D Word* for *Dyke TV* (1993–2007), a magazine-style public access cable program televised in seventy-eight US cities and considered "the first and longest running show by, and for, queer women" (Dyke TV 2010; "About *The D Word*" 2010). Viacom (Showtime's parent company) got wind of *The D Word* project and threatened *Dyke TV* with a cease and desist letter while auditions for the parody were still in process. The half-hour television show *Dyke TV*, produced by an all-volunteer staff in New York City and operating on an annual budget of around $100,000, often struggled to find outside funding. Due to these factors, it is surprising that the weekly show survived as long as it did, fourteen years, while reaching so many public access affiliates nationally (Sebek 2004: 61). Dasha Snyder, who produced material for the show, decided to separate the production and funding of *The D Word* from *Dyke TV* to protect the organization. She chose instead to edit *The D Word*'s six short episodes, originally designed to run as comedic segments within the cable access show, together into an hour-long film. As a film, *The D Word* went on an international tour in 2005 and 2006, earning invites to the major American LGBTQ film festivals (Frameline, Outfest, Newfest, etc.) and screenings in Israel, New Zealand, and throughout Europe. According to Snyder, *The D Word* has never been "aired on TV, released on DVD, or digitally for sale," due to potential legal issues with Viacom (Snyder 2010). However, parodies such as *The D Word* potentially shaped aspects of *The L Word*'s legacy, as they prompted producers of the show to theatricalize fan and critical reactions to earlier seasons, textually acknowledging suggestions and critiques articulated in the LGBT press and circulated through queer fansites. Later seasons of *The L Word* increasingly included varied perspectives concerning sexuality, race, class, and gender that *The D Word* and similar critical discourses pointed out as lacking from the original TV text. *The L Word*'s focus noticeably shifted from erotically titillating crossover viewers to dialoguing dynamically with queer fans (Moore 2007: 3–23).[1] Through adding new characters, themes, and self-referential narratives, seasons two through six of *The L Word* exhibited the producers' self-consciousness and the pretense of being informed by fan culture.

This chapter focuses on how *The L Word* incorporates many of the interventions and revisions put forth in parody by *The D Word*, namely: a critique of the class and racial privilege of the main characters, including an FTM character as part of an otherwise queer female community, a roast of Jenny's self-importance, and, most significantly, the very act of parody itself. This is not to suggest that Showtime consciously copied elements of *The D Word*. Rather, the parody (released shortly after the show's first season) represented a zeitgeist of common criticisms levied at the show that *The L Word*'s producers were made aware of and likely influenced by. Because *The D Word*'s revisions seem trenchant and largely representative, I use descriptions of scenes from *The D Word* as a structuring device for my argument about *The L Word*'s accumulative tactics with regards to critiques. This chapter also tracks assorted critical and fan discourses that weighed in on *The L Word*'s perceived representational diversity, burden, lack, and mistakes, demonstrating that many of these perspectives were later folded into the television text in some form.

Directly following the reception of its first season, *The L Word* adopted self-reference, topicality, and pastiche as sly antidotes to questions over whether the show accurately portrayed the community it purported to. *The L Word*'s second season demonstrated the quick responsiveness of the show's producers, who clearly registered a complaint aimed at the debut season by lesbian fans and critics—that the series seemed designed to arouse straight men—and worked to redirect this viewership's ire through a plotline featuring the downfall of a misguided male voyeur, Mark. As John Caldwell has argued, self-referentiality and television have been inseparable from the beginnings of television history. *The L Word*'s tendency to underscore its own constructedness and thematize media-making are not new to television and in fact, as Denise Mann argues, instances of self-referentiality in television serve to draw viewers in by offering them the illusion of transparency (Mann 1992: 41–69). We must not forget that the show became, and still is, a media franchise, spurring a major networking website, revenue through syndication on Logo, and a spin-off series presently on Showtime (as of 2011), *The Real L Word*. Thus, self-reference is doubly self-promotion (Caldwell 1995). Whereas *The L Word* punctuated its meta moments, using reflexivity as part of an implicit claim to offering artistic, "quality television" while playing to Showtime's largely educated, middle- and upper-class pay cable subscribers, *The D Word* openly mocked its host television text, seeing assimilation as *The L Word*'s main goal.

D for dyke

Interviewed about what motivated her to spoof *The L Word* with her film *The D Word*, Snyder described viewing the show and not seeing her circle of queer friends reflected:

> I just think that [the characters of *The L Word*] represent a small slice of privileged beautiful, skinny, mostly Caucasian Los Angelenos. I'm a big butch woman from New York City. You don't see anyone who looks like me or my friends on the show. So *The L Word* inspired me to show a slice of my multicultural, varied body type, LGBTQ part of the world. (Kilchenmann 2005: 10)

The parody Snyder created in response puts into relief the particular way in which, even as *The L Word* arguably queers certain scenarios to allow for ambiguities, the series also inscribes "lesbian" as a category with specific class-based, racial, and gendered elements. *The D Word*'s abbreviated letter references lesbian's sister term, dyke, historically used as a negative slur and self-adopted by queer women to indicate radicalism and pride. Offering loosely disguised and playfully silly D-named versions of *The L Word*'s characters, *The D Word* takes *The L Word* to task for playing to straight viewers and maintaining unspoken classism and conservative representational choices, among other perceived missteps. For instance, when *D Word* lesbian couple Dot (comedienne Marga Gomez) and Dina (Jessica Horstman) catch neighbor Dim (Sergei Burbank) masturbating to their image across the way, they ask him to make a sperm donation to their cause. Dim agrees, granted that they make out for him; "Dude, you've been watching too much cable," Dot chastises, alluding to the failed threesome—between couple Bette and Tina and a male artist they seduced—that capped *The L Word*'s pilot.

Actress Marga Gomez describes *The D Word* as "*The L Word* through a fun house mirror in Coney Island" and thought Showtime

> should be flattered. All [the parody] does is create an energy for them—not saying that this is *The Rocky Horror Picture Show*, but *Rocky Horror* did really well by people dressing up as the characters and going up on the stage at midnight and throwing toast. So this is all part of making *The L Word* bigger. (Moore 2005)

Showtime did not reportedly see the spoof as the good-natured, auxiliary public relations booster for *The L Word* that Gomez implied it could be. Snyder admitted that "Showtime, who make *The L Word*, have commented that they're not thrilled to have a parody out there, but so far all is civil and quiet" (Kilchenmann 2005: 10). While network executives may not have been "thrilled" at this somewhat scathing imitation, they did not pursue legal action beyond the initial cease-and-desist letter sent by Showtime's parent company, Viacom (Snyder 2010). Even though Snyder felt *The D Word* received a form of "anti-support" from Viacom's legal department, she relayed that *L Word* director and executive producer Rose Troche (*Go Fish*) reportedly "loved it … We've received great support from the creative people at *The L Word*" (Grubb 2005: 15). Troche's girlfriend at the time, Cherien Dabis, even directed portions of *The D Word*, suggesting that certain personnel of Showtime's lesbian soap opera were at least aware of, if not struck by, the spoof. In an article on *The D Word* in lesbian glossy *Curve*, Dabis remarked that Troche "has a sense of humor about her work. She thought it [*The D Word*] was funny" (Gilchrist 2005: 17).

Marked by a few major differences from its mainstream predecessor, *The D Word* takes place in New York instead of Los Angeles; its characters live in tiny walk-up tenements rather than sprawling sunny bungalows and ride subway lines instead of tooling around in product-placed PT cruisers or muscle cars. Women of color and assorted body types comprise the majority rather than the minority of *The D Word*'s cast. The show includes two Latino characters—Dani and Dot—and two black characters—Daynisha and Daria. Not everyone on *The D*

Word shares the same fashion preferences and gender presentations, nor are they all stick thin.

In these ways and others, *The D Word* represented aspects of diversity that some viewers found lacking in *The L Word*'s initial season. A Washington D.C. fan of the show, Lisbeth Meléndez Rivera, told the *Washington Blade*, for example, that she found it "ridiculous that you would have a series [like *The L Word*] set in West Hollywood and not include a Latina character" and added that "she also would like to see 'The L Word' include characters from working-class backgrounds as well as someone in an obviously butch role. 'Not just a fleeting character ... but someone who's going to stay there and talk about the reality of what we as butches represent'" (Smith 2005: 51–6). Echoing Dasha Snyder's characterization of *The L Word*'s cast of characters as "skinny," Constance Reeder wrote an entire article on the subject in the feminist news journal *Off Our Backs*, entitled "The Skinny on the L Word." In her piece, Reeder describes each *L Word* character with the adjective skinny and then rhetorically asks, "[a]re you starting to see a pattern develop?" (Reeder 2004: 51). Salon.com columnist Thomas Rogers described his sense that fans held *The L Word*'s main creator/ executive producer responsible for the show's perceived homogeneity: "one of the show's creators, Ilene Chaiken faced criticism for [*The L Word's*] seeming willingness to cater to straight male viewers and its narrow representation of lesbian life. To quote a friend of mine, 'Have all the butch women in L.A. been murdered by femmes?'" (Rogers 2010). Examining *The L Word*'s representations of class, British columnist Liz Hoggard singled in on the image of the "[financially] loaded" "Power Lesbian" that she sees the series promoting: "*The L Word*, a glossy American soap, is peopled by wealthy lesbians in designer clothes bathing in palm-fringed pools" (Hoggard 2005).

In an article published in *The Chronicle of Higher Education* immediately following *The L Word*'s pilot episode, the late queer theorist Eve Kosofsky Sedgwick made her own extensive character wish list:

> I would like to order up some character with body hair, ungleaming teeth, subcutaneous fat, or shorter-than-chin-length haircuts. Oh, and maybe with some politics. I would like to see a lot more of Pam Grier. I hope—especially in a West Coast production—that the show's sense of race will extend beyond black and white ...

I will be relieved when the writers decide they have sufficiently interpellated straight viewers and can leave behind the lachrymose plot of Jenny's Choice. I want to see the range of ways in which gay men function in this (West Hollywood) lesbian ecology. I want the generational span to widen enough so that some of the sex can fully engage with pedagogy and maternality. (Sedgwick 2004: 10)

Bourgie ass girls

The L Word's producers integrated some of the constructive elements of such public commentary on what the show lacked into the series, not only to take the power out of these critiques but also to encompass the savvy and relevant visions of queer life that critics suggested needed representation. In response to criticisms of *The L Word* (clearly represented within *The D Word*) that the show primarily centered around well-off, femme white women, the fourth season introduced a character—"Papi"—who served as a composite for certain elements of diversity found slight in the show's early seasons.

Season four episode "Livin' La Vida Loca" (4:2) opens with Alice moving hesitantly through a queer dance club full of people of color and transfolk, searching for Papi, a womanizing lesbian who crashed OurChart.com, Alice's social networking website, with her many connections with the women of Los Angeles.[2] Visibly uncomfortable and conspicuously out of place in her whiteness and gender normativity, Alice spends the night meeting assorted individuals who claim to be Papi, feeling foolish after learning that the name is so prevalent because it means "daddy" in Spanish. Alice's search next takes her to a taqueria with velvet paintings and Latino men playing pool, where her face registers how out of place she feels. She's finally directed to a limo parked outside driven by the Papi she seeks, who takes charge, bedding Alice in the back of the limo tricked out with seats that convert into a mattress. Papi, who corrects Alice on the pronunciation of her name, adds that it is a "little more Latina than your tongue is used to." *The L Word*'s narrative introduces Papi as the Latina "version" of Shane, who operates in an ethnic world set to salsa music, laced with tequila, and foreign to the show's major characters. Thus, *The L Word* contrasts Papi's quality of being "more Latina" than its characters are "used to" with Carmen's more assimilated Latina character, part of the show's main cast from seasons two to three. Upon meeting Shane, who she sees as her competition, Papi declares, in concert with critical descriptions of Shane as "not butch enough": "You're just a skinny little white girl!" to which Shane replies, "Yeah, I guess I am." Papi continues to reference Shane's whiteness in interactions with her, dubbing Shane "Vanilla Spice," "'cause she's like me but in a different flavor."

Rather than incorporating Papi as an ongoing character of *The L Word*, the show uses Papi as an exotic and stereotyped side note, exaggerating her difference from the main characters. The producers ascribe cockiness, street vernacular, womanizing, and access to "another" Los Angeles to a Latina lesbian, who acts as a "portal" (in Alice's words) to new "places to meet girls." When Papi tells Alice about her favorite spot to meet women ("Every Sunday there's a lesbian pick-up basketball game at West Hollywood Park—all different kinds of girls, all sweaty"), she jokes: "What are you going to call your team? Shit!—The Bourgie Ass Girls?" In this dialog, Papi calls attention to the differences in class and race between *The L Word*'s "lesbian bourgeoisie" and the "different kinds of girls," mostly women of color, who show up on the court to play as part of Papi's team in "Layup" (4:4). Papi brags to Alice that her team is going to "whip your asses back to Rodeo Drive so you can go shopping, which is probably the only sport you can play." Papi's exchanges with the main characters before and during the basketball game mark a decidedly self-conscious moment of *The L Word* in which the show acknowledges that its characters live in a privileged and—despite its few characters of color—primarily white and insular community. For instance, while facing off against Bette, Papi calls her "Brown Barbie" and "Rodeo Drive," implying that, regardless of Bette's skin color, she represents mainstream, assimilated, upper-middle-class privilege. Papi remains an auxiliary character, brought onto *The L Word* in order to poke fun at the homogeneity of the show's featured characters while also allowing the series to display its attempts at diversity and convey a sense of humor about its own dominant narrative framework.

For the most part, early seasons of *The L Word* did not critique the class or racial privilege of its characters or provide significant explorations of certain masculinities—butch, transgender, and gay male—that are integral or complementary to lived queer female lives.[3] This caused some admonishment of the series in the LGBT press. In a 2006 *Girlfriends* magazine article entitled "I Love Not *The L Word*:

Who's Afraid of the Big, Bad Butch," Judith Halberstam called *The L Word* "positively phobic about butchness in its zeal to put positive and non-stereotyping images of lesbians on TV" and begged "the producers of this wildly successful lesbian soap [to] venture into the uncharted territory of butch-femme erotics and transgender identity," adding, furthermore, that "we can only hope that at some point the show will turn away from its lousy yuppie premise" (2006: 38).

The trouble with Max

In the vanguard of such critical responses to *The L Word*, *The D Word* included elements of queer culture that *The L Word*'s first season arguably neglected: including butch gender presentation, BDSM, strap-on sex, and transgenderism. Womanizing lothario Drea (played by *Big Gay Sketch Show*'s Julie Goldman), *The D Word*'s version of soft butch Shane, presents clearly as a butch lesbian with her short hair, broad build, and menswear. Predating Alice and Dana's purchase of a dildo in *The L Word*'s season two and Shane's strap-on sex scene with Cherrie Jaffe in season three, *The D Word* features two scenes featuring explicit strap-on sex. Additionally, the parody's stand-in for Alice, Dixie (Victoria Soyer), writes professionally for *Fetish Quarterly* rather than the popular media and ridicules her boyfriend shamelessly for having no passion for kink.

The D Word also portrays FTMs as dyke allies who may have identified as lesbians prior to transitioning and often continue to participate in some of the same social circles afterwards. Notably, *The D Word* replaces *The L Word*'s sole straight female character, Kit, with Dex (Geo Wyeth), a transman, a full year before *The L Word* introduced Max. A singer like Kit, Dex used to front a band called The Cunning Linguists. When a music fan exclaims that she thought Dex was "a dyke," Dex replies snappily, "so did I for a long time." Dialog with and about Dex attempts to educate viewers who may not have encountered transgender individuals or be familiar with their experiences. Dex, who brags he is "almost shaving," takes testosterone but does not plan on having bottom surgery. In an expository moment, one of the characters explains why Dex feels genital reconstruction is not necessary for him: "actually the clitoris becomes greatly enlarged when on testosterone." The inclusion of a transgender character within *The D Word*'s group of friends attempts to closely represent contemporary urban queer communities, which often include transfolk; at the same time, the parody gestures to the relative gender normativity of *The L Word*'s traditionally feminine ensemble cast in season one.

The L Word's transmale character Max offers an answer of sorts to *The D Word*'s inclusion of Dex, who's unabashedly out and comfortable about his transition from female to male. Snyder spoke of her desire to cast a trans actor in Dex's role in contrast to popular culture's all-too-often tendency to cast cis-women or men in transgender roles. She mentions that initially it was "tough to find an actor who would play that role, but we lucked out" (Grubb 2005: 15). In contrast, *The L Word*'s producers seemed to not quite know how to handle trans, butch, and non-normative genders, particularly as they began to work a broader spectrum of topics and characters into the show's repertoire. Max, a character introduced in season three, undergoes a transition from working-class Midwesterner to professional LA technology worker at the same time as he transitions from a butch-identified female (Moira) to a transman, becoming the series' touchstone for representing trans experiences and, later, queer male sexuality as he starts to date men.

Max's character arc becomes a source of gender trouble for *The L Word*, particularly because he represents the show's exoticized and abjected other, made to bear the responsibility of representing multiple constituencies. An allegorical figure, Max marks a main point of engagement with many experiences: butch, rural, working class, trans, gay male, and, in an unfortunate plot twist, a pregnant FTM. In this way, Max not only becomes a composite figure, like Papi, utilized to diversify the show, but his character moreover exemplifies *The L Word*'s attempts to keep apace with cultural shifts as well as the show's tendency to scavenge the headlines for storyline fodder. *The L Word*'s producers lifted an unusual true story about an FTM, Thomas Beatie—who purposefully stopped taking testosterone so that he could bear a child after his wife had a hysterectomy—from the headlines; they then transformed this anomalous incident into Max's season six pregnancy plot.

In a previous essay on *The L Word*, I suggested that Jenny's character—who discovers homoerotic curiosity and then full-fledged desire—stands in for touristic viewers of the show. She operates as an insider-outsider figure: the traveler of queer female culture who eventually becomes a local (Moore 2007: 3–23). Rather than being brought inside the show's queer female community, Max's narrative works in contrast to Jenny's as he moves from insider to outsider position, becoming increasingly excluded from the central group. By coupling Max and Jenny, *The L Word* pairs its previously confused femme with a newly confused butch, whose identification as a lesbian is "fleeting," though one would not suspect so based on Chaiken's public assurance before the third season première that: "[Moira is] our first real butch on the show—a fabulously attractive butch, but nonetheless a real butch" (AfterEllen.com 2006).

A blogger for AfterEllen.com, a website that tracks lesbian and bisexual representation in media, took Chaiken to task for the prejudices potentially underlying this particular comment as well as for the show's handling of Moira's transition to Max:

> Even though Chaiken's statement revealed that she actually felt that few butches were attractive, at least she admitted that *The L Word* had never before had a "real" butch on the show. Nope, not even Shane counted. Could this mean that Chaiken and the producers of *The L Word* actually knew what a real butch was? It's too bad that as soon as that "real butch" sauntered onto the scene, she transitioned from female to male in a clumsy storyline that reduced the complexity of transgender issues to a stereotypical war between the sexes. To make matters worse, Moira's transition into Max was written in a way that not only dismissed the possibility of butch identity, it ridiculed it. (AfterEllen.com 2006)

Even within a show about a queer female community, the butch, it seems, gets canceled. Max, who previously took part in a "dyke community in Wilmette," his hometown, enters into *The L Word*'s group of friends while still identifying as a butch female. As Moira, Max is accepted as an "insider" inasmuch as Moira is read as lesbian, yet treated as an "outsider" based on a masculine, Midwestern, and working-class self-presentation.

The L Word's move to represent an FTM main character, coming a year after *The D Word*'s pointed revision, does more than diversify the program's scope. Certainly, the introduction of Max was strategically topical given increasing attention in LGBT communities on FTM transsexuals' continued and honorary roles within queer female communities. The increased availability of access to hormone and surgical therapies, a trend towards transitioning with fewer or no surgeries, and the gradual destigmatization of transexuality over the last few decades have all led to a noticeable increase in gender transitions from female to male, compared to previous generations. *The L Word* was not merely responding to this phenomenon and trying to keep their show current about issues affecting LGBT life—although of course this too was the case. Rather, by focusing gender transgression on a character who comes to understand himself as male, the show polices borders between concepts of lesbian and transgender identities.

Paul Vitello from *The New York Times* describes this particular policing tendency by some lesbian-identified women who see straight transmen as deserters of their cause, transitioning to seek male and heterosexual privilege. He writes:

> Among lesbians—the group from which most transgendered men emerge—the increasing number of women who are choosing to pursue life as a man can provoke deep resentment and almost existential anxiety, raising questions of gender loyalty and political identity, as well as debates about who is and who isn't, and who never was, a real woman. (Vitello 2006)

The L Word uses its one primarily straight character, Kit, as a mouthpiece for this anti-trans perspective in a scene that finds Kit referring to Max as a "girl" ("Lead, Follow, Or Get Out of the Way," 3:9). "I'm not a girl, Kit," Max bristles. "It's not cool. It's like if someone's trying to change their name and someone refuses to call them by their new one." Kit responds patronizingly, "I'm just worried about you." Kit pathologizes Max, suggesting he may have "problems" that will not necessarily be solved through gender transition. She also acts as a spokeswoman for the queer female community: "So removing your breasts and changing yourself into a man is going to change all your problems? It just saddens me to see so many of our strong butch girls giving up their womanhood to be a man. We're losing our warriors—our greatest women—and I don't want to lose you." *The New York Times* ran a story on Internet backlash against *The L Word*'s Moira-to-Max storyline, quoting Kit's dialog in this scene and characterizing her sentiment as

> [a] tamer version of what many other women wrote on lesbian blogs and Web sites in the weeks after the episode was broadcast

last spring. Many called for the Max character to be killed off next season. One suggested dispatching him "by testosterone overdose." The reaction to the fictional character captured the bitter tension that can exist over gender reassignment. (Vitello 2006)

The *L Word*'s producers position Kit as a mouthpiece for affective reservations about female-to-male gender transition, potentially because of her character's generational, sexuality, and racial differences from the majority of the main characters. In her speech to Max, Kit compares his gender transition from female to male to racial passing—specifically to an African-American choosing to live as a white person, suggesting that Max's transition is a form of minority desertion with privilege as its goal: "What if I lived my life feeling white inside and then the next day I woke up and I could change the color of my skin, the features on my face to become white? Would you encourage me to do that?" The comparative nature of Kit's reaction underlines an acknowledgment of how different types of embodiment come with different culturally reinforced levels of access to power and relationships to complicated histories. This scene casts Kit's reaction as highly personal to her character's experience rather than "representative" of the opinions of the show's producers or other characters. As the visibly black half-sister of a character, Bette, who is often accused of attempting to pass as white, Kit is portrayed as sensitive about the idea of downplaying or erasing one's born identity. The main major character of the second-wave feminist generation who also lived through civil rights era struggles for racial equality, Kit seems bestowed with credibility when discussing both gender and race, especially since she is played by actress Pam Grier, a woman of color famous for her roles in films like *Coffy* (1973) and *Foxy Brown* (1974). Kit's role in this exchange, however, arguably operates to deflect any sense that this disapproval of transgenderism is coming from either the producers or the young, white, lesbian perspective inhabited by the majority of the characters.

We can easily interpret Kit's perspective as representing those viewers made uncomfortable by the inclusion of a transmale character. Just as convincingly, however, we can also see Kit's character articulating common linkages between the experiences of oppression and misunderstanding that people of color, queers, and transgender individuals face, bridges that lay the groundwork for thinking coalitionally. As transgender theorist Sandy Stone argues,

> [*passing* is] not an activity restricted to transsexuals. This is familiar to the person of color whose skin is light enough to pass as white, or to the closet gay or lesbian ... or to anyone who has chosen invisibility as an imperfect solution to personal dissonance. In essence I am rearticulating one of the arguments for solidarity which has been developed by gays, lesbians and people of color. (Stone 2006: 232)

Like Kit, Stone suggests that transgender individuals should problematize passing as their end goal: "To deconstruct the necessity for passing implies that transsexuals must take responsibility for *all* of their history, to begin to rearticulate their lives not as a series of erasures" (Stone 2006: 232).

As one cultural critic pointed out, the experience among some lesbian women of feeling betrayed by transgender men may not be quite as prevalent in younger generations:

> How uncomfortable are the architects of *The L Word* with the growing trans movement? Squirmy enough to drop a tortured character (Max) into the proceedings as a cautionary male. The ultimate after-school-special message reads: Dude, don't go there— total downer. To which we say: Out of touch, much? Any queer in a major city who's under 30 knows that trans men are the rock stars of the scene. (Brooks 2009)

The inclusion of an FTM character in *The L Word* allows the producers to demonstrate that the series is as up to date with "trans chic" as *The D Word*. Yet, true to *The L Word*'s tendency to equivocate, Max's character suffers through an unstable plot arc and fellow characters who fail to understand him, allowing the show room for varying audience perspectives, including punishing ones. In an interview for *Diva* magazine, actress Daniela Sea suggested while playing Max, "[It was hard] to make these abrupt transitions from butch to transman; from shy guy to the testosterone-fueled straight man, from the passing straight man to the toned-down gender-queer" (Halberstam 2008).

Though *The L Word* stages scenes that border on the transphobic, the show also attempts to self-correct potentially discriminatory representations after they occur (thus framing transphobia as such) and to stretch viewers' assumptions about transmen's experiences of their community affiliations, bodies, and sex. Max quits a job where he is afforded male privilege, coming out as trans to express solidarity with a woman mistreated in the workplace. After being told he is getting "off topic" by discussing trans issues on an OurChart.com podcast and reminded that it is a "lesbian site," Max, wearing a "Womenswork" T-shirt to prove his feminist "cred," chews Alice out: "you can't segregate trans people out of the lesbian community!" Alice later apologizes to Max publicly over a podcast, admitting she "said some things that were uncool." In a sense, Alice's season five apology to Max for discriminating against him and attempting to exclude his voice from OurChart.com does double duty as an apology to viewers who may have expressed or felt disappointment with *The L Word*'s handling of its transmale character.

Later seasons see Max as developing a nuanced, personal understanding of his identity and body rather than reciting the "born in the wrong body" narrative season three originally offers him. Max comes to understand himself as male not because his body is naturally or surgically constructed as such (he decides he "felt enough of a guy without the surgery"), but because he feels and experiences it as such.

Killing Jenny softly

While Papi allows the show to rib itself for the class and racial privilege of its main characters and Max becomes the show's trans straw man, Jenny is the former protagonist who quickly becomes untenable for the text. Released directly after *The L Word*'s first season, which framed Jenny as a major (if not the main) character, fan parody *The D Word* makes an early start of poking fun at Jenny's pretentiousness and her overwritten memoir-based writing projects, often superimposed as typed words on the screen in *The L Word*. Dani (*The D Word*'s version of Jenny, played by Meeni Naqvi) types heavy-handed, flowery treatises on the most banal elements of her life, which float similarly on-screen in courier font. Dot, who works as the manager of a theater collective, ends up producing Dani's self-absorbed play about her affair with female bar owner Daria (Mellyss'ah Mavour) telling Dani she is "glad [her] personal life is such a mess. Otherwise we wouldn't have this play."

The D Word translates Bette and Tina's backyard swimming pool into a *mise-en-scène* appropriate to New York: the rooftop of the main characters' apartment complex. During the finale of The D Word's play-within-the-show, performed in its last episode, the character based on Dani takes a suicidal leap from this roof, presaging Jenny's death (by drowning in the pool) in the last season of The L Word as well as The L Word's creation of a similarly meta film-within-the-show. Outside the theater, an audience member shouts praise: "I love what you did with the roof! There's just not enough roof jumping!" implying, perhaps, that more of the main characters (of The L Word) should meet their demises.

At the beginning of the show's second season, Matthew Gilbert of The Boston Globe singled out Jenny as a "dreary, confused introverted narcissist ... played with irritating realness by Mia Kirshner" (Gilbert 2005). Reacting to growing sentiments among viewers of profound disidentification with one of The L Word's founding characters, The L Word's producers accentuated Jenny's unlikable character attributes, refashioning the character into a parodic caricature very much like The D Word's. Once the naive newbie with writerly dreams, Jenny shifts noticeably in season three, her self-absorption and conceited qualities becoming more exaggerated as her writing becomes better received. In season four, Jenny cruelly adopts (and puts to sleep) a sickly dog to seduce a literary critic's veterinarian girlfriend in revenge for a bad book review. In season five, she takes on a personal assistant, Adele, who she thanklessly treats like a servant, having her fulfill ridiculous requests. Kirshner admitted that Jenny "isn't loved by the gay community at all, because of her duplicity and confusion" (Sloane 2010). *New York* magazine's Kera Bolonik reports that "Jenny-bashing became a spectator sport almost from the moment she arrived in Season 1." Bolonik breaks Jenny's negative characteristics down into categories: selfish, victimized, heartless, vindictive, bitch, narcissistic, ending with "dead": "she's found floating in a pool, and everyone on the show is a murder suspect. Okay, we confess" (Bolonik 2009).

The final season of The L Word literalizes The D Word's staged death of character Dani as well as a renegade sticker campaign waged by fans to "Kill Jenny" by transforming season six into a faux whodunit to solve her very murder. T-shirts produced by the company Girlfriends Events after Jenny was revealed dead at the beginning of season six read, "I would have killed Jenny in Season One" ("*The L Word* Gifts" 2010). By drowning Jenny in the pool where she first observed and became fascinated with lesbian sex, the producers signpost the show's dénouement while over-meeting fans' pleas. Merchandise (buttons, T-shirts, and stickers) bearing the slogan "I Killed Jenny" circulated to and among fans, offering multiple confessions. Fans (rather than the diegetic suspects) might certainly be held culpable in this particular charactericide.

Harnessing the content of fan-generated criticism and showcasing their awareness of the content of those critiques, the producers of *The L Word* produced their own parodies both outside of and within the show. *The L Word* constantly restaged the show's landmark first season, for example, at fan events, online, and in later seasons. Capitalizing on productive fan practices, which often revisit and re-author popular episodes of television, Showtime sponsored events such as 2007's "Be Scene" held in Palm Springs, where attendees acted out season one scenarios while being judged by a panel of *L Word* actresses (Jenkins 1992). Fans' renditions were then webcast on OurChart.com, a now-defunct site partly owned by Showtime Networks. Downloadable, these amateur versions were presented as authorized parodies framed by star hosts who compared the fan performances to their originals.

Similarly, season five recycled earlier *L Word* scripts through staging the adaptation and film production of Jenny's autobiographical serial novel *Lez Girls*. In *Lez Girls'* alternate universe, characters acted more salaciously than their L Word counterparts while mouthing nearly identical lines. Mimicking *The D Word*'s play on *The L Word*'s characters' names, *Lez Girls* featured barely disguised versions of *The L Word*'s characters: Shaun instead of Shane, Helen instead of Helena, Bev instead of Bette, etc. Jenny's memoir versions of *The L Word*'s previous scenes, reconstructed in a variety of ways on the show (through words typed into screenplay format or read in voiceover and through imagined, dramatic, and filmed scenes), place Jenny as the writer/producer/director (rather than show-runner Ilene Chaiken) in charge and thus liable for criticism. Jenny's arc from unsure aspiring writer to conceited Hollywood player (whose creation is eventually maligned) and the series' at-times-scathing "behind the scenes" versions of Hollywood production cultures tell a fairly unveiled tale of a Hollywood success story gone wrong and a media representation of lesbian culture mishandled by the whims of its large distributor. The gradual narrative collapse and arguable suicide of this series becomes personified through the Jenny character, who, in a sense, doubly represents the text and its author. The final two seasons of the show thematize the selling of narratives about a lesbian community to the media, the act of "selling out" and the experience of one's ideas being twisted. Framing *Lez Girls* as a film production rather than a television show underscores the fictional remove of these representations of homophobic media executives, pampered, self-important stars, and double-crossing assistants from the actual people involved with creating *The L Word*. Just as *The D Word*'s sarcastic ribbing of *The L Word*'s homogeneity served a political as well as a humorous purpose, *The L Word* similarly destabilizes its own fiction in later seasons, thus becoming a show about its own fraught mode of production as well as the impossibility of fully inclusively representing a sexual minority group.

Notes

1 Though girl-on-girl sex continued undiminished, the series retired season one's somewhat expository structure.

2 OurChart.com was both a website referred to within the fiction of *The L Word* and an actual lesbian social networking and blogging site (promoting *The L Word*, among other things) that operated from 2006–2009 and was partly owned by Showtime Networks.

3 Shane's briefly mentioned back-story did include living in a homeless shelter as a kid and working as a gay male prostitute.

Why *The Real L Word* Matters: Community and Lesbian Sex, in the Flesh

Tara Shea Burke

I'm a poet. I believe in language and words, in their ancient, civilization-forming powers, and in their beautiful and harmful effects on human beings. Because of this, as a graduate student in an MFA program, I'm not supposed to like television much, and for a while I told my colleagues and fellow creative writers that I rarely turned the thing on. This is a lie I'm ready to let go of, because some TV shows have become such important parts of my life that they have defined or redefined how I think of myself as I watch them in secret in my apartment after three-hour literature seminars or writing workshops, alone with take-out and beer. This is important and necessary to admit; most of us feel there is something shameful about connecting to a character on television because of the lasting stigma between what is considered refined culture and what is trash. I'm finally coming to a place where I think it's okay to write poetry, watch classic "cinema," and still turn on trash shows when my brain is too full of analysis, literature, craft, and theory. There is a reason entertainment is such a rich part of American culture—most of us live on treadmills, and the pleasure we derive from whatever we watch, listen to, or read is often more important to our contemplative lives than we think. We should admit to and explore what we love about television because most of us watch something. Even those that claim never to watch TV use their laptops to stream shows on Hulu or Netflix; when they have the time, of course.

Not only am I poet who believes in the power of words, I am also a lesbian, a feminist, an aspiring queer theorist. I'm also a fan of a pretty bad reality show that is stirring up a bit of controversy in lesbian America. *The Real L Word*, created by Ilene Chaiken for Showtime, makes me cringe and sometimes bores me, like much reality television, and when my girlfriend and I watch it, we sometimes shake our heads in disbelief more than we engage, but there is something here to defend. I feel a deep need to defend *The Real L Word*'s uncomfortably drunken sex scenes, its misrepresentation of lesbians, its hacksaw edits and poor use of the word "real," its live sex, the community conversation it supports, and did I mention the sex? The second season of *The Real L Word* began airing on Showtime just a few weeks ago, despite the first season's bad ratings and harsh reviews. Why? Why are lesbians still watching it, despite obvious moments of infuriating misrepresentation, and near pornographic exploitation?

The *Real L Word* is deeply connected to my life. I have to watch it. A bit of back-story is important here because I know my story is not mine alone. I grew up in a house where the TV was never turned off, even at night, and as soon as I got to college in 2001 and lived on my own, I promised myself I'd spend little time watching television. It worked for a while, and I didn't miss it at all, though I'll admit when I went home to visit my parents for holidays, the remote rarely left my hand. It was like a drug that I allowed myself a few times a year to avoid flashbacks or withdrawal symptoms. Between 2003 and 2004, I was working full time at a restaurant, trying not to fail out of college, writing poetry, battling depression, and discovering my sexuality. My manager at the time, Carrie, became my best friend, partly because of Ilene Chaiken's first show. One Sunday, we were hanging out after work drinking beer and blowing off steam, and *The L Word*, season two, was on in the background. Carrie and I both considered ourselves "open" sexually, but had never engaged in relationships with women or talked about it much to anyone.

That night, we drank too many beers and watched in awkward silence while Shane seduced Carmen and Jenny did things that newly out lesbians do. Every time there was an intimate moment between two characters, we were quiet and the air in the room thinned. We discussed the politics of Bette and Tina's affairs and why we didn't think Alice was bisexual. Then we really started sharing, courtesy of the alcohol. She told me about her experiences with women at college parties, and how she had a quiet, sexual relationship with one of her sorority sisters. Around the same time, she'd fallen in love with her boyfriend and never looked back. I told her of a close friend who was an out lesbian, and who was falling in love with me, causing some first-time questions concerning my own identity. I shared my tragic bisexual experiences in high school, and how I had always considered myself "open" but with no opportunity to explore in a small town. I told Carrie that if I could allow myself to fall in love with a woman, my friend would be it, but I couldn't bring myself to take that step. This was my excuse. Eventually we focused back on the show, and started talking about who we were attracted to, and whom we most identified with. For me, it was Jenny, the writer who was a newly out lesbian and didn't know how to fit it into the new world around her. This process of identifying with characters on *The L Word* is something I'm sure almost everyone who watched the show did, whether gay, straight, or out-and-coming like us. We felt like we were sharing something secret, dark, but revolutionary, and there were women doing the same thing all over the country, because this was one of the first times that lesbians had this opportunity to see themselves on television in this way: sexual, multitudinous, and real.

Less than a week later, I was bartending and Carrie came to me with exciting news. She took me aside and told me about her experience buying a car the day before. An obvious, sexy, butch lesbian was her salesperson and was openly flirtatious during the sell. Carrie said she'd felt something she had never felt before and left with a new car, a phone number, and a nervous smile. I was surprised at how immediately encouraging I was, not because I had any prejudices (I was raised by free-loving hippies), but because I had never been so excited for someone else's love connections. More importantly, I never knew someone as they were coming out. I laughed while urging her to call April. Carrie was afraid that her other friends wouldn't accept her change in lifestyle, so I think that's why we became close. I supported her immediately and quickly offered to be her supportive friend at any event where there would be lesbians. This was my in.

Carrie and April dated for a while, split up, and then April moved across the country. They met again a few years later and have been together ever since. During the time they were dating and after April moved, Carrie and I frequented the few local gay clubs and bars in our area, and I confessed that I, too, thought I was coming out. We cut our hair, hit on all the wrong women, watched *The L Word* and were generally a mess that summer. Figuring out how to be something you have been your entire life is exhilarating and exhausting. I had a few flings, and then my first relationship. We were stereotypically intense and serious by month three, and by the fifth, I was dumped. That's when I signed up for cable television again, the first time since I'd moved out of my parents' place that I had television at home. I watched *The L Word* by myself and would call Carrie, who had since moved to Washington D.C. to work and seek love in a new city. We would talk after the episodes, always debating the issues. Sometimes we would get online together while on the phone and look at the websites associated with the show. Though it seemed juvenile, it felt thrilling, new, and real. I loved having TV again because I didn't love being dumped and I wasn't sure what to do next with my life or my newfound outness. Carrie and I would frequent a few sites to catch up on *L Word* gossip and read about lesbian culture both on Showtime's main page, AfterEllen.com, and on thelwordonline.com. This is where we discovered Riese and her recaps.

Online, Marie Lyn Bernard goes by the name of Riese, and at the time she had her own personal blog and wrote hilariously critical and at times quite lovely recaps of each episode of *The L Word*. I read her recaps religiously as soon as they were posted, and though I'd like to think that my opinions are always my own, Riese was able to articulate how I felt about *The L Word* and lesbian life in a way I wasn't quite sure how to do yet, even with my academic training in feminism and queer theory. I wasn't the only one, either. Women across the country of all ages would log on each Monday after the show, read, and comment under her recaps. Riese had a brilliant way of recapping while highlighting aspects that were flawed, making audiences laugh at our devotedness to the show, and illuminating why we kept watching, even as we learned more about the creator, the writers' power over us, and lesbian representation. Her recaps were often beautifully written, snarky and critical, funny and intelligent all at once. I watched and read, as she became a small, but popular online voice for lesbian representation in popular culture because of *The L Word*. More people began following her personal blog, the popular and historic AfterEllen.com linked to her recaps, and she met several other women with similar interests in writing about "girl-on-girl culture," as she soon came to call it. Eventually, with these other women, and because of her popular recaps, she compiled a small following of devoted readers, myself and Carrie included, and created Autostraddle.com. The site today still has links to the original recaps. In addition, it has become a well-known place for commentary on anything in popular culture related to lesbians and the greater LGBT community. The site's mission statement defines its values and goals:

> Founded in March 2009 and still run by a dedicated team of indentured masochists, Autostraddle is an intelligent, hilarious & provocative voice and a progressively feminist online community for a new generation of kickass lesbian, bisexual & otherwise inclined ladies (and their friends) … Autostraddle is owned, run & operated by an all-volunteer army. It's a serious labor of love—a personal dream that one day became a start-up and then somehow became the world's most popular independently-owned lesbian website … Autostraddle's girl-on-girl culture is rooted in basic social values and ideals—we want women to feel good about themselves, we want equality and visibility for all marginalized groups and ultimately, we'd like to change the world. We seek to be a fresh, energizing voice for queer women, one that takes the reader seriously and encourages intelligent discourse, one that entertains with funny, uncensored & brutally honest conversation & content and one that provides photos of hot girls. (Quoted in Bernard 2011d)

Riese, in her personal blog, fancied herself a young creative writer, a feminist, and someone who didn't watch much television until *The L Word* aired. This might be why I loved her; I felt connected to her life and brain because it was similar to mine, and I agreed with and felt deeply connected to almost everything she wrote. Others felt the same. Through recaps that she enjoyed writing and their online popularity, assumedly because audiences wanted more community than just banter about *The L Word*, Riese and her staff have made a tangible, virtual space for the discussion of lesbian culture. It is here that hundreds of thousands, both celebrities and real people, stay up to date on lesbian popular culture, LGBT world news, art, television, public policy, and everyday life. This is why this site is so important to the understanding of how *The Real L Word* is received and why it is quietly and powerfully influential.

The Real L Word is *The L Word* 2.0. After *The L Word* ended, the American lesbian community was left with Callie and Arizona on *Grey's Anatomy*, a boring couple who rarely kiss on prime-time, and a few other similar characters on an otherwise heterocentric web of TV networks. Riese, though hesitant at first, continued recapping every episode of *The Real L Word*. At first she was skeptical of the show's potential, but she decided that since she had begun with recaps of the show's predecessor, she had to go on with the spin-off. Her fans, even if they hate the show, need the discussion, and this is where the power of *The Real L Word*'s audience proves to be more than what we may think. These women are not damaged because of the show; they are smart and funny viewers who create and strengthen their own identities both in relation to and in opposition to what is portrayed. They also come together to discuss the only show on television that has an all-lesbian cast, even if they dislike most of it. Autostraddle is important to understanding why we care even when we don't have to. The power button is always there and television isn't supposed to be about us, but at this moment in history, how can it not be saying something meaningful about us?

So this is why I need to watch *The Real L Word*. Even though I'm one of those readers that rarely comments online, I feel like a part of this community of queer women from all over the world who have come together to form Autostraddle's readership. I support every one of the women who comes online after an episode to read a recap, even if it is solely to vent about her frustrations. Riese faithfully recaps what she can, makes jokes, and critically compares *The Real L Word*'s representation of lesbians to other lesbian images in pop culture, like one of the girls from *America's Next Top Model*. All of this not without an editor's note as the first thing we read:

> Editor's Note: I've been totally stalled on recapping this thing, because Dinah Shore only lasts for five days for a reason. Girl drama gets boring real fast, unless a writer writes it better than it is in real life—much like straight drama. At some point I could no longer take it. Yell at me, tell me I can't spell, it's okay, I want more than this MORE THAN THIS I want us all to have fun, I want life to be full of fun, and heart, and peace, and things that matter, and good education & free health insurance & a better economy and The Nicest Thing the Movie Dot Com and equal rights, and that's what I want. I want love, a farm, and mountains. xoxo] (Quoted in Bernard 2010b)

We can already tell what the coming recaps will be: critical and demanding for more depth. It's hard to argue with that. It's clear that the author wants more for lesbian representation, but powers through it, hilariously.

I think one of the reasons audiences are drawn to reality TV is that, even though we understand that televisual reality is always obscured by corporations, directors, and the disconnect the camera brings to people's lives, we still watch with hopes of seeing pieces of ourselves. I think that's why lesbians kept watching *The Real L Word*. There were nice, seemingly normal women in the first season that some of us desperately wanted to relate to. Still, it was the wild, seemingly hypersexual Whitney that kept us watching, even if her choices disgusted us. During the first episode, in between scenes, the audience was introduced to all of the characters, their personalities that got them there, and who they were romantically or sexually involved with through the typical reality television off-set interviews. It is important to note that there were no completely single lesbians as main characters in the first season. The main characters included Tracy, a model and sweet woman trying to come out to her mother, and her girlfriend Stamie, an out comedian and real estate agent with two children from a past partnership. Jill and Niki are two very rich, very thin lesbians who have been together for some time and knew each other as children at summer camp. Their purpose on the show was to exemplify how lesbian couples can be "just like everyone else" through the planning of their wedding. Jill still didn't consider herself a lesbian and Niki was super controlling. Mikey was a butch lesbian who wouldn't take her sunglasses off and was running LA's first fashion week. The entire season revolved around her stressful life, her power as head of LA Fashion Week, and her girlfriend, hairdresser Raquel, who was rarely around. This, like the tensions introduced in the other relationships, created added drama. Rose was the Latina "butch" but came across as femme to the Autostraddle audience. Rose was there to party, wildly and in your face, and treat her mousy blonde, newly out girlfriend Natalie, like crap. And then there was Whitney. In the first episode, viewers are supposed to be drawn to Whitney because she's a player, supposedly like the popular character, Shane, on *The L Word*. We are introduced to at least three different women she is involved with in the first few episodes. The viewers and Autostraddle members almost unanimously felt like this show was more unreal than anything they had ever seen, and in a historic time of LGBTQ progress in politics, rights, and representation, the show didn't seem to be helping.

Interestingly enough, something real finally did happen, and it stirred up the most controversy and discussion.

In episode 107 of *The Real L Word*, Whitney and one of the women she was involved with, Romi (a side character for the first season, but a main character in the upcoming second), had too much to drink and were filmed having sex with a strap-on. There had already been one sex scene in the shower, but this went further. Way further. Unlike the "sex" that occurs on other American reality television shows, the audience could actually see this happening. Everything. Usually, there are dark rooms, subtitles and blankets covering the action, and the audience is aware but cannot see. In this episode, the audience saw everything short of Romi and Whitney's internal organs. As a viewer, I was surprised not to see this on the front-page news the next day. Surely, this was the first time for American television in general, let alone lesbians, and though I wasn't sure how I felt about it yet, I knew it was really raw territory. I read nothing in the news, even on popular television blogs, so I logged on to Autostraddle, where the girl-comments were on fire. This was the first time that *The Real L Word*'s audiences were torn, and, to me, this is where the show may have gone too far, but for some good reason. Riese interviewed Romi, the side character who seemed to be quite drunk on the show, and this is what she released to the public:

> First of all, Whitney and I were extremely intoxicated at the party and we weren't even really aware that the cameras had followed us in the room. We had already been very comfortable sleeping with each other and it's not a secret that this is one of the ways lesbians have sex. I'm not ashamed of having sex with Whitney or using a strap-on – because we do. That having been said, it was very difficult for me to see it on television because I am not a porn star. It's not something I wanted out there for my friends and family to see in that graphic detail. I have no choice but to own it now, because it happened, it's done, and I'm just trying to get through the hype of everything. Straight sex is everywhere, in the movies, on TV and I guess it's good for these walls to be broken down and hopefully remove the mystery of it … but it's a little uncomfortable to personally be the one breaking those walls down. I'm not part of the main 6 cast members, I have no power whatsoever in what airs, so having it removed from the episode was not an option and

that is hurtful – because it is ME out there. Do I regret mine and Whitney's actions – no. We're two adults comfortable with our sexuality. Am I upset that it is in the public eye – yes. I just hope my family isn't disappointed in me or feels like I let them down. (Quoted in Bernard 2010c)

There are over 100 posts from commenters who expressed mixed feelings about what happened during that episode. Some felt sorry for Romi; since she was not a main character with a contract, she had no control over what aired. Some felt that the scene bordered on pornography and was in bad taste. Others felt that it was a huge step forward for queer television and that those involved should be proud. Still others thought is was sexy and wished the show would give us more, insisting that it was high time for lesbian sex to be made visible and legitimate. Some compared reality television in the United States to British reality programming and said it's about time the US caught up and gave audiences a real representation of what it means to be a lesbian sexual being. Riese was torn, but wanted people to talk seriously and sensitively about the issue, particularly since, at this point, the actual stars of *The Real L Word* read her posts every week. The cast were able to make fun of themselves, but Riese wanted us, the audience, to be aware that real lives were involved.

Regardless of commenters' views, the discussion about the border between pornography and sex was long and varied, and could point the way towards the future of lesbian televisibility. Let's face it, most lesbian characters on television, like Callie and Arizona on ABC's *Grey's Anatomy*, are monogamous and rarely even kiss on-scene. Long-term relationships ostensibly exist, but sex is invisible, and one could argue that this invisibility has been a necessary step towards making the general public more comfortable with lesbians on TV sets and therefore, in life.

In an interview with Ilene Chaiken on Movieline.com by Kyle Buchanan, the producer states that she definitely wanted the camera to be everywhere, and hoped to catch steamy sex scenes, but never asked for it or pushed it. She wanted all actresses to set their own boundaries but was clear to say that she cast some women because she knew they'd go all the way given the chance (Buchanan). Even in the world of "quality" subscription cable television, sex still sells and Chaiken knew this when she began her first show. *The L Word* tried to appeal to all audiences, not just lesbians. Some Internet reviewers have said that *The Real L Word* was just a straight male fantasy (a criticism that was similarly leveled against *The L Word*), but a quick search online shows that not too many straight males were online talking about Niki and Jill's wedding venue, Rose and Natalie's constant drama, or Tracy and Stamie's fight to win Tracy's mother's acceptance. There is little significant evidence that a straight male viewership existed even for the sex scenes. So what is the point of strapping it on for the camera?

When I first started writing about *The Real L Word*, I thought that the critically engaged Autostraddle community was the most important aspect, the thing that would ultimately prove that *The Real L Word*, no matter how terrible, is an important series in the history of queer television. However, after looking through the recaps and re-reading the commentary from the episodes from the first season, I've come to another realization. Yes, this community is important, but what may be more important is the live-sex, full-frontal portrayed on *The Real L Word*. This sex is what got the series to be renewed for a second season, and it is Whitney's body (and her sexual partners') that we will be watching again when we tune in. All the other seemingly more interesting characters from the first season are not returning. The nice, normal-ish characters that Autostraddle's members liked the most in the beginning are gone.

In the postings responding to Riese's recaps from season one of *The Real L Word*, readers mostly agreed that the show wasn't always terrible, it was just boring and had no structure or characters with which they could easily identify. However, as soon as Whitney and Romi's sex scene was aired, the comments went wild and Autostraddle's recap readership grew. We wanted to see what Whitney would do next. She's complicated, messy, and doesn't apologize, which is something lesbians still do too much to keep the greater heterosexual community happy, and us safe. The sex scene was powerful and uncomfortable. It kept a small audience engaged, and it is now clear that what stirs up the most controversy and discussion among lesbian audiences will be what keeps the show alive.

Autostraddle posted a few quickies about the upcoming second season, wherein Riese tells us that Showtime promises a better season. She claims that she will continue to hate it because she hates most reality television, but she's hopeful, as I think we always will be when lesbians are on TV. She then quotes Showtime president David Nevins to explain his decision for renewing the series despite bad ratings:

> I think there is an interesting version of the show that we didn't quite get last year. I think we can make the show feel more Showtime, more premium and exclusive. We're going to make some real cast changes. We're going to focus it somewhat around Whitney and her friends, who I found are the most authentic, young 20-something lesbians in Los Angeles. And I think we can do a better job at sort of capturing that sub culture. (Quoted in Bernard 2011c)

In the end, the "authentic" women are the hyper-sexualized women, the ones who don't apologize for the sex they have. This label—"authentic"—felt dangerous to me at first. In my defense, I can still be critical of *The Real L Word* and love and defend it at the same time; we all should. Indeed, there are queer theorists and LGBTQ activists who fear the only thing gay people are defined by is what they do with their bodies. However, we as a community may be the only ones, besides the forever-fearful religious right wing, who are talking about queer sex and why what we do with our bodies is important. I don't want to be defined by what I do with my body, but then again, some of the best poetry I'm working on right now is almost as graphic as Whitney and Romi's sex scene. My mentors are pushing me to get deeper into this body-centric poetry, and it may be time for a television culture that is more body centered, especially for women and lesbians. Why can't we talk about both? Whitney, though not always proud of her decisions, is never sorry and seems to love her life. She signed on to let cameras into her bedroom, and now she is letting them in again. Let them have sex on television if they want to, and let's talk about it. There's no reason why we shouldn't talk about the theory and the flesh, because one does not live strongly or in balance without the other.

On Autostraddle, readers and commenters are getting excited for season two, and I hope the conversation gets even deeper and more risky. I promise to watch with hope of a better, more interesting season, and then if hope fails, to at least read recaps and comment with others, enhancing again the community that this show is keeping alive, no matter how bad and unreal. In these new threads about season two, there is an Ilene Chaiken-bashing party, as many fans apparently feel that Chaiken hates all lesbians except for LA lesbians. I highly recommend the comments under the post "Real L Word Picked Up For Season Two: Ilene Chaiken Hates Us" to liven up a boring day. They are spirited and intense. My favorite comments about season two include one that says even if the show doesn't improve, there will be more pretty lesbians having sex, and "there ain't nothing wrong with that." And finally, a commenter who says what I think sums up my defense: "I really think Season 2 of the real L Word is going to do wonders for lesbian visibility … A deep, thought provoking study of queer women struggling to find their place in a heterosexist society" (Quoted in Bernard 2011b). Halleluiah, sister. Part of me is afraid that I might have missed some sarcasm here, but I'm sincerely going with it. Our bodies still make us uncomfortable, no matter how much power we have or don't have over them, and maybe *The Real L Word* is just a little groundbreaking because it makes us watch and face our own discomfort. This show is the only one that creates this kind of a space right now, and until there are more I say let's watch it with our friends, let's debate and be disgusted, let's laugh and love *The Real L Word*.

The second season aired two weeks ago, and there has already been a live sex scene and a masturbation scene where the subject spoke to the camera while pleasuring herself. I watched. I was uncomfortable, but damn, I love this show. And something tells me this is different from season one. It doesn't feel pornographic. These are different bodies, and they want to be filmed doing what they do, their way. The male gaze is always a question, but are they even watching, and does it even matter? It is unclear how far this season will go, but its aim is clear, and the advance reviews prove it: *The Real L Word*'s second season will contain an epic amount of real lesbian sex and masturbation, on camera, in full lighting. Part of me still wonders if this might be damaging. Is there such a thing as too much visibility? What will people say? Is this just a way to win over heterosexual audiences? Is this what we want? Is it exploitation? In the end it is probably all these things, and I believe Riese sums up my ambivalence when she writes:

Because the lesbian media universe is so teeny-tiny, *The Real L Word* presents a really special challenge to the lesbian media— chances are good that anyone writing about the show knows one or all of the cast members and/or has friends who are friends with one or all of the cast members. I already feel weird making fun of actual people to begin with. Also chances are good you've been to these bars and to these restaurants and to Dinah Shore. Chances are good you see enough of this kind of dyke drama in your own life that you're not really compelled to witness similar exploits on television. When Claire & Francine start fighting my #1 feeling is "I'm gonna go inside and drink some vodka, you girls work your shit out and let me know when it's time for Yogurt Stop." I mention this 'cause I'm trying to figure out why this show, though seemingly far better this season, still ranks somewhere between "counting potatoes" and "painting my toenails" on my excitement scale. In addition to obvious reasons like "I hate reality teevee," I think this might be 'cause the show's primary selling point, like *The Hills & The Real Housewives* (which I've never seen), is the exoticism of good looking people living sexy sex lesbian sex glamour fashion sunshiney California lives. ... This isn't without merit—once upon a time *The L Word* was that kind of show for me and it changed my life by showing me people that seemed more like my friends than lesbians I'd seen in the media before *The L Word*. For lesbians not lucky enough to live in a gayborhood, it's not just the sunny sexification that seems out of reach but the concept of having a lesbian network so large and diverse to begin with. When you're the only gay in the village, finding one girl to bed let alone three is challenging. So that's a value. Reality TV isn't ever about our actual lives—it's exotic/aspirational (*The Hills*) or completely bizarre (*Storage Wars*)—and I suspect part of the lesbian critical disdain for this show comes from the fact that the show is kinda like our actual lives except you know, prettier. (Quoted in Bernard 2011a)

I completely agree, and though some cast members this season seem to be more than sex puppets—like Sadjah who is young, African-American, fresh and politically active, and a new couple, Cori and Kacy, who are trying to have a baby and actually seem to love each other—I'm sure we'll all get fired up about the sex and wind up agreeing that these more interesting, well-rounded characters are boring. Nevertheless, I'll be watching with my girlfriend all summer. We'll get together with Carrie and April for viewing parties and I'll smile because these women in the room and on the television are all very connected to my identity and my life, no matter how silly that may seem. This is where the reality happens. We need to connect and define ourselves in this world, and part of that definition may be related to the only television show out there trying to say something about what it really means to be a lesbian.

Character/Actor Guide

Marcus Allenwood (Marcus Gibson), season one

Andrew (Darrin Klimek), season one

Kate Arden (Annabella Sciorra), season four

Ivan Aycock (Kelly Lynch), seasons one and two

Billie Blaikie (Alan Cumming), season three

Charlotte Birch (Sandra Bernhard), season two

Sunset Boulevard (Roger Cross), season six

Adele Channing (Malaya Drew), season five

Jamie Chen (Mei Melançon), season six

Slim Daddy (Snoop Dogg), season one

Carmen de la Pica Morales (Sarah Shahi), seasons two and three

Dawn Denbo (Elizabeth Keener), season five

Gabby Deveaux (Guinevere Turner), seasons one and two

Dana Fairbanks (Erin Daniels), seasons one–three

Marina Ferrer (Karina Lombard), season one

Grace (Simone Bailly), seasons four and five

Timothy "Tim" Haspel (Eric Mabius), season one (with minor appearances during seasons two, three, and six)

Cherie Jaffe or Cherie Peroni (Rosanna Arquette), seasons one, three, and four

Candace Jewell (Ion Overman), seasons one and two

Tina Kennard (Laurel Holloman), main character

Molly Kroll (Clementine Ford), seasons five and six

Phyllis Kroll (Cybill Shepherd), seasons four and six

Jodi Lerner (Marlee Matlin), seasons four, five, and six

Lei Ling (Taayla Markell), season one

"Lisa" the lesbian-identified man (Devon Gummersall), season one

Tom Mater (Jon Wolfe Nelson), seasons four, five, and six

Gabriel McCutcheon (Eric Roberts), season three

Shane McCutcheon (Katherine Moennig), main character

Shay McCutcheon (Aidan Jarrar), seasons three and four

Stacey Merkin (Heather Matarazzo), season four

Dylan Moreland (Alexandra Hedison), seasons three, four, and six

Angus Partridge (Dallas Roberts), seasons three–six

Helena Peabody (Rachel Shelley), seasons two–six

Peggy Peabody (Holland Taylor), seasons one–six

Lara Perkins (Lauren Lee Smith), seasons one–three

Alice Pieszecki (Leisha Hailey), main character

Angelica Porter-Kennard (Olivia Windbiel), seasons two–six

Bette Porter (Jennifer Beals), main character

Kate "Kit" Porter (Pam Grier), main character

Marci Salvatore (Katharine Isabelle), season six

Jenny Schecter (Mia Kirshner), main character

Jared Sobel (Jackson Allan), season four

Paige Sobel (Kristanna Loken), season four

Niki Stevens (Kate French), seasons five and six

Moira/Max Sweeney (Daniela Sea), seasons three–six

Tonya (Meredith McGeachie), seasons one–three

Eva Torres, "Papi" (Janina Gavankar), seasons four–six

Beatie Mark Wayland (Eric Lively), season two

Kelly Wentworth (Elizabeth Berkley), season six

Tasha Williams (Rose Rollins), seasons four–six

Joyce Wischnia (Jane Lynch), seasons two–six

Complete Episode Guide

Season one

US première: Sunday January 18, 2004, Showtime

1:1 "Pilot" (1h 36m) Writer: Ilene Chaiken; Director: Rose Troche

1:2 "Let's Do It" (46m) Writer: Susan Miller; Director: Rose Troche

1:3 "Longing" (50m) Writer: Angela Robinson; Director: Lynne Stopkewich

1:4 "Lies, Lies, Lies" (50m) Writer: Josh Senter; Director: Clement Virgo

1:5 "Lawfully" (54m) Writer: Rose Troche; Director: Heike Brandstatter

1:6 "Losing It" (49m) Writer: Guinevere Turner; Director: Clement Virgo

1:7 "L'Ennui" (52m) Writer: Ilene Chaiken; Director: Tony Goldwin

1:8 "Listen Up" (48m) Writer: Mark Zakarin; Director: Kari Skoglan

1:9 "Luck, Next Time" (51m) Writer: Rose Troche; Director: Rose Troche

1:10 "Liberally" (48m) Writer: Ilene Chaiken; Director: Mary Harron

1:11 "Looking Back" (46m) Writer: Guinevere Turner; Director: Rose Troche

1:12 "Locked Up" (45m) Writer: Ilene Chaiken; Director: Lynne Stopkewich

1:13 "Limb from Limb" (59m) Writer: Ilene Chaiken; Director: Tony Goldwyn

Season two

US première: Tuesday February 15, 2005, Showtime

2:1 "Life, Loss, Leaving" (56m) Writer: Ilene Chaiken; Director: Daniel Minahan

2:2 "Lap Dance" (56m) Writer: Ilene Chaiken; Director: Lynne Stopkewich

2:3 "Loneliest Number" (56m) Writer: Lara Spotts; Director: Rose Troche

2:4 "Lynch Pin" (59m) Writer: Ilene Chaiken; Director: Lisa Cholodenko

2:5 "Labyrinth" (55m) Writer: Rose Troche; Director: Burr Steer

2:6 "Lagrimas de Oro" (45m) Writer: Guinevere Turner; Director Jeremy Podeswa

2:7 "Luminous" (55m) Writer: Ilene Chaiken; Director: Ernest Dickerson

2:8 "Loyal" (57m) Writer: A. M. Homes; Director: Alison Maclean

2:9 "Late, Later, Latent" (57m) Writer: David Stenn; Director: Tony Goldwyn

2:10 "Land Ahoy" (57m) Writer: Ilene Chaiken; Director: Tricia Brock

2:11 "Loud and Proud" (49m) Writer: Elizabeth Turner; Director: Rose Troche

2:12 "L'Chaim" (44m) Writer: Ilene Chaiken; Director: John Curran

2:13 "Lacuna" (Season Finale) (56m) Writer: Ilene Chaiken; Director: Ilene Chaiken

Season three

US première: Sunday January 8, 2006, Showtime

3:1 "Labia Majora" (57m) Writer: Ilene Chaiken; Director: Rose Troche

3:2 "Lost Weekend" (52m) Writer: A. M. Homes; Director: Bille Eltringham

3:3 "Lobsters" (49m) Writer: Ilene Chaiken; Director: Bronwen Hughes

3:4 "Light My Fire" (46m) Writer: Cherien Dabis; Director: Lynne Stopkewich

3:5 "Lifeline" (51m) Writer: Ilene Chaiken; Director: Kimberly Peirce

3:6 "Lifesize" (50m) Writer: Adam Rapp; Director: Tricia Brock

3:7 "Lone Star" (53m) Writer: Elizabeth Ziff; Director: Frank Pierson

3:8 "Latecomer" (56m) Writer: Ilene Chaiken; Director: Angela Robinson

3:9 "Lead, Follow, or Get Out of the Way" (54m) Writer: Ilene Chaiken; Director: Moisés Kaufman

3:10 "Losing the Light" (48m) Writer: Rose Troche; Director: Rose Troche

3:11 "Last Dance" (44m) Writer: Ilene Chaiken; Director: Allison Anders

3:12 "Left Hand of the Goddess" (56m) Writer: Ilene Chaiken; Director: Ilene Chaiken

Season four

US première: Sunday January 7, 2007, Showtime

4:1   "Legend in the Making" (56m) Writer: Ilene Chaiken; Director: Bronwen Hughes

4:2   "Livin' La Vida Loca" (56m) Writer: Alexandra Kondracke; Director: Marlene Gorris

4:3   "Lassoed" (44m) Writer: Ilene Chaiken; Director: Tricia Brock

4:4   "Layup" (50m) Writer: Elizabeth Ziff; Director: Jessica Sharzer

4:5   "Lez Girls" (52m) Writer: Ilene Chaiken; Director: John Stockwell

4:6   "Luck Be a Lady" (56m) Writer: Angela Robinson; Director: Angela Robinson

4:7   "Lesson Number One" (50m) Writer: Ariel Schrag; Director: Moisés Kaufman

4:8   "Lexington and Concord" (48m) Writer: Ilene Chaiken; Director: Jamie Babbit

4:9   "Lacy Lilting Lyrics" (53m) Writer: Cherien Dabis; Director: Bronwen Hughes

4:10 "Little Boy Blue" (45m) Writer: Elizabeth Ziff; Director: Karyn Kusama

4:11 "Literary License to Kill" (54m) Writer: Ilene Chaiken; Director: John Stockwell

4:12 "Long Time Coming" (55m) Writer: Ilene Chaiken; Director: Ilene Chaiken

Season five

US première: Sunday January 6, 2008, Showtime

5:1   "LGB Tease" (54m) Writer: Ilene Chaiken; Director: Angela Robinson

5:2 "Look Out, Here They Come!" (50m) Writer: Cherien Dabis; Director: Jamie Babbit

5:3 "Lady of the Lake" (53m) Writer: Ilene Chaiken; Director: Tricia Brock

5:4 "Let's Get This Party Started" (49m) Writer: Elizabeth Ziff; Director: John Stockwell

5:5 "Lookin' at You, Kid" (56m) Writer: Angela Robinson; Director: Angela Robinson

5:6 "Lights! Camera! Action!" (58m) Writer: Ilene Chaiken; Director: Ilene Chaiken

5:7 "Lesbians Gone Wild" (49m) Writer: Elizabeth Ziff; Director: Angela Robinson

5:8 "Lay Down the Law" (52m) Writer: Alexandra Kondracke; Director: Leslie Libman

5:9 "Liquid Heat" (58m) Writer: Ilene Chaiken; Director: Rose Troche

5:10 "Lifecycle" (56m) Writer: Angela Robinson; Director: Angela Robinson

5:11 "Lunar Cycle" (55m) Writer: Ilene Chaiken; Director: Robert Aschmann

5:12 "Loyal and True" (66m) Writer: Ilene Chaiken; Director: Ilene Chaiken

Season six

US première: Sunday January 18, 2009, Showtime

6:1 "Long Night's Journey into Day" (55m) Writer: Ilene Chaiken; Director: Ilene Chaiken

6:2 "Least Likely" (50m) Writer: Rose Troche; Director: Rose Troche

6:3 "LMFAO" (49m) Writer: Alexandra Kondracke; Director: Angela Robinson

6:4 "Leaving Los Angeles" (54m) Writer: Ilene Chaiken; Director: Rose Troche

6:5 "Litmus Test" (55m) Writer: Angela Robinson; Director: Angela Robinson

6:6 "Lactose Intolerant" (58m) Writer: Elizabeth Ziff; Director: John Stockwell

6:7   "Last Couple Standing" (51m) Writer: Ilene Chaiken; Director: Rose
       Troche

6:8   "Last Word" (64m) Writer: Ilene Chaiken; Director: Ilene Chaiken

Film and TV Guide

Films

Better than Chocolate (Anne Wheeler, 1999)

Boys Don't Cry (Kimberly Peirce, 1999)

Charlie and the Chocolate Factory (Tim Burton, 2005)

Chasing Amy (Kevin Smith, 1997)

Coffy (Jack Hill, 1973)

The D Word (The D Word LLC/Dyke TV, 2005)

Danny: Escaping My Female Body (BBC, 2007)

Foxy Brown (Jack Hill, 1974)

The Good, the Bad, and the Ugly (Sergio Leone, 1966)

Morocco (Josef von Sternberg, 1930)

Opposite Sex: Jamie's Story (Josh Aronson, Showtime, 2004)

Opposite Sex: Rene's Story (Josh Aronson, Showtime, 2004)

Queen Christina (Rouben Mamoulian, 1933)

The Rocky Horror Picture Show (Jim Sharman, 1975)

Shane (George Stevens, 1953)

TV

America's Next Top Model (10 by 10 Entertainment/Pottle Productions/Ty Ty Baby Productions/CW, 2003–)

Big Love (Anima Sola Productions/HBO, 2006–2011)

Boy Meets Boy (Evolution Film & Tape/Bravo, 2003)

Buffy the Vampire Slayer (Mutant Enemy Productions/WB Television Network, 1997–2001; UPN, 2001–2003)

CSI (Anthony E. Zuiker/CBS, 2000–)

Desperate Housewives (Cherry Alley Productions/ABC, 2004–2012)

Dirty Sexy Money (Berlanti Television/ABC, 2007–2009)

Ellen (Touchstone Television/ABC, 1994–1998)

ER (Constant c Productions, Amblin Entertainment, Warner Brothers Television/CBS, 1994–2009)

Flipping Out (Authentic Entertainment/Bravo, 2007–)

Friends (Warner Bros. Television/NBC, 1994–2004)

Glee (20th Century Fox Television/Fox, 2009–)

Grey's Anatomy (Shondaland/ABC, 2005–)

Jersey Shore (495 Productions/MTV, 2009–2012)

The L Word (Anonymous Content/Showtime, 2004–2010)

LA Law (20th Century Fox Television/NBC, 1986–1994)

Law and Order: Special Victim's Unit (Wolf Films/NBC, 1999–)

Modern Family (Levitan Lloyd/20th Century Fox Television/ABC, 2009–)

Nurse Jackie (Caryn Mandabach Productions/Showtime, 2009–)

The Oprah Winfrey Show (October 12, 2007)

Project Runway (Bravo, 2004–2009)

Queer as Folk (Cowslip Productions/Showtime Networks Inc., 2001–2005)

Queer Eye for the Straight Guy (Scout Entertainment/Bravo, 2003–2007)

The Real Housewives of … (True Entertainment/Bravo, 2006–)

The Real L Word (Magical Elves Production/Showtime, 2010–)

Roseanne (ABC, 1988–1997)

Sex and the City (Sex and the City Productions/HBO, 1998–2004)

Sister Wives (Puddle Monkey Productions/TLC, 2010–)

Skins (Company Pictures/E4, 2007–)

The Sopranos (HBO, 1999–2007)

Sugar Rush (Shine Limited/Channel 4, 2005–2006)

Tabatha's Salon Makeover (Reveille Productions/Bravo, 2008–)

There's Something About Miriam (Remy Blumenfeld/SKY 1, 2004)

Thirtysomething (The Bedford Falls Company/ABC, 1987–1991)

Top Chef (Magical Elves Productions/Bravo, 2006–)

Top Design (Bravo Cable, 2007–)

Transamerican Love Story (World of Wonder/Logo, 2008–2009)

Transgenerations (Sundance Channel, 2005)

True Blood (Your Face Goes Here Entertainment/HBO, 2008–)

Twin Peaks (Lynch/Frost Productions, ABC, 1990–1991)

Two and a Half Men (Chuck Lorre Productions/CBS, 2003–)

Ugly Betty (Silent H Productions/ABC, 2006–2010)

Watch What Happens Live (Bravo, 2006–)

Work Out (Bravo, 2006–2008)

Xena: Warrior Princess (MCA Television Entertainment Inc./Universal TV, 1995–2001)

Young Americans (Columbia Tristar Television/WB, 2000)

Bibliography

Abelkop, Gina. "R.I.P. Jenny Schecter: In Memory of a TV Lesbian." Jewcy.
com, March 2, 2009.

"About *The D Word*" [online]: http://www.thedword.com/about.html.
Accessed October 17, 2010.

AfterEllen.com. "Gender Trouble on '*The L Word*.'" April 6, 2006: http://
www.afterellen.com/TV/2006/4/butches.html. Accessed October 15,
2010.

Akass, Kim and Janet McCabe. "What is a Straight Girl to Do? Ivan's
Serenade, Kit's Dilemma." Kim Akass and Janet McCabe, eds. *Reading*
The L Word: *Outing Contemporary Television*. London and New York:
I.B.Tauris, 2006 (2006b): 143–56.

——— eds. *Reading* The L Word: *Outing Contemporary Television*. London
and New York: I.B.Tauris, 2006 (2006a).

Allen, Robert C. and Annette Hill, eds. *The Television Studies Reader*.
London and New York: Routledge, 2004.

Anderson, Benedict. *Imagined Communities*. London and New York: Verso,
1983.

Apollonia-6. "Disappointed with the L Word (But Not Entirely)." *Showtime
Message Boards*. September 30, 2004: http://www.sho.com/site/
message/thread.do?topicid=97261&boardid=268&groupid=12.

Arkaycee. "More Black Lesbian Couples." *Showtime Message Boards*. July 7, 2005:
http://discussion.l-word.com/viewtopic.php?t=12203&highlight=race.

Baber, P. Ryan. "Trans America." *Hollywood Reporter – International Edition*
25, April 2008: http://search.epnet.com. Accessed January 10, 2010.

Bagemihl, Bruce. *Biological Exuberance: Animal Homosexuality and Natural
Diversity*. New York: St Martin's Press, 1999.

Barrett, Tom. "Hard Questions and Unexpected Answers in Papou TV
Special," *Vancouver Sun*. October 24, 1995: C6.

Beatie, Thomas. "Labor of Love: Is Society Ready for this Pregnant
Husband." *The Advocate*. April 8, 2008: 24L: http: www.advocate.com/
article.aspx?id=22217. Accessed April 3, 2009.

Beck, Ulrich. "Cosmopolitan Realism: On the Distinction between
Cosmopolitanism in Philosophy and the Social Sciences." *Global
Networks*. 4. 2004: 31–156.

Becker, Ron. *Gay TV and Straight America*. Brunswick, NJ: Rutgers
University Press, 2004 (2004a).

————. "Prime-time Television in the Gay Nineties: Network Television, Quality Audiences, and Gay Politics." R. C. Allen and A. Hill, eds. *The Television Studies Reader.* London and New York: Routledge, 2004 (2004b): 373–88.

Beinin, Joel. "The New American McCarthyism: Policing Thought about the Middle East." *Race and Class.* 46. 2004: 101–15.

Beirne, Rebecca. "Fashioning *The L Word.*" *Nebula.* 3. 4. 2006: http://www.nobleworld.biz/.

————. "Dirty Lesbian Pictures: Art and Pornography in *The L Word.*" *Critical Studies in Television.* 2. 1. 2007 (2007a): 90–101.

————. "Lesbian Pulp Television: Torment, Trauma and Transformations in *The L Word.*" *Refractory: A Journal of Entertainment Media.* 11. 2007 (2007b): http://blogs.arts.unimelb.edu.au/refractory/2007/09/04/lesbian-pulp-television-torment-trauma-and-transformations-in-the-l-word-rebecca-beirne/.

————. *Lesbians in Television and Text after the Millenium.* New York: Palgrave Macmillan, 2008 (2008a).

————. *Televising Queer Women: A Reader.* New York: Palgrave Macmillan, 2008 (2008b).

Berger, John. *Ways of Seeing.* London: Penguin Books, 1972.

Berlant, Lauren. *The Queen of America Goes to Washington City: Essays on Sex and Citizenship.* Durham, NC: Duke University Press, 1997.

Bernard, Marie Lyn, ed. "Real L Word Needs Lesbian Executive Realness: Context, Depth: How We'd Fix It." Autostraddle.com. August 21, 2010: http://www.autostraddle.com/the-real-l-word-final-thoughts-57192/. Accessed January 14, 2013 (2010a).

————. "*Real L Word* Recap: Episode 101 – The Power of the Clam is Overrated." Autostraddle.com. June 23, 2010: http://www.autostraddle.com/real-l-word-recap-epiosde-101-the-power-of-the-clam-49427/. Accessed April 25, 2011 (2010b).

————. "Romi Tells Us What It's like to Be in *Real L Word*'s Lesbian Strap-On Scene." Autostraddle.com. August 3, 2010: http://www.autostraddle.com/real-l-word-lesbian-sex-romis-statement-54423/. Accessed April 25, 2011 (2010c).

————. "*Real L Word* Returns for Season 2 with Extra Sexy Lesbian Sex." Autostraddle.com. May 31, 2011: http://www.autostraddle.com/real-l-word-returns-for-season-2-with-extra-sexy-lesbian-sex-90794/. Accessed June 1, 2011 (2011a).

————. "*Real L Word* Season 2: Behind the Scene: Sex, Sex & Rock 'n' Roll." Autostraddle.com. May 23, 2011: http://www.autostraddle.com/real-l-word-season-2-behind-the-scenes-sex-90027/. Accessed June 1, 2011 (2011b).

————. "*Real L Word*'s Second Season Will Definitely Suck Less than the First." Autostraddle.com. January 15, 2011: http://www.autostraddle.com/real-l-word-2-it-gets-better-73423/. Accessed April 25, 2011 (2011c).

————. "What is Autostraddle?" Autostraddle.com: http://www.autostraddle.com/about/. Accessed April 25, 2011 (2011d).

Bianco, David. "The Heyday of Lesbian Pulp Novels." Planet Out.com. July 19, 1999: www.planetout.com/news/history/archive/07191999.html.

Bignell, Jonathan. *An Introduction to Television Studies*. London, Routledge, 2004.

Bigsmooches. "So, We're Not Supposed to Say Anything about the Racism?" *Showtime Message Boards*. January 14, 2004: http://www.sho.com/site/message/thread.do?topicid=45925&boardid=212&groupid=12.

Binnie, Jon, Julian Holloway, Steve Millington, and Craig Young, eds. *Cosmopolitan Urbanism*. London: Routledge, 2006.

Bolonik, Kera. "The Life and Aggravating Times of Jenny Schecter." *The New York Times*. January 11, 2009.

————."*The Real L Word* Creator Ilene Chaiken on the Reality Spinoff of Her Insane Lesbian Drama." *New York Magazine*. June 18, 2010: http://nymag.com/daily/entertainment/2010/06/ilene_chaiken_on_the_real_l_wo.html.

Bonsu, Samuel K. and Aron Darmod. "Co-creating Second Life: Market Consumer Cooperation in Contemporary Economy." *Journal of Macro-marketing*. 28.4. 2008: 355–68.

"Bravo." NBC Universal Cable Networks. May 1, 2007: http://www.nbc.com/nbc/NBC_Universal_Cable_Networks.

Brooks, Caryn. "*The L Word*: Sad Max." NYmag.com, February 9, 2009: http://nymag.com/daily/entertainment/2009/02/the_l_word_sad_max.html. Accessed October 15, 2010.

Brown, Mary Ellen. *Television and Women's Culture: The Politics of the Popular*. Sydney, Australia: Currency Press, 1990.

Brunsdon, Charlotte and Lynn Spigel, eds. *Feminist Television Criticism: A Reader*. New York: Open University Press, 2008.

Buchanan, Kyle. "*The Real L Word* Creator Ilene Chaiken on Showtime's Gentrification and Filming Real Love Scenes." Movieline.com. August 2, 2010: http://movieline.com/2010/08/02/the-real-l-word-creator-ilene-chaiken-on-showtimes-gentrification-and-filming-real-love-scenes/. Accessed April 25, 2011.

Burns, Kellie. "Cosmopolitan Sexual Citizenship and the Project of Queer World Making at the Sydney 2002 Gay Games." *Sexualities*. 15. 3–4. 2012a: 314–35.

————. "Lesbian Mothers, Two-headed Monsters and the Televisual Machine." K. H. Robinson and C. Davies, eds. *Queer and Subjugated Knowledges: Generating Subversive Imaginaries*. UAE: Bentham, 2012b: 56–73.

Burns, Kellie and Cristyn Davies. "Producing Cosmopolitan Sexual Citizens on *The L Word*." *Journal of Lesbian Studies*. 13. 2009: 174–88.

Butler, Judith. *Gender Trouble: Feminism and the Subversion of Identity*. London and New York: Routledge, 1990.

———. *The Psychic Life of Power: Theories in Subjection.* Stanford, CA: Stanford University Press, 1997.

———. *Undoing Gender.* New York: Routledge, 2004.

Byfield, Ted. "Odd that a National Bank should have the Courage the Rest of Us Lacked." *Alberta Report*, November 6, 1995: 44.

Cain, Patrick. "Companies are Finding Second Life." *Investors Business Daily.* February 21, 2007: http://www.investors.com/editorial/IBDArticles.asp?artsec=17&issue=20070221. Accessed March 22, 2008.

Caldwell, John. *Televisuality: Style, Crisis, and Authority in American Television.* New Jersey: Rutgers University Press, 1995.

Califia, Pat. "Doing it Together: Gay Men, Lesbians, and Sex." *The Advocate.* July 7, 1983: 24.

———. *Public Culture.* 1984: http://suif.stanford.edu/~jeffop/WWW/unmonogamy.html.

Calvert, Ben, Neil Casey, Bernadette Casey, Liam French, and Justin Lewis. *Television Studies: The Key Concepts.* London: Routledge, 2008.

Campbell, John E. "Outing PlanetOut: Surveillance, Gay Marketing and Internet Affinity Portals." *New Media & Society.* 7. 5. 2005: 663–831.

Capsuto, Steven. *Alternate Channels: The Uncensored Story of Gay and Lesbian Images on Radio and Television, 1930s to the Present.* New York: Ballantine, 2000.

Chaiken, Ilene. "She is *The L Word.*" Interview with Laura Conway, June 14, 2005; file:///Users/user/Documents/Publications/The%20L%20Word/Queering%20Feminism%20on%20The%20L%20Word/New%20York. webarchive. Accessed May 10, 2010.

Chambers, Samuel A. "Heteronormativity and *The L Word*: From a Politics of Representation to a Politics of Norms." Kim Akass and Janet McCabe, eds. *Reading* The L Word: *Outing Contemporary Television.* London and New York: I.B.Tauris, 2006: 81–98.

———. "'An Incalculable Effect': Subversions of Heteronormativity." *Political Studies.* 55. 2007: 656–79.

———. *The Queer Politics of Television.* London: I.B.Tauris, 2009.

Chasin, Alexandra. *Selling Out: The Gay and Lesbian Movement Goes to Market.* New York: St Martin's Press, 2000.

Cole, Pam. "Season 3 Ratings Up." *L Word Fan Site News Flash.* February 8, 2006: www.l-word.com/news/s3_ratings.php.

Cossman, Brenda. *Sexual Citizens: The Legal and Cultural Regulation of Sex and Belonging.* Stanford, CA: Stanford University Press, 2007.

D'Acci, Julie. "Television, Representation and Gender." Robert C. Allen and Annette Hill, eds. *The Television Studies Reader.* London: Routledge, 2004: 373–88.

Davies, Cristyn. "Disturbing the Dialectics of the Public Toilet." *Hecate: An Interdisciplinary Journal of Women's Liberation.* 33. 2. 2007: 120–34.

———. "Becoming Sissy: A Response to David McInnes." Bronwyn Davies, ed. *Judith Butler in Conversation: Analyzing the Texts and Talk of Everyday Life*. New York: Routledge, 2008a: 117–33.

———. "Proliferating Panic: Regulating Representations of Sex and Gender During the Culture Wars." *Cultural Studies Review*. 14. 2. 2008b: 83–102.

———. "It's Not at All Chic to be Denied Your Civil Rights: Performing Sexual Citizenship in Holly Hughes' *Preaching to the Perverted*." *Sexualities*. 15. 3/4. 2012: 277–96.

Davies, Faye. "Paradigmatically Oppositional Representations: Gender and Sexual Identity in *The L Word*." Rebecca Beirne, ed. *Televising Queer Women*. New York: Palgrave Macmillan, 2008: 179–94.

Davis, Glyn and Gary Needham, eds. *Queer TV: Theories, Politics, Histories*. London: Routledge, 2009.

Dean, William. "Out of the Shadows: An Interview with Ann Bannon." *Clean Sheets Magazine*. Online edition: www.cleansheets.com/articles/dean_01.08.03.shtml.

D'Emilio, John. "Capitalism and Gay Identity." Ann Snitow, Christine Stansell, and Sharon Thompson, eds. *Powers of Desire: The Politics of Sexuality*. New York: Monthly Review Press, 1983 (1983a): 100–13.

———. *Sexual Politics, Sexual Communities: The Making of a Homosexual Minority in the United States, 1940–1970*. Chicago: University of Chicago Press, 1983 (1983b).

Doty, Alexander. *Making Things Perfectly Queer: Interpreting Mass Culture*. Minneapolis: University of Minnesota Press, 1993.

Dow, Bonnie. "Ellen, Television and the Politics of Gay and Lesbian Visibility." *Critical Studies in Mass Communication*. 18. 2. 2001: 123–40.

Duggan, Lisa. *The Twilight of Equality: Neoliberalism, Cultural Politics, and the Attack on Democracy*. Boston: Beacon Press, 2003.

Duggan, Lisa and Nan D. Hunter. *Sex Wars: Sexual Dissent and Political Culture*. New York: Routledge, 1995.

Dyke TV [online]: http://www.myspace.com/dyketv. Accessed October 17, 2010.

Esposito, Jennifer and Bettina Love. "The Black Lesbians are White and the Studs are Femmes: A Cultural Studies Analysis of *The L Word*." *Gender Forum: An Internet Journal for Gender Studies*. 23. 2008: http://www.genderforum.org/index.php?id=155.

Evans, David T. *Sexual Citizenship: The Material Construction of Sexualities*. London: Routledge, 1993.

Faderman, Lillian. *Odd Girls and Twilight Lovers: A History of Lesbian Life in Twentieth Century America*. New York: Penguin, 1991.

Fannie, Grace. "Stuff One Lesbian Likes: Jenny Schecter." *Grace the Spot*. February 5, 2009.

Faulkner, Amy, Daniel Fedrizzi, and Jeffrey Garber. *2006 Top Brands for Gay and Lesbian Consumers Report*. OpusCommGroup and Scarborough

Research. Syracuse: Scarborough Research, 2006: 1–27: http://www. scarborough.com/press_releases/GLBT%20Brands%20FINAL%20 6.22.06.pdf.

Ficera, Kim. "The Chart." Kim Akass and Janet McCabe, eds. *Reading* The L Word: *Outing Contemporary Television*. London and New York: I.B.Tauris, 2006: 111–14.

Fiske, John. *Television Culture*. London: Methuen, 1987.

Fonseca, Nicholas. "Return of the Pink Ladies." *Entertainment Weekly*. February 18, 2005: 39–41.

———. "*The L Word* Series Finale: Who Killed Jenny Schecter? And does it Even Matter?" *Popwatch. EW.Com*. March 9, 2009: http://popwatch. ew.com/2009/03/09/the-l-word-seri/.

Forrest, Katherine V., ed. *Lesbian Pulp Fiction: The Sexually Intrepid World of Lesbian Paperback Novels 1950–1965*. San Francisco: Cleis, 2005.

Foucault, Michel. *The History of Sexuality: An Introduction Volume 1*. Robert Hurly, trans. New York: Random House, 1990 [1978].

———. *Discipline and Punish: The Birth of the Prison* (2nd edition). Alan Sheridan, trans. New York: Random House, 1995 [1975].

Gilbert, Matthew. "'Word' has it Jenny Set to Take Her Lumps," *The Boston Globe*, February 17, 2005.

Gilchrist, Tracy E. "TV Gets *The L Word* and *The D Word*." *Curve*. December 1, 2005: 17.

Glock, Alison. "She Likes to Watch." *The New York Times*. February 6, 2005: 38.

Godley, Elizabeth. "Laurie Papou." *Vancouver Sun*. April 15, 1989: D1.

Goodman, T. "Showtime's *The L Word* Goes Boldly Where Other Series have Only Flirted – to Love and Sex among L.A. Lesbians." *San Francisco Chronicle*. January 16, 2004: http://www.sfgate.com/cgi-bin/ article.cgi?f=/c/a/2004/01/16/DDGFQ4A4V11.DTL.

———. "Time for a Change of Direction at Showtime." *The Hollywood Reporter* [online]. May 23, 2011: http://www.hollywoodreporter. com/bastard-machine/time-a-change-direction-at-191173. Accessed December 21, 2011.

Gorton R. Nick, Jamie Buth, and Dean Spade. *Medical Therapy and Health Maintenance for Transgender Men: A Guide for Health Care Providers*. Lyon-Martin Women's Health Services. San Francisco, CA, 2005.

Gould, Claudia. "Screwing it on Straight." Lisa Yuskavage and Katy Siegel, eds. *Lisa Yuskavage*. Philadelphia: University of Pennsylvania, 2000: 9–14.

Grubb, R. J. "Double Up With *The D Word*." *Bay Windows*. May 12, 2005: 15.

Guidotto, Nadia. "Cashing in on Queers: From Liberation to Commodification." *Canadian Online Journal of Queer Studies in Education*. 2. 1. 2006 [online]: https://jps.library.utoronto.ca/index.php/jqstudies/article/viewFile/ 3286/1415. Accessed June 8, 2011.

Halberstam, Judith. *Female Masculinity.* Durham, NC: Duke University Press, 1998.

————. *In a Queer Time and Place: Transgender Bodies, Subcultural Lives.* New York: New York University Press, 2005.

————. "I Love Not *The L Word*: Who's Afraid of the Big, Bad Butch." *Girlfriends.* January 2006: 38, 40, 41.

————. "Daniela Sea: *The L Word*'s Trans Pioneer." *Diva.* August 2008: 52–7.

————. "Global Female Masculinities." *Sexualities.* 15. 3/4. 2012: 336–54.

Hall, Marcia B. "Lisa Yuscavage's Painterly Paradoxes." Lisa Yuskavage and Katy Siegel, eds. *Lisa Yuskavage.* Philadelphia: University of Pennsylvania, 2000: 23–30.

Hall, Stuart. *Representation: Cultural Representations and Signifying Practices.* London: Sage, in association with the Open University, 1997.

————. "Race, Articulation and Societies Structured in Dominance." Malcolm Cross, ed. *The Sociology of Race and Ethnicity.* Cheltenham, UK: Edward Elgar Publishing, 2000: 40–80.

————. "Encoding/decoding." M. G. Durham and D. Kellner, eds. *Media and Cultural Studies: Keyworks.* Rev. edn. Malden, MA and Oxford: Blackwell, 2006.

Hammond, Harmony. *Lesbian Art in America,* New York: Rizzoli, 2000.

Haralovich, Mary Beth and Michael W. Trosset. "Expect the Unexpected: Narrative Pleasure and Uncertainty Due to Chance in *Survivor.*" Susan Murray and Laurie Ouellette, eds. *Reality TV: Remaking Television Culture.* New York: New York University Press, 2004: 75–96.

Hart, Lynda. *Fatal Women: Lesbian Sexuality and the Mark of Aggression.* Princeton, N.J.: Princeton University Press, 1994.

Hector, Alley. "Pregnant Man is Just Another Life in the Life …" March 25, 2008: http://qpdx.com/2008/03/pregnant-man-is-just-another-day-in-the-life/. Accessed December 20, 2010.

Hekman, S. J. *Feminist Interpretations of Michel Foucault.* University Park: Pennsylvania State University Press, 1996.

Heller, Dana. "How Does a Lesbian Look? Stendahl's Syndrome and *The L Word.*" Kim Akass and Janet McCabe, eds. *Reading the L Word: Outing Contemporary Television.* London and New York: I.B.Tauris, 2006: 55–68.

Hennessy, Rosemary. "Queer Visibility in Commodity Culture." *Cultural Critique.* 29. 1995: 31–76.

Herman, Andrew, J. Rosemary, and Kaye Lewis. "Your Second Life? Goodwill and the Performativity of Intellectual Property in Online Digital Gaming." *Cultural Studies.* 20. 2–3. 2006: 184–210.

Herring, Scott. *Another Country: Queer Anti-Urbanism.* New York: New York University Press, 2010.

Hibberd, James. "Lights! Camera! 'L Word' Action!" *Television Week.* May 12, 2005: http://search.epnet.com. Accessed January 10, 2010.

Hills, Matt. *Fan Cultures.* London: Routledge, 2002.

Hoggard, Liz. "*The L Word*: Lesbian. Loaded. Loving It." *The Independent,* November 20, 2005: http://www.independent.co.uk/news/uk/this-britain/the-l-word-lesbian-loaded-loving-it-516111.html.   Accessed January 25, 2012.

hooks, bell. *Black Looks: Race and Representation.* Boston, MA: South End Press, 1992.

Howe, Delmas. "Stations: A Gay Passion" [online]: www.delmashowe.com/stations.html.

Hutcheon, Linda. *The Politics of Postmodernism.* London: Routledge, 1989.

IloveBette. "What the Show has Done for Me." *Showtime Message Boards.* April 17, 2006: http://www.sho.com/site/message/thread.do?topicid=1 82788&boardid=107&groupid=12.

Jacky. "Fan Mail." *The L Word Complete Second Season.* DVD edition. Showtime, 2005.

Jeffreys, Sheila. *Unpacking Queer Politics: A Lesbian Feminist Perspective.* Malden, MA: Blackwell Publishers, 2003.

Jenkins, Henry. *Textual Poachers: Television Fans & Participatory Culture.* New York: Routledge, 1992.

———. *Convergence Culture: Where Old and New Media Collide.* New York: New York University Press, 2006.

Jenkins, Tamara. *Lisa Yuskavage: Small Paintings, 1993–2004,* New York: Harry N. Abrams, 2004.

Jensen, Elizabeth. "The L Word Spins Off Its Chart." *New York Times.* December 18, 2006: C5.

Johnson, K. "Tele-branding in TVIII: The Network as Brand and the Programme as Brand." *New Review of Film and Television Studies.* 5. 1. 2007: 5–24.

Johnson, Merri Lisa. "L is for 'Long Term': Compulsory Monogamy on *The L Word*." Janet McCabe and Kim Akass, eds. *Reading* The L Word: *Outing Contemporary Television.* London and New York: I.B.Tauris, 2006: 115–37.

——— ed. *Third Wave Feminism and Television: Jane Puts It in a Box.* London: I.B.Tauris/Palgrave Macmillan, 2007.

Keen, Lisa. "Frank Introduces Trans-Inclusive ENDA." *Bay Windows.* 27/28. June 25, 2009: 13.

Keller, Yvonne. "Pulp Politics: Strategies of Vision in Pro-Lesbian Pulp Novels, 1955–1965." Patricia Juliana Smith, ed. *The Queer Sixties.* New York: Routledge, 1999.

———. "'Was It Right to Love Her Brother's Wife So Passionately?' Lesbian Pulp Novels and U.S. Lesbian Identity, 1950–1965." *American Quarterly.* 57. 2005: 385–410.

Kilchenmann, Jennifer. "LLGFF 2005: Chick Flicks." *G3 Magazine.* March 2005: 10.

Kline, Stephen, Nick Dyer-Witherford, and Greig de Peuter. *Digital Play: The Interactions between Technology, Culture and Marketing.* Kingston, Ontario: McGill/Queen's University Press, 2004.

Kregloe, Karman and Jane Caputi. "Supermodels of Lesbian Chic: Camille Paglia Revamps Lesbian/Feminism (while Susie Bright Retools)." Dana Heller, ed. *Cross Purposes: Lesbians, Feminists, and the Limits of Alliance*, Bloomington: Indiana University Press, 1997: 136–54.

"*The L Word* Gifts": www.zazzle.co.uk/the+l+word+gifts. Accessed October 17, 2010.

"*The L Word*: Ilene Chaiken. The Final Word: Part One." Showtime: The L Word: http://www.sho.com/site/lword/home.do. Accessed October 21, 2010.

"The L-Word Wiki: Who on *The L Word* is Gay?" Question 10. Retrieved June 8, 2011, from Showtime.com: http://lwordwiki.sho.com/page/10c.

Lacan, Jacques. "The Signification of the Phallus." *Ecrits: A Selection.* Bruce Fink, trans. New York: Norton, 1977: 271–80.

Ladson-Billings, G. "Just What is Critical Race Theory and What's it Doing in a Nice Field Like Education?" *Qualitative Studies in Education.* 11. 1. 1998: 7–24.

Lavery, David. *Full of Secrets: Critical Approaches to Twin Peaks.* Detroit, MI, Wayne State University Press, 1995.

Lévi-Strauss, Claude. *The Elementary Structures of Kinship.* James Harle Bell and John Richard von Sturmer, trans. Boston: Eyre & Spottiswoode, 1969.

Lewis, Reina and Katrina Rolley. "Ad(dressing) the Dyke: Lesbian Looks and Lesbian Looking." Peter Horne and Reina Lewis, eds. *Outlooks: Lesbian and Gay Sexualities and Visual Cultures.* New York: Routledge, 1996: 178–90.

LilWannaB3_R0cK$t@R. "Has *The L Word* Affected Your Sexuality or Coming Out?" *Showtime Message Boards.* March 7, 2005: http://www. mediablvd.com/forums/index.php?showtopic=13355&st=20.

Lorde, Audre. *The Audre Lorde Compendium: Essays, Speeches, and Journals.* London: Pandora, 1996.

Lotz, Amanda. *Redesigning Women: Television after the Network Era.* Urbana: University of Illinois Press, 2006.

Malou. "Has *The L Word* Affected Your Sexuality or Coming Out?" *Showtime Message Boards.* March 13, 2005: http://www.mediablvd.com/ forums/index.php?showtopic=13355&st=60.

Mann, Denise. "The Spectacularization of Everyday Life: Recycling Hollywood Stars and Fans in Early Television Variety Shows." Lynn Spigel and Denise Mann, eds. *Private Screenings: Television and the Female Consumer.* Minneapolis: University of Minnesota Press, 1992: 41–69.

Mayberry, C. "An 'L-Word' Script Hits the Fans: Online Contest Lets Viewers Pen 'Fanisode,' a TV First." *The Hollywood Reporter.com* [online]. April 24, 2006: http://business.highbeam.com/2012/article-

1G1-145930601/lword-script-hits-fans-online-contest-lets-viewers. Accessed December 21, 2011.

Mayne, Judith. *Framed: Lesbians, Feminists and Media Culture.* Minneapolis: University of Minnesota Press, 2000.

McCroy, Winnie. "L is for Invisible." *The New York Blade Online,* October 31, 2003.

McFadden, Margaret T. "We Cannot Afford to Keep Being so High-minded: Fighting the Religious Right on *The L Word.*" James R. Keller and Leslie Stratyner, eds. *The New Queer Aesthetic on Television.* Jefferson, N.C.: McFarland, 2006: 113–29.

"Memorable Quotes: Showtime: The L Word Wiki: Daniela Sea." Showtime *The L Word:* http://lwordwiki.sho.com/page/Daniela+Sea.

Meyer, Richard. *Outlaw Representation: Censorship and Homosexuality in Twentieth-Century Art.* Oxford: Oxford University Press, 2002.

Mflover. "What Do You NOT Like about The L Word?" *Showtime Message Boards.* December 9, 2004: http://www.sho.com/site/message/thread.do?topicid=105879&boardid=268&groupid=12.

Miklitsch, Robert. "Shot/Countershot: Sexuality, Psychoanalysis, and Postmodern Style in *The Sopranos.*" *Roll Over Adorno: Critical Theory, Popular Culture, Audiovisual Media.* Albany: State University of New York Press, 2006.

Moody, Glyn. "The Duplicitous Inhabitants of Second Life." *Guardian.* November 23, 2006: http://www.guardian.co.uk/technology/2006/nov/23/secondlife.web20.

Moore, Candace. Interview with Marga Gomez, April 2005.

———. "Having it All Ways: The Tourist, the Traveler, and the Local in *The L Word.*" *Cinema Journal.* 46. 4. Summer 2007: 3–23.

Morrison, Toni. *Sula.* New York: Alfred A. Knopf, 1992. Available at www.sovo.com/print.cfm?content_id=2172. Accessed May 12, 2007.

Mulvey, Laura. "Visual Pleasure and Narrative Cinema." *Screen.* 16. 3. 1975: 6–18.

Munger, Kel. "Paperback Writer." *Sacramento News and Review.* April 7, 2005. Online edition: www.newsreview.com/sacramento/Content?oid=oid%3A34731.

Muñoz, José Esteban. *Disidentifications: Queers of Color and the Performance of Politics.* Minneapolis: University of Minnesota Press, 1999.

Nanda, Serena. "Sex/Gender Diversity in Euro-American Cultures." *Gender Diversity: Crosscultural Variations.* Long Grove, IL: Waveland Press, Inc., 2000: 87–100.

Nealon, Christopher. "Invert-History: The Ambivalence of Lesbian Pulp Fiction." *New Literary History.* 31. 2000: 745–64.

Newcomb, Horace, ed. *Television: The Critical View.* Oxford: Oxford University Press, 1994.

Newman, M. Z. "From Beats to Arcs: Toward a Poetics of Television Narrative." *The Velvet Light Trap.* 58. 2006: 16–28.

Nys Dambrot, Shana. "Interview: Catherine Opie." *Artkrush*. 36. July 12, 2006.

Ondrejka, Cory. "Aviators, Moguls, Fashionistas and Barons: Economists and Ownership in Second Life": http://www.papers.ssrn.com/sol3/papers.cfm?abstract_id+614663. Accessed November 20, 2009.

Opie, Catherine. *American Photographer*. New York: Guggenheim Foundation, 2008.

Phoenix, A. *Young Mothers*. Cambridge, UK: Polity Press, 1991.

Posener, Jill. *Spray It Loud*, London: Routledge and Kegan Paul, 1982.

Powers, Alan. *Front Cover: Great Book Jackets and Cover Design*. London: Mitchell Beazley, 2001.

PR Newswire. "Announcements: Showtime Networks and Electric Sheep to Launch *The L Word* in Second Life" [press release]. Retrieved January 22, 2007 from http://www.prnewswire.com/news-releases/showtime-networks-and-electric-sheep-to-launch-the-l-wordr-in-second-life-53677687.html.

Raymond, Janice. *The Transsexual Empire*. London: The Women's Press, 1980.

Reed, Jennifer. "Reading Gender Politics on *The L Word*: The Moira/Max Transitions." *Journal of Popular Film and Television*. 37. 4. 2009: 169–78.

Reeder, Constance. "The Skinny on *The L Word*." *Off Our Backs*, January/February 2004: 51.

Reilly, Maura. "The Drive to Describe: An Interview with Catherine Opie." *Art Journal*. 60. 2. 2001: 82–95.

Renshaw, Sal. "The F Word on *The L Word*: And By That We Mean Feminism." *Ms Magazine*. Winter 2009 (2009a): 59–60.

———. "A Lipstick Stained Farewell." Online Update February 2009 (2009b). *Ms Magazine Online*: http://www.msmagazine.com/winter2009/TheLWordUPDATE.asp.

Renshaw, Sal and Laura Robinson. "Fictions of Our Own Creation: Season One of *The L Word* and the Limits of Representation." Kylo-Patrick R. Hart, ed. *Mediated Deviance and Social Otherness: Interrogating Influential Representations*. Newcastle: Cambridge Scholars Publishing, 2007: 258–72.

Rich, Adrienne. "Compulsory Heterosexuality and Lesbian Existence." Barbara Charlesworth Gelpi and Albert Gelpi, eds. *Adrienne Rich's Poetry and Prose*. N.Y.: Norton, 1993 [1980]: 203–24.

Riese. "*Real L Word* Needs Lesbian Executive Realness, Context, Depth: How We'd Fix It." *Autostraddle*. August 21, 2010: http://www.autostraddle.com/the-real-l-word-final-thoughts-57192/.

Rigney, Melissa. "Brandon Goes to Hollywood: Boys Don't Cry and the Transgender Body in Film." *Film Criticism*. 28. 2. 2003: 4–23.

Robinson, Frank M. and Lawrence Davidson. *Pulp Culture: The Art of Fiction Magazines*. Portland: Collectors Press, 2001.

Rodríguez, Clara E., ed. *Latin Looks: Images of Latinas and Latinos in the U.S. Media*. Boulder, CO: Westview Press, 1997.

Rogers, Thomas. "'The Real L Word': Will TV Ever Get Lesbian-ism Right?" Salon.com, July 16, 2010: http://mobile.salon.com/ent/tv/2010/07/16/ilene_chaiken_interview/index.html. Accessed October 15, 2010.

Rooney, Monique. "Networking in Fortress Los Angeles: Sexuality, Race and the Postmodern Metropolis in *The L Word*." *Australian Humanities Review*. 38. April 2006.

Rose, Nikolas. *Powers of Freedom: Reframing Political Thought*. Cambridge, UK: Cambridge University Press, 1999.

Rosenduft, Raimy. "Now It's Our Party." *Velvet Park*. Winter 2005: 19–27.

Russo, Vito. *The Celluloid Closet: Homosexuality in the Movies*: New York: Harper & Row, 1987.

Schneider, Michael. "'L Word' Gets Real this Time." *Daily Variety*. September 1, 2009: 1–10.

Schwartz, Shauna. "The Other 'L' Word: Representing Latina Identity." K. Akass and J. McCabe, eds. *Reading* The L Word: *Outing Contemporary Television*. London and New York: I.B.Tauris, 2006: 177–81.

Scott, Michael. "Uncaging the Sexual Animal." *Vancouver Sun*. September 3, 1997: C5.

Seajay, Carol. "Pulp and Circumstance." *Women's Review of Books*. 23. 2006: 18.

Sebek, Anezka. "Dyke TV: A Study in Lesbian Media Activism Project Thesis." New School University, April 19, 2004.

"Second Life: Community: The L Word." Linden Labs and Linden Research, Inc. March 24, 2007: http://secondlife.com.

Sedgwick, Eve Kosofsky. *Epistemology of the Closet*. Berkeley, CA: University of California Press, 1990.

———. "Axiomatic." Simon During, ed. *The Cultural Studies Reader*; 2nd edition. London: Routledge, 1999: 320–39.

———. "Paranoid Reading and Reparative Reading, or You're So Paranoid, You Probably Think This Essay is About You." *Touching Feeling: Affect, Pedagogy, Performativity*. Durham: Duke University Press, 2003: 123–51.

———. "*The L Word*: Novelty in Normalcy." *Chronicle of Higher Education*. January 16, 2004: B10–B11.

———. "The Letter L." Kim Akass and Janet McCabe, eds. *Reading* The L Word: *Outing Contemporary Television*. London and New York: I.B.Tauris, 2006: xix–xxiv.

Sender, Katherine. "Sex Sells: Sex, Class, and Taste in Commercial Gay and Lesbian Media." *GLQ: A Journal of Lesbian and Gay Studies*. 9. 3. 2003: 331–65.

———. *Business, Not Politics: The Making of the Gay Market*. New York: Columbia University Press, 2004.

Shelby. "Heterosexual Male Fans of the Show." *The L Word Online Message Boards*. February 6, 2008: http://www.mediablvd.com/forums/index. php?showtopic=14138&st=0.

Showtime (2009a). "*The L Word*: The Final Word": http://www.sho.com/ site/lword/interrogation.do. Accessed March 1, 2010.

————— (2009b). "A Closer Look at Season 6": http://www.youtube.com/ watch?v=r9Lwt2IgOK4&feature=related. Accessed March 1, 2010.

Siegel, Katy. "Local Color." Lisa Yuskavage and Katy Siegel, eds. *Lisa Yuskavage*. Philadelphia: University of Pennsylvania, 2000: 15–22.

Silverstone, Roger. *Television and Everyday Life*. London: Routledge, 1994.

Sitemeter.com. September 1, 2006 and February 20, 2010: http://www. sitemeter.com/?a=stats&s=s17lwordonline.

Sloane, Ivana. "Mia Kirshner: Jenny's Nice Side." *Diva*: http://www.divamag. co.uk/diva/features.asp?PID=43682. Accessed October 24, 2010.

Smith, Anna Marie. "The Feminine Gaze." *The Advocate*. November 19, 1991: 83.

Smith, Barbara. *Toward a Black Feminist Criticism*. Brooklyn: Out & Out Books, 1981.

Smith, Rhonda. "L Word Mixing its Message." *Washington Blade*. February 18, 2005: 51–6.

Smith, Roberta. "A Painter Who Loads the Gun and Lets the Viewer Fire It." *The New York Times*. January 12, 2001: E53.

Snyder, Dasha. Email to Candace Moore (October 17, 2010).

Spigel, Lynn. *Make Room for TV: Television and the Family Ideal in Postwar America*. Chicago: University of Chicago Press, 1992.

Steinert-Threlkeld, Tom. "Don't Write Premium TV's Obituary: Showtime Chief Sees Growth in Subscription Model." *Multichannel News*. April 10, 2006: http://www.multichannel.com/article/122888-Blank_Don_t_ Write_Premium_TV_s_Obituary.php. Accessed June 8, 2011.

Stelter, Brian. "Gay Characters on Television at a New High, Study Says." *The New York Times*. September 29, 2010: http://artsbeat.blogs.nytimes. com/2010/09/29/record-high-for-gay-characters-on-tv-study-says/.

Stillinside. "Thanks to *The L Word*." *Showtime Message Boards*. November 3, 2007: http://www.sho.com/site/message/thread.do?topicid=236020&b oardid=226&groupid=12.

Stockwell, Anne. "Burning Questions." *The Advocate*. January 31, 2006: 48–9.

Stone, Sandy. "The *Empire* Strikes Back: A Posttranssexual Manifesto." Susan Stryker and Stephen Whittle, eds. *The Transgender Studies Reader*. New York and London: Routledge, 2006: 232.

Streitmatter, Rodger. *From "Perverts" to "Fab Five": The Media's Changing Depiction of Gay Men and Lesbians*. New York: Routledge, 2008.

Taylor, Valerie. *The Girls in 3-B*. Femme Fatales Edition. New York: Feminist Press, 2003.

Tenderwolf. "My Lesbian Role Models on *The L Word*." *Showtime Message Boards*. February 2, 2004: http://www.sho.com/site/message/thread.do?topicid=48385&boardid=218&groupid=12.

Topor, Joanna. "Sapphic Strife: Interview with Ilene Chaiken." *Screen Talk*: www.screentalk.biz/interviews/ilenechaiken_interview.php.

Tropiano, S. *The Prime Time Closet: A History of Gays and Lesbians on TV*. New York: Applause Theater and Cinema Books, 2002.

Trumbach, R. "London's Sapphists: From Three Sexes to Four Genders in the Making of Modern Culture." G. Herdt, ed. *Third Sex, Third Gender: Beyond Sexual Dimorphism in Culture and History*. New York: Zone Books, 1994: 111–36.

Turner, S. Derek and Mark Cooper. "Out of the Picture: Minority and Female TV Station Ownership in the United States – Current Status, Comparative Statistical Analysis and the Effects of FCC Policy and Media Consolidation." Free Press, 2006: http://www.benton.org/initiatives/ownership.

Vance, Carole S. "The War on Culture." *Art in America*. 77. 9. September, 1989: 39–45.

Vitello, Paul. "The Trouble When Jane Becomes Jack." *The New York Times*. August 20, 2006.

Walters, Suzanna Danuta. "As Her Hand Crept Slowly Up Her Thigh: Ann Bannon and the Politics of Pulp." *Social Text*. 23. Autumn–Winter. 1989: 83–101.

Warner, Michael. *Fear of a Queer Planet*. Minneapolis: University of Minnesota Press, 1993.

———. *The Trouble with Normal: Sex, Politics, and the Ethics of Queer Life*. New York: Free Press, 1999.

———. *Publics and Counterpublics*. New York: Zone Books, 2002.

West, Celeste. *Lesbian Polyfidelity: A Pleasure Guide for the Woman Whose Heart Is Open to Multiple, Concurrent Sexualoves, or How to Keep Non-Monogamy Safe, Sane*. San Francisco: Booklegger Publishing, 1996.

Westerburg, Arboriasha. "Interview: Cory Linden on IP Issues in Second Life." *The Second Life Herald*. 2004: http://www.alphavilleherald.com/archives/000372.html.

Wheeler, Lorna and Lara Raven Wheeler. "Straight-up Sex in *The L Word*." Kim Akass and Janet McCabe, eds. *Reading* The L Word: *Outing Contemporary Television*. London and New York: I.B.Tauris, 2006: 99–110.

Williams, Linda. "Melodrama Revised." Nick Browne, ed. *Refiguring American Film Genres: Theory and History*. Berkeley: University of California Press, 1998: 42–88.

Wilton, Tamsin, ed. *Immortal Invisible: Lesbians and the Moving Image*. London, Routledge, 1995.

Wittel, Andreas. "Toward a Network Sociality." *Theory, Culture and Society*. 18. 6. 2001: 51–76.

Wolfe, Susan J. and Lee Ann Roripaugh. "The (In)visible Lesbian: Anxieties of Representation in *The L Word*." Kim Akass and Janet McCabe, eds. *Reading* The L Word: *Outing Contemporary Television*. London and New York: I.B.Tauris, 2006: 43–54.

YouAreSoAnalog. "Why Does Everyone Hate Max?" *Showtime Message Boards*. March 27, 2006: www.sho.com/site/message/thread.do?topici d=198625&boardid=4644&groupid=12.

Yuskavage, Lisa and Katy Siegel. *Lisa Yuskavage*. Philadelphia: University of Pennsylvania, 2000.

Zimet, Jaye. *Strange Sisters: The Art of Lesbian Pulp Fiction 1949–1969*. New York: Viking Studio, 1999.

Zita, Jacquelyn N. "Male Lesbians and the Postmodernist Body." *Hypatia*. 7. 4. 1992: 106–27.

Index